The Jewish Spiritual Path

THE JEWISH
SPIRITUAL
PATH

THE WAY OF THE NAME

JOSHUA GOLDING

URIM PUBLICATIONS
Jerusalem • New York

The Jewish Spiritual Path:
The Way of the Name
by Joshua Golding

Copyright © 2019 Joshua Golding

Typeset by Ariel Walden

Printed in Israel
First Edition

ISBN 978-1-60280-311-4

Urim Publications
P.O. Box 52287
Jerusalem 9152102
Israel
www.UrimPublications.com

Library of Congress Cataloging-in-Publication Data
Names: Golding, Joshua L., author.
Title: The Jewish spiritual path : the way of the name / Joshua Golding.
Description: New York, NY : Urim Publications, [2019]
Identifiers: LCCN 2018024357 | ISBN 9781602803114 (hardcover : alk. paper)
Subjects: LCSH: Spiritual life—Judaism. | Prayer—Judaism. | Cabala.
Classification: LCC BM723 .G63 2018 | DDC 296.7—dc23
LC record available at https://lccn.loc.gov/2018024357

Dedicated in loving honor of
My mother in law
Miriam Pollak

מרים בת עזריאל זאב הלוי

A survivor of the Holocaust
A woman of valor
Generous, compassionate, devout
Mother, Grandmother, and Great Grandmother
May she see many years of continued
happiness and blessing!

——≋€——

And
Dedicated in loving memory of
My father in law
Ithamar Ephraim Pollak

איתמר אפרים בן חיים אברהם הלוי ז"ל

A survivor of the Holocaust
A righteous, straight, and true person
A learned man, who loved to teach
An inspiration to many
Father, Grandfather, and Great Grandfather
May his soul be bound up in the bond of eternal life!

מכתב מאת הרב יחיאל ברלב שליט"א,
מחבר ספרי קבלה, ידיד נפש, באור על הזוהר, ועוד

בס"ד יום רביעי ערב ראש השנה תשע"ח

זכינו שבדור הזה יותר יהודים לומדים יותר דפי גמרא מאשר אי פעם
בהיסטוריה. אנו רואים עשרות אלפי אנשים משתתפים בשיעורי גמרא והלכה
בבתי כנסת, בישיבות, ברכבת תחתית, במשרדים, בכל אתר ואתר. חלק
מההצלחה הגדולה הזאת בלימוד התורה יש לזקוף לרב הגאון מאיר שפירא
זצ"ל מלובלין הוגה הרעיון של לימוד "הדף היומי." בעת רצון זו קמו חכמי
תורה והוציאו לאור את הש"ס עם באורים שהופכים את הלימוד בסוגיות
הגמרא לחוויה מרגשת ומהנה.

בד בבד עם התפשטות הלימוד בתורת הנגלה, גברה בדור האחרון הנטייה
ללמוד בתורת הנסתר. גם בנושא זה התפרסמו פרושים על ספר הזוהר בשפה
שמובנת לאלה שמוכנים להתעמק בדבה. בעבר, הלימוד בתורת הנסתר היה
מוגבל רק למתי מעט. בדור הזה אנו עדים לאלפים שעוסקים בלימוד בתורת
הנסתר.גם בנושא זה זכינו לראות ספרים רבים שמסבירים בלשון נקייה את
הרעיונות העמוקים שבתורת הנסתר.

הרב פרופסור יהושע גולדינג שליט"א עומד להוציא לאור ספר שיהיה כתוב
בשפה ברורה וידידותית, ואשר יתרום להפצת הלימוד בתורת הנסתר. שמעתי
כמה הקלטות מהספר שהוקלטו על ידי הרב יהושע גולדינג והתרשמתי מאד
מהשפה הנקייה והצחה שמסבירה את המושגים העמוקים ביותר בתורת
הנסתר ותורמים לחיזוק האמונה, הבנת הדרך בה הקב"ה מנהיג את העולם.
והחשוב מכולם שתורמת להבנה עמוקה למשמעות התפילה.

אני מאחל לרב יהושע גולדינג שליט"א שיזכה להפיץ את ספריו ויביא לידי
הגברת האמונה והתחזקות בעבודת ה.

בברכת כתיבה וחתימה טובה לכל כלל ישראל,

בידידות רבה,

הרב יחיאל ברלב

RABBI YECHIEL BARLEV
Author of numerous Kabbalistic works including *Yedid Nefesh*,
Commentary on the Zohar, and Introduction to Kabbalah
Translation by the Author

BS"D
Wednesday, Eve of Rosh Hashanah, 5778
[September 20, 2017]

We have merited in our generation that more Jews are learning more pages of Talmud than any other time in history. We see tens of thousands of people participating classes in Talmud and halachah [Jewish law] in synagogues, seminaries, [even] in the subway, in offices [at work], and many other places. Part of this great success in Torah study may be attributed to Rav Hagaon Meir Shapiro of blessed memory from Lublin, who conceived the notion of the *daf yomi* [daily page of study]. At this auspicious time, Torah sages took the initiative and published the Talmud with [extensive] translation and commentary, thus turning the study of Talmud into a lively and enjoyable experience.

Together with the spread of the study of the "revealed" Torah, in the last generation there has grown an inclination toward the study of the "hidden" Torah, or Kabbalah. In this area also, commentaries on the Zohar have been published in a language that is comprehensible to those who are able to delve into such matters. In the past, study of Kabbalah was confined to a select few. In this generation, we are witnesses to thousands who delve into the study of Kabbalah. Here too, we have merited seeing many books that explain in plain and clear language the deep ideas of the Kabbalah.

Rabbi Professor Joshua Golding has written this book in a clear and user-friendly style, which will contribute to the spread of the study of Kabbalah. I have listened to several audio recordings from the text of the book made by Rabbi Golding and I am impressed with the clear and fine way in which the book explains the deepest concepts of Kabbalah. [The book] contributes to the strengthening of faith, and to the understanding of the ways in which the Holy One Blessed Be He conducts the affairs of the world. Most importantly, this book contributes toward a deep understanding of the meaning of the prayers.

I wish Rabbi Golding success in the publication and dissemination of his work. May it lead to an increase in faith and a strengthening of the worship of the Lord.

With blessings for a good inscription and seal for the New Year for all Israel,

With great affection,
Rabbi Yechiel Barlev

CONTENTS

INTRODUCTION

OPENING THE DOOR
TO THE WAY OF THE NAME

THE TORAH TEACHES THAT the essential or proper name of
God is the Tetragrammaton, or four-lettered name, י-ה-ו-ה. Jews regard
this name with such reverence that they do not even attempt to pronounce it, but instead often use the word *Hashem*, which means, *the
Name*. A central teaching in the Kabbalah, or Jewish mystical tradition,
is that a proper understanding of the Name is the key to living a rich and
meaningful spiritual life. The four-lettered name signifies the ways in
which the infinite essence of God is manifest in reality, and, in order to
"walk in the way of God," we must understand and implement the meaning of the Name. For the Kabbalist, this understanding illuminates and
energizes our fulfillment of the commandments, or *mitzvot*, and especially our practice of *tefillah*, that is, prayer and meditation. Indeed, the
Jewish spiritual path may be neatly summarized in one simple phrase:
Derech Hashem, or the Way of the Name.[1]

The leading idea of this book is that the Jewish spiritual path has four
major stages, which correspond to the four letters of the Name. The
structure of this book follows this four-fold pattern. In doing so, this
book combines a theoretical presentation of some of the basic elements
of Kabbalah, with the practical aim of offering a guide that can be used
in "real time" to energize and enrich one's spiritual life. We shall find that
the four-fold Way of the Name is closely linked with the daily Morning
Service, or *Shacharit*. Those who are familiar with *Shacharit* will find
that their service will be energized by studying and following the Way

---

1. *Derech Hashem* is also the name of a work by Rabbi Moshe Chaim Luzzatto
(Ramchal). Much of the present book is inspired by and based on that classic. See
below, note 21.

of the Name. Those who are not familiar with *Shacharit* may be encouraged to adopt it or something similar as a regular morning practice. The appendix to this book provides sample exercises for meditation; all of them center on the Name.

In recent years, there has been a resurgence of interest in Kabbalah. Many people have discovered some of the powerful spiritual ideas and teachings in this part of the Jewish tradition. Yet, even many Jews are woefully unaware of the rich treasures taught in Kabbalah regarding the Way of the Name.[2] This is unfortunate, because those who succeed in studying and following the Way of the Name are aware of its intellectual depth and the tremendous power it brings to their spiritual lives. In fact, the Kabbalists teach that the study and application of the Kabbalah will help bring about the Messianic age of world peace, harmony, and unity between man and man, and between man and God. Hence the present book, which utilizes basic teachings from Kabbalah, to illuminate the spiritual path. To apply the insights of the Kabbalah is not to engage in superstitious practices, but rather to employ the insights of Kabbalah as a way of structuring one's moral, intellectual and spiritual development, and as a way of infusing it with cosmic significance.

This book aims to articulate the Way of the Name in a rational and systematic manner. Some people have the misconception that Kabbalah is anti-rational, and that it is filled with anthropomorphisms and downright weird views about God. In fact, Kabbalah is a complex theoretical structure that meets a high degree of intellectual rigor, and indeed the Kabbalists were quite anxious to dispel literal readings of their highly metaphorical language used to describe God. The classic sources of Kabbalah place a high premium on wisdom and understanding. As we shall see in this book, there is a logical flow to the four stages of spiritual growth. Nevertheless, it cannot be denied that Kabbalah also teaches

---

2. Some religious Jews are hesitant to study Kabbalah at all, based on the belief that study of Kabbalah is suitable only for rare individuals. The modern day Kabbalist R. Yaakov Moshe Hillel discusses this issue at length in his book, *Petach Sha'ar Hashamayim* (see especially page 69). His relevant conclusions are as follows. While intensive study of Kabbalah is suitable only for certain individuals, some study of the basics of Kabbalah is appropriate for any religious Jew, if it is grounded in halachic observance and geared toward the purpose of improving one's relationship with God. Anyone is permitted to study books such as *Derech Hashem, Tanya* and *Nefesh Hachayim*, which utilize Kabbalistic teachings to illuminate the spiritual path. The present book, which relies heavily on such classics, is an attempt to contribute toward this same genre, with the goal of reaching a contemporary audience.

that there is an aspect of God and our commitment to God that goes beyond, or "transcends" reason. One of the goals of this book is to clarify the extent to which Kabbalah – and indeed Judaism itself – is rational, and to what extent it involves a non-rational or "trans-rational" element. We shall also try to clarify to what extent Kabbalistic doctrines are based on ordinary experience, and to what extent they are teachings based on the *mesorah,* or Jewish tradition.

This book adopts what may be called a Kabbalistic approach on how to understand the very idea of God. Many people think of God as *a being* or *an entity,* that is, a very special, non-physical being, but an entity nonetheless. This entity is conceived as having certain divine attributes or qualities, such as power, justice, providence, mercy, and so forth. On this conception, to believe in God is to believe that there exists such an entity (and, to disbelieve in God is to believe that such an entity does not exist.) If this being exists, it stands "over and against" the world or reality, and so, to have a good spiritual life is to have a good relationship with this entity. This is what might be called the *pashut,* or widespread, common conception of God.

However, based on Kabbalistic sources, this book proposes that we may think of God's essence as *Being,* and we may think of the divine attributes of God as the *ways in which Being is manifest in our world.* To say that this view is Kabbalistically based is not to imply that *every* Kabbalist would endorse it. Still, such a conception seems more prevalent among those who are known as "mystics." On this conception, God's essence is not *a* being; rather, God's essence *is* Being. All beings that exist have something in common, namely, that they express or manifest Being. Thus, all things that exist are expressions or manifestations of God's essence. On this conception, to have a good spiritual life is not to develop a relationship with some entity that is *outside* of oneself, but rather to become continually more aware of and in tune with the ways in which Being is manifest in the world. The Torah, as filtered through the lens of Kabbalah, teaches us what are those "ways" in which God is manifest, and what path we must follow to achieve a good relationship with God. The Name itself is the key to that path.

At first glance, it may seem that this way of thinking of God is not compatible with the Biblical conception of God. It may seem that if God's essence is identified with Being itself, then God cannot be *a person,* that is, a rational agent. In turn, this seems to imply that God does not guide the world with intentional providence (*hashgachah*). However, in the course of this introduction and throughout this book, we shall see how Kabbalah provides a framework for understanding how this conception of God is entirely compatible with Biblically based, halachic[3] Judaism. It is also entirely compatible with the belief in divine personhood and divine providence. Moreover, we shall find that this way of thinking about God opens wide the door to the spiritual path, that is, the Way of the Name.

This book also addresses the question of to what extent is the Way of the Name available to those do *not* believe in divine providence or other traditional or "masoretic" teachings of Judaism, such as God's special relationship with Israel, the claim that the Torah is God's revealed way, and so on. It seems that some people are under the impression that one could be a Kabbalist or make use of Kabbalistic insights without accepting the major doctrines of Judaism. Indeed, we shall find that that there are *some* lessons of the Jewish spiritual path that are available to those who do not accept the traditional doctrines of Judaism. Yet, equally importantly, this book will show that, especially in its more advanced stages, the Jewish spiritual path is integrally connected with certain traditional Jewish doctrines. In fact, we shall find that the Jewish spiritual path is *itself* a way to attain knowledge of the God of Israel, that is, a God who is providential and has the character that is taught by the traditional doctrines of Judaism.

Much of the material in this book is based on classic texts of Kabbalah, *Chassidut*, Jewish Philosophy, and *Mussar*.[4] Through reading this book, those who wish to learn about Kabbalah without ever implementing its rich treasures in their spiritual life will at the very least gain a better understanding of Kabbalah. Yet, the main thrust of this book is to serve as a practical guide. An alternative title for this book might have been, *How*

---

3. Halachic Judaism upholds the doctrine that there is a divinely ordained law, as interpreted and filtered through the rabbinic tradition to the present day. Halachic Judaism is based on the Talmud and subsequent rabbinic literature including the classic "codes" of practical everyday law, such as Rabbi Moses Maimonides' *Mishneh Torah*, Rabbi Yosef Karo's *Shulchan Aruch*, and subsequent commentaries.

4. Kabbalistic sources of this book include the *Zohar*, the *Shaarei Orah* of Rabbi Yosef Gikatillia, the works of Rabbi Moshe Cordovero (known as Ramak), Rabbi Isaac Luria (the Ari), Ramchal, and Rabbi Chaim of Volozhin's *Nefesh Hachayim*. Chassidic works include the *Tanya* of Rabbi Schneur Zalman of Liadi (the first Lubavitcher Rebbe) and more recent works such as *Netivot Shalom* of Rabbi Sholom Noach Berzovsky (the late Slonimer Rav). Philosophical works include Moses Maimonides' *Guide to the Perplexed* and the works of the Maharal of Prague. The word *mussar* means discipline. Briefly, *mussar* refers to a body of Jewish literature that concentrates on the ethical and spiritual values or virtues of Judaism. Such works often contain practical advice and strategies for improving one's character. Classics are Bahya Ibn Pakuda's *Chovot Halevavot*, and Ramchal's *Mesilat Yesharim*.

to Energize Your Spiritual Life in Four (not so) Easy Steps. The parenthetical phrase is meant to indicate that the four steps are in some respect easy, but yet in another way, not easy. In some way, the four stages are relatively simple, both in theory, and practice. On a deeper level, the four stages require a great deal of devotion and effort. So, this book may be useful to two different groups of readers in two different ways. For those readers who wish to expand their spiritual life by adapting certain general aspects of the Way of the Name, the four-fold path may be relatively easy. But, for those readers who wish to follow closely the Way of the Name, especially in a rigorously traditional Jewish manner, the path requires a good deal of effort and devotion. The "easy" way is perhaps somewhat superficial, but still worthwhile. The "not so easy" way is more demanding, but in the end, it is deeper and far more rewarding. Of course, it is up to the reader to make use of the Way of the Name in whatever way he or she sees fit.

The prospective audience of this book includes anyone who is interested in spirituality, and especially those who are interested in the spiritual path taught by Judaism and Kabbalah. This includes Jews and non-Jews; both those who are devout or not devout. This includes beginners as well as those who are already deeply committed to some spiritual tradition. This includes people who are already knowledgeable about Kabbalah to some extent, as well as those who are not knowledgeable about Kabbalah. No prior knowledge is assumed. References and technical points will be relegated to footnotes. It is hoped that even the scholar of Judaism and Kabbalah will find something novel in this book. But this book does not speak exclusively to scholars. With some patient reading, any serious spiritual seeker will be able to learn and grow from this book.

Our first step is to reflect on the Name itself. Although the main purpose of this book is to serve as a spiritual guide, it is necessary first to lay the groundwork by describing the basic elements of the Kabbalistic understanding of the Name. This understanding is not merely a prelude– it is part of the Way. Judaism teaches that the spiritual journey involves not only one's actions and emotions, but also the mind or the intellect. While some of the material in this introduction may seem abstract and difficult to grasp, many things will become clearer as the book goes on. The very reading of this book is itself part of the Jewish spiritual path. I invite the reader to embark on the journey.

THE NAME י-ה-ו-ה
AND THE MYSTERY OF BEING

WHO, OR WHAT, IS GOD? We can learn something profound about God by reflecting on the proper Name of God. In the Torah, God has many names. For example, God is referred to as *elohim* and *adon*. These "epithets" or descriptive names mean Judge and Lord. But the only proper name of God is the Tetragrammaton or י-ה-ו-ה . While on occasion angels and even human beings are referred to as *elohim* or *adon*,[5] there is not a single occasion when a human or angel is referred to as י-ה-ו-ה. This name is uniquely used to refer to God alone.

Somewhat paradoxically, a great mystery surrounds this name. Surely, the single most important name in the Torah is God's proper name. Although the Torah often takes a verse or two to explain the derivation of an important name (as in the case of Adam, Chavah, Noach, Avraham, Yitzchak, Yaakov, and Moshe) the Torah avoids any explicit explanation of the meaning of the Name. Moreover, according to Jewish tradition, the proper pronunciation of the Name was kept hidden; at the present stage in history, it seems no one knows definitively how to pronounce the Name. The commonly used pronunciation *Ye-ho-v-ah* is quite dubious and almost certainly incorrect. The mystery of the Name calls out to us as a riddle to be pondered.

Despite the mystery, within the Jewish tradition it is almost universally accepted that the Name, י-ה-ו-ה, has something to do with *Being*.[6]

---

5. Genesis 6:4, 32:5; Exodus 22:8.

6. Rabbi Yosef Karo writes that when we say blessings or pray, we should have in mind that the plain meaning of the Name is that *God was, is,* and *will be.* See *Shulchan Aruch: Orach Chaim* (hereafter, SA:OC) 5:1. See also *Tanya, Shaar Hayichud,* chapter 7. See also Exodus 3:13ff., where Moshe asks God, what is his name. At first,

This approach is both linguistically and conceptually plausible. It is linguistically plausible because the Hebrew words for "was, is, and will be" are, respectively היה, הוה, and יהיה. No other Hebrew words are so similar to the Name. In fact, some Jews use the word *Havayah* (Hebrew: ה-ו-י-ה) in place of the more common *Hashem* (the name) when speaking of God. The word *Havayah* means Being. Moreover, since the Torah teaches that God is eternal and that God is the source of all things that exist, it is conceptually plausible to think that the essential name of God must have something to do with the very idea of Being itself. We tend to think of God as the most basic or fundamental being or reality. Now, what could be more basic or more fundamental than Being itself? When we think about things or beings in the world – planets, trees, animals, and humans – we are thinking about specific or particular things or beings. And, when we think about Being in general we are thinking of that which is most basic and fundamental. We can conceive of a universe without trees, planets, animals, or humans. Yet, can we conceive of a world without Being? In a way, the most obvious thing about reality is . . . that there is Being! Hence, it stands to reason that the Name of God would have something do with Being.

There is something puzzling and mysterious about the idea of Being. In thinking about Being itself, we are implicitly thinking about an endless or infinite number of all possible beings or things. For there are an infinite number of possible beings which one can think of, and all of these possibilities are in some way inherent in the very idea of Being. Yet, at the same time, the mind draws a blank when contemplating Being itself. Precisely because it is so fundamental and general, there is nothing specific that the mind thinks of when it thinks of Being. Thus, the verbal mystery of the Name points to another, deeper, metaphysical mystery: the mystery of Being. The mystery of being is that it is at once so familiar yet so elusive.

Let it be emphasized that the suggestion here is only that the Name י-ה-ו-ה has *something to do* with Being, and not that the Name should be *translated* as "Being." In the following section, based on Kabbalistic teachings, we shall make progress on how to understand better the relationship between י-ה-ו-ה and the notion of Being.

God responds by saying that his name is *Ehyeh asher ehyeh* ("I will be what I will be"). Shortly thereafter, God refers to himself simply as *Ehyeh* (*I will be*). Subsequently, God tells Moshe that his name is י-ה-ו-ה. This intimates that the Tetragrammaton is linked to the name *Ehyeh*, which clearly stems from the Hebrew word for *being*.

THE INFINITE ESSENCE
(*ATZMUT EIN SOF*)

KABBALAH MAKES A DISTINCTION between the *essence* of God and God's *ways*. The essence, or *atzmut*, of God is God's true nature, in and of itself. On the other hand, the *sefirot* have to do with the ways in which the essence or *atzmut* of God is manifest or expressed in our universe.

Let us focus first on the Kabbalistic notion of God's essence. The Kabbalists refer to the essence, or *atzmut*, as *ein sof*, i.e., infinite; that is, without limit or definition. It is probably best to understand "infinite" here to mean unbounded, or undefined, rather than as infinite in some kind of mathematical sense. The essence is nameless or indefinable, or at least, it is very difficult to speak much about it.[7] We cannot directly know or experientially grasp the essence of God. In some respect, the essence of God always eludes our grasp. Kabbalah teaches that although we can know that *ein sof* is a reality of some sort, we do not, and cannot, have a direct, unmediated experiential knowledge of *ein sof*. The Kabbalists note that precisely because *ein sof* is so obscure, it is never explicitly mentioned in the Torah. The doctrine of *ein sof* is taught to us by the oral tradition of the Kabbalah, which reveals certain hidden or "esoteric" teachings.

Still, we may press the question, what more, if anything, can be said about the mysterious *ein sof*? Following an approach found in some

---

7. Moses Maimonides, the great Jewish philosopher, also regards God's essence as unknowable. See *Mishneh Torah, Hilchot Yesoday Hatorah*, I:10. This is a major theme in his *Moreh Nevuchim* (*Guide to the Perplexed*). The nameless quality of the divine essence or ultimate reality is a well-known theme throughout many great world traditions.

Kabbalistic sources, we may understand the notion of God's *atzmut*, or essence, as *Being itself*.[8] On this approach, the very essence of God is Being itself, and the world that we live in, as well as all the various beings and things that exist in the world, are *manifestations* or *expressions* of God's essence, that is, Being. Anything and everything that exists, from a tiny pebble to a massive planet, is to some degree a manifestation or expression of Being, that is, God's essence. The Kabbalistic notion of *tzimtzum*, or "self-contraction," is relevant here. If God's essence is conceived as Being itself, the idea of self-contraction may be understood in the following way. Any particular thing or being that exists (or that might exist) is bound to be a *limited* expression or manifestation of Being. Whether it is a pebble or a planet – or even something imaginary such as a unicorn – any particular thing or being *has* certain properties, but *lacks* other properties. Thus, it will express or manifest Being in some respect, but not in other respects.

Indeed, even the entire universe, that is, the sum total of all things that exist, does not and cannot *totally* express or manifest Being. No matter how complex and populated our universe may be, there will always be an infinite number of possible things that do *not* exist, and so, no universe can ever totally express Being. Now, we shall see later that Kabbalah teaches that there are some things that express God's essence *more fully* than do other things. In particular, there is something very special about human persons, and there is also something very special about the Torah, both of which represent unique manifestations of God's essence. It is also part of the divine plan that God's essence will be manifest or expressed *as fully as possible* in the world at some future time (in the Messianic age and the World to Come). We shall return to this notion later in this book. The important point here is that one must always bear in mind that nothing that exists can *totally* express God's infinite essence, that is, Being itself.

Much of what the Kabbalists say about *atzmut ein sof* applies to the idea of Being. Although we can certainly formulate the idea of Being itself, we cannot know or experientially grasp Being itself. It is impossible to experience pure Being itself; one can only have an experience of some particular manifestation or expression of Being. Moreover, as noted above, Being itself is, in a way, infinite, or *ein sof*. The very idea of Being contains within itself limitless possibilities of the various ways in which

---

8. See Rabbi Schneur Zalman of Liadi in *Sha'ar Hayichud* and Rabbi Chaim of Volozhin in *Nefesh Ha-Chaim*. For these thinkers, God is reality, and everything that exists is a manifestation of God.

Being can be expressed. On the other hand, our mind draws something of a blank when contemplating Being, for there is no specific content to this idea. Thus, it is plausible to identify the Kabbalistic notion of God's infinite essence, or *atzmut ein sof*, with the idea of Being itself.

It is important here to forestall a potential misunderstanding. It may seem that if we identify God's essence as Being itself, we are then committed to *pantheism*, that is, the view that God *is* everything. This is a mistake, which rests on an ambiguity in the word, "Being." If we use the word "Being" to mean "everything that exists" then, of course, if we say that "God is Being" we are indeed saying that "God is everything that exists." However, in this book we are using the word "Being" to mean that very essence which is common to all things that exist – and even those possible things that do not actually exist. Understood in this way, the view that God's essence is Being is *not* tantamount to pantheism. As an analogy, consider the idea of Love. Love is found or expressed or exhibited in all examples of love, including, loving actions and loving people. Yet, love is not *identical* with the sum total of all examples of love. Rather, Love is that very essence which all those examples, and indeed many other possible examples, have in common. Similarly, here we are thinking of Being as that essence which all beings have in common.

This way of thinking about God's essence has the following advantage over the common, or *pashut*, conception. On the common conception, God's essence is *a being* or *an entity*, so in order to believe in God, one must believe that there exists a non-physical entity who, as it were, stands over and against the universe. Depending on one's background and philosophical temperament, one may or may not have difficulty believing that there is such a being. However, on the present approach, where one thinks of God's essence as *Being itself*, the matter is quite different. There can be no reasonable doubt that there is a universe, and that there are things that exist. Furthermore, even though it is somewhat mysterious, the idea of Being itself is one we can readily formulate, and there is no doubt that the things in this world in some way manifest or express Being. On this approach, it is incorrect to say that "God's essence *exists*," as if God's essence were just another being among many that exist.[9] A being or an entity is something that can exist, or fail to

9. The word "exist" comes from the Latin *existare*, which literally means, *to stand out*. A thing that exists is something that stands out as a particular thing among many others. But in Hebrew, the word that is often used to describe some reality is *matzuy* or *nimtza*, which literally means, "that which is found." God's essence is *nimtza*; it is found or discovered. Thus, the Kabbalists refer to God's essence as a *metziut*, or something which is found or uncovered. This should not be taken to

exist; but, on the present approach, God's essence is not *a* being; rather God's essence is Being itself.[10] Nothing could be more self-evident than the fact that there are things that exist, and, that all things manifest or express Being.

There is another advantage of this approach to understanding God's essence. If we think of God's essence as Being itself, the idea of God's "omnipresence" makes perfectly good sense. To say that God is omnipresent is to say that God is "everywhere." If God is *a being*, what does it mean to say that God is everywhere? It would have to mean something like the idea that God is *available* everywhere or that God has *control* or *power* over any domain in the universe. However, if God is Being itself, it makes good sense to believe that "God is everywhere," for, as stated earlier, Being is manifest in all things or beings that exist. Anywhere and everywhere one can go in this universe, one cannot get away from that which manifests or expresses Being! As we shall see later, this aspect of God is symbolized by the last ה in God's name, which represents the *Shekhinah*, or divine presence.

Still another difference between this way of thinking about God and the *pashut* conception is as follows. On the *pashut* conception, God is an entity who existed before the world, and who caused the world to exist. He also sustains the world in being. Indeed, this is the way the Biblical creation story seems to read if taken at face value. But on the present Kabbalistic conception, that reading is not entirely correct. God's essence is not an entity, so it cannot properly be said that God existed before the world. Instead, God's essence is Being itself. On this approach, although it is incorrect to say that God brought the world into existence, it is rather the case that God or Being itself is the "explanatory ground" of the world, for everything is an expression or manifestation of Being.

Some readers may resist this way of thinking about God's essence, for it seems to violate the plain meaning of the Hebrew Scriptures. Surely, on the surface, the Scriptures speak as if God is *a* being. However, there are a number of passages in the Scriptures that plainly indicate that God

---

imply that the Kabbalists think of God's essence as a being that *exists*.

10. Ontology is the branch of philosophy that studies the nature of being, and that seeks to determine what kinds of being or beings there are. Using philosophical terms, we may say that this way of understanding God's essence is more "ontologically parsimonious" than the common, or *pashut*, way of understanding God's essence. It is ontologically parsimonious because, unlike the common understanding of God's essence, it does not require the postulation of an entity or a being.

is radically different from everything else.[11] The common, or *pashut*, reading simply cannot suffice even on its own terms. Especially in the creation story itself, it is obvious that certain passages cannot be taken literally. For example, what does the Torah mean when it says that "God said, let there be light?" Surely, this does not mean that God uttered words with a mouth. Indeed, God does not literally have a mouth, eyes, ears, etc. even though on many occasions Scripture speaks as if God does. Many sages in both the Kabbalistic and philosophical traditions have insisted that the Torah speaks metaphorically to express certain profound teachings.[12] So, the fact that the plain, or *pashut*, meaning of the text reads as if God is an entity does not rule out other interpretations. Just because the plain or common meaning of the Scriptures seems to indicate that God is *a* being, this does not rule out the notion that we may think of God's essence as Being itself.

However, another problem is that if we think of God's essence as Being itself, it seems to follow that God is *impersonal*. For, it seems that, Being itself cannot be characterized as a person, that is, a rational agent, who is capable of communicating with persons, or engaging in such activities as issuing commands, responding to prayer, rewarding the righteous, punishing the wicked, and engaging in relationships of mutual love and respect. Putting the point bluntly, it seems that Being is an "It" rather than a "He." If one insists that God is an It rather than a He, one would thereby depart radically from traditional Judaism. According to Kabbalah, the answer to this question lies in the teaching of the *sefirot*, which complements the teaching of *atzmut ein sof*. Kabbalah teaches that through the doctrine of *sefirot* it becomes feasible to understand *ein sof* as personal. Let us turn then to the doctrine of the *sefirot*.

11. Deuteronomy 4:12, 4:15; Isaiah 40:18–26.
12. Maimonides, *Mishneh Torah, Hilchot Yesodai Hatorah* I:9; *Tikkunei Zohar* 42:7 (82a).

THE DIVINE WAYS (*SEFIROT*)

KABBALAH TEACHES THAT ALTHOUGH *ein sof* is not directly accessible, it is manifest or expressed in certain general ways, and those ways are indeed accessible to us. These "ways" are called *sefirot* (in the singular, *sefirah*). The term *sefirah* is related to the word for *counting*. Whereas *ein sof* connotes infinity, *sefirah* connotes something countable or definite. Still, while each *sefirah* has a distinctive character, all the *sefirot* are interrelated or interdependent. Kabbalah also teaches that the name י-ה-ו-ה represents the sum total of all those ways in which the essence is manifest.[13] There are precisely ten *sefirot*, and they are divided into four groups; each group is symbolized by one letter of the Name. Unlike the term *ein sof*, the name י-ה-ו-ה occurs explicitly and prominently in the Hebrew Scriptures, and, as mentioned earlier, it is the proper name of God. The other names of God refer to certain specific aspects of God's ways. Only the Tetragrammaton refers to the sum total of all those ways at once.

Kabbalah teaches that it is in virtue of the *sefirot* that we can describe God as a Person, and that we can have an interpersonal relationship with God, that is, a relationship of mutual love, respect, and dialogue. It is in virtue of the *sefirot* that we may speak of God as providential. The *sefirot* are the ways in which God's essence is manifest, and, by knowing the *sefirot*, we can in some fashion know God, and, through imitating or following in God's ways, we can become, in some respect, God-like. Through the *sefirot*, the *ein sof* is accessible to us, if only indirectly.

If we understand *atzmut ein sof* as Being itself, we may also under-

---

13. For a basic summary of the Kabbalistic approach to the Name, see *Tanya: Iggerret Hatshuvah*, chapter 4.

stand the *sefirot* as the *general ways in which Being is manifest in the world*. On this approach, the Name represents the general ways in which Being itself is manifest in the world.[14] In other words, the *sefirot* are the guiding principles in accord with which the universe operates. In effect, Kabbalah is the study of Being and the basic ways in which Being is manifest or expressed in the universe. In studying the significance and meaning of the Name of God, we are engaged in the most fundamental and profound study of all – the study of Being and the ways in which Being is manifest or expressed in the world. Thus it has been said that the entire Kabbalah is really one long commentary on God's Name.

In the course of this book, the reader will learn more about the *sefirot*, and about how each of the *sefirot* corresponds to certain steps along the Jewish spiritual path. At this stage, only a brief introduction is in place. The ten *sefirot* are *shekhinah, yesod, hod, netzach, rachamim, din, chessed, binah, chochmah,* and *keter*. Roughly, these terms may be translated as *presence, foundation, majesty, victory, compassion, justice, benevolence, understanding, wisdom,* and *will*. One must bear in mind that there are many alternative names for each of the *sefirot*, and that these English translations have misleading connotations. It is best to think of each *sefirah* as connoting several closely related aspects of God or God's manifestation. All the *sefirot* are interrelated; they are not conceptually separable. The following table displays the ten *sefirot* and their correspondence to the four letters of the Name:

The Ten *Sefirot* and י-ה-ו-ה

י	*Keter, Chochmah*
ה	*Binah*
ו	*Chessed, Din, Rachamim, Netzah, Hod, Yesod*
ה	*Shekhinah*

---

14. Kabbalists differ on how to understand the "ontological status" of the *sefirot*. Are the *sefirot* entities or beings that exist? Alternatively, are the *sefirot* rather to be understood as the ways in which God's essence manifests or expresses itself? In this book, we understand the *sefirot* as the *ways* in which the *ein sof* is expressed. To believe in the doctrine of *sefirot* is to believe that there are certain "structural patterns" which the world follows, and it is these structural patterns that we can know at least to some degree, and which describe the ways in which the essence of God is expressed in the universe. Using philosophical terms, this view of the *sefirot* is more "ontologically parsimonious" than the alternative view. It requires less postulation of entities in the universe. See note 10 above.

Note that the *last* letter of the Name corresponds to the *last* of the ten *sefirot*, and the *first* letter of the Name corresponds to the *first* two of the *sefirot*. The underlying idea is that the last letter represents the most *outward* or *lowest* level of God's expression in the world, whereas the first letter represents the *highest* level of God's expression. Since there are two *heh*s in God's Name, the Kabbalists refer to the last *heh* as the "lower *heh*" and the first *heh* as the "upper *heh*." At this stage, a very brief discussion of two *sefirot* will be helpful, in order to illustrate how the teaching of the *sefirot* allows us to depict God as a Person.

As noted, one of the *sefirot* is *chessed*. When we speak of *chessed* as an attribute of a human being, we have in mind the quality of generosity or benevolence, that is, *the sharing of undeserved good things*. Kabbalah teaches that one of the ways in which *ein sof* is manifest is through the *sefirah* of *chessed*. In other words, the universe is such that undeserved good things happen all the time. Crops grow, humans and animals are nourished, societies thrive, people live, love, reproduce, nurture the next generation, and so on. Indeed, the existence of human beings who are themselves generous or benevolent is itself a remarkable fact of our world. For the Kabbalist, this is not a cosmic accident, but rather a result of the fact that the *sefirah* of *chessed* is operative in the universe. The Kabbalist would say that the existence of our earth and solar system is an expression of the *ein sof* as it manifests itself through the *sefirah* of *chessed*. Thus, although the *ein sof*, or essence, of God is in and of itself inscrutable, one of the ways in which it is manifest is through the *sefirah* of *chessed*. Now, since *chessed*, or benevolence, is something that human persons engage in, we can, in virtue of the *sefirah* of *chessed*, refer to God as having this person-like quality. Of course, this does not mean that God is a person *just exactly as we are*. Rather it means that there is something true about God – indeed, something true about *ein sof* – which bears a resemblance to what people do when they act benevolently. While strictly speaking it is incorrect to say that God's essence is a person, there is a deep parallelism between the way God's essence is manifest and the benevolent activities of a human person.

Another *sefirah* is *binah*. In a human person, *binah* is the quality of *understanding* or *intelligence*. Again, this is one of the ways in which *ein sof* is manifest or expressed. The world that we live in exhibits *binah* in that the world has a structure, an organized plan. When we examine our world, we find that the world has a great deal of order. There are certain natural laws or at least regularities in nature which it is the aim of natural science to discover. The fact that the universe has this order is an expression of divine *binah*. But, Judaism teaches that not only does the world have a *natural order*; it also has a *providential order*. In other words, there is a cosmic process going on, such that things are happening in accordance with a divine plan, such that human history is heading toward some great end. It is also part of the order of things that human activity can help bring about (or delay) that great end. The nature of that end will be addressed later in the chapters on the upper *heh* and the *yod*. The point here is that there is an end toward which cosmic and especially human history is heading. For the Kabbalist, the order in the world is not a cosmic accident, but an expression of *binah*. More precisely stated, the order in the world is an expression of the *ein sof*, and we can speak about this order by using the term, *binah*. It is in virtue of the *sefirah* of *binah* that we can relate to God as an intelligent agent or a person, who communicates with people, and who guides the universe toward some great end.[15] On this approach, although strictly speaking it is incorrect to say that the infinite essence, or *atzmut ein sof*, is a being who has a mind like ours, the fact is that the universe is orderly, and there is a master-plan according to which the universe runs.

We have seen some sampling of how the doctrine of *sefirot* enables us to understand God as a person. A more thorough explanation will take place in the course of this book. At this stage, another point needs to be addressed. The Torah and especially Kabbalah speak not only as if God is a person but also as if God has *gender*. Often, God is referred to in masculine terms but occasionally in feminine terms. Evidently, God has masculine and feminine aspects. Of course, taken literally, this becomes problematic. For if God does not have bodily parts, how can he or she have a gender? We turn to this issue in the next section.

---

15. Intelligence alone is not a sufficient condition for personhood, nor is benevolence. Arguably, a machine could be both "intelligent" and "benevolent" but that would not make it a *person*. Toward the end of this book we shall discuss the *sefirah* of *keter*, which is related to the notion of will or choice. It is in virtue of this *sefirah* that God may be described as volitional. However, one cannot have volition without intelligence as well.

י-ה-ו-ה AND THE HUMAN BEING: MASCULINE AND FEMININE ASPECTS

THE TORAH (*GENESIS* 1:27) teaches that God "created the human being in his own image, masculine and feminine he created them." This indicates that God is in some way similar to the human being, or rather perhaps that the human being is in some special way a reflection of God, and that God has both masculine and feminine aspects. Kabbalah offers a detailed interpretation of what this means. We have already said that the *sefirot* are the general ways in which God's essence is expressed or made manifest. Kabbalah teaches that the ten *sefirot* are paralleled or mimicked by ten aspects of the human being.[16] Each of the ten *sefirot* corresponds to a certain specific part of the human being, as indicated by the diagram on the next page.

The basic idea is that the *sefirot* correspond to certain aspects of the human being. This is what the Torah means when it says that God created the human being "in the divine image" (*betzelem elokim*). In addition, Kabbalah teaches that in virtue of the *sefirot*, God has certain characteristics which are designated as masculine and others as feminine. This does not mean that God has a body or that God literally has male and female anatomy. Rather, there is a parallelism between certain ways in which God's essence is manifest in the world, and certain aspects of the human being, including the masculine and feminine aspects of the human. We shall find this theme recurring throughout this book. A brief discussion of this topic is in place here.

---

16. See the section from *Tikkunei Zohar* 17a known as *Patach Eliahu*. This is printed at the beginning of some *siddurim* (prayer books).

THE HUMAN BODY AND THE *SEFIROT*

Head: Will, Wisdom, Intelligence

Left Arm: Justice   **Right Arm:** Benevolence

Chest: Compassion

Left Thigh: Majesty   **Right Thigh:** Victory

Sexual Organ: Foundation

Feet: Presence

First, note that certain *sefirot* are on the right side, others are on the left, and still others are central. This positioning is not accidental. Kabbalah teaches that the *sefirot* on the right side designate aspects of God that are "positive" or "expansive" whereas the *sefirot* on the left side designate aspects of God that are "negative" or "restrictive." For example, God's benevolence is on the right side whereas God's justice is on the left side. There is a certain tension between the left side and the right side; they are in a sense opposites. The central *sefirot* represent a balance or harmony between the two sides. For example, as explained later in this book, compassion is regarded as a balance between benevolence and justice. Periodically, we shall return to this theme in the ensuing chapters.

The Name is made up of two *heh*s, a *vav* and a *yod*. Kabbalah teaches that the *heh*s in God's name represent feminine aspects, whereas the *vav* and *yod* represent masculine aspects. The feminine aspects have to do with *receptive aspects* of reality, and the masculine aspects have to do with *active aspects* of reality.[17] When we look around the world, we find certain features that are receptive, and certain features that are active. Using the approach adopted in this book, we may say that Being is manifest or expressed in certain ways that are receptive, and in certain other ways that are active. In one way or another, all things in this world are *receptive* in the sense that they are *affected by things that happen to them*. On the other hand, all things in the world have certain *active* properties in that *they can have effects on other things*. For example, the soil of the earth is receptive, in that it can take in seeds and water; but it also has an active aspect in that it brings forth grass and vegetation. Water has an active aspect in that it can serve as a catalyst to make things grow; but it also has a receptive aspect in that it can easily change composition depending on whether it is boiled or frozen.

In certain cases, the receptive nature of one being or thing may be more notable, especially when compared to another being or thing. In contrasting a woman with a man, a woman is in certain ways more of a receiver whereas a man is more of an actor. A woman is a creature who receives seed from a man, and in that sense a woman is a receiver whereas a man is an actor or an agent who gives the seed. It has also been said that women tend to be more psychologically "receptive" whereas men tend to be "active" or aggressive or "headstrong." Perhaps this is a stereotype; certainly there are aggressive women and receptive men. Nevertheless, Kabbalah uses the term "feminine" to designate those characteristics that are receptive, and "masculine" to designate those that are active.

The Kabbalistic teaching that the feminine aspects of the Name are symbolized by the two *heh*s and the masculine aspects are symbolized by the *vav* and the *yod* dovetails with certain features of Hebrew grammar. In Hebrew, the feminine ending for verbs and for indicating feminine possession for nouns is a *heh*. On the other hand, the ending for masculine third person singular is a *vav*, and the masculine indicator for future verbs is a *yod*. The Kabbalists take this a step further, by teaching that the very shape of the letters hints at these aspects.[18] The *heh* (ה) is

---

17. A similar notion is found in other traditions; for example, consider the Chinese concept of Yin and Yang.

18. The notion that the appearance and sound of the Hebrew letters correspond to aspects of divinity is expressed succinctly in *Tanya, Shaar Hayichud ve-ha'emunah,* chapter 12 in the *hagaah* (note).

an "open" letter, both on the bottom, and on the top. The openness of the letter symbolizes *receptive* features of reality. As we shall see later, the *two* openings of the *heh* – one on the bottom and one toward the top – symbolize two different kinds of receptivity, both of which apply to the human and to God. One is a more physical type of receptivity; the other is more of an intellectual or psychological type of receptivity. On the other hand, the *yod* (י) and the *vav* (ו) are not "open" letters. The *vav* may be looked at as an extended version of a *yod*. The *yod* represents the potential for action, and the *vav* represents the actualization of that potential. The *vav* is viewed as symbolic of a pipeline through which energy or activity is transmitted. The *vav* is not round or open, it is rather closed and focused, like a pencil or writing instrument. This symbolizes the active aspect of reality.[19]

We have seen that there are certain features or aspects of reality that are receptive and certain others that are active. A guiding notion of this book is that we may think of God's essence as Being itself. Now, the essence of God is neither masculine nor feminine; it transcends this distinction. Yet, insofar as God or Being is manifest in the world, there are certain aspects of reality as we know it that are masculine and certain that are feminine. To say that God has a "masculine" character is simply to say that certain aspects of being or reality are active and to say that God has a "feminine" character is to say that certain aspects of reality are receptive. Similarly, there are certain aspects of the human being that are receptive and others that are active. In the course of this book, we shall find that the Jewish spiritual path involves the cultivation of certain virtues that involve *receptivity*, and certain others that involve *activity*, and still certain other qualities that harmonize those two. Both receptive and active virtues are necessary for developing a rich and wholesome Jewish spiritual life. Both involve ways of "engaging" with God or Ultimate Being.

Another Kabbalistic teaching which plays a role in this book is that the human soul has five parts or aspects. Certain aspects of the soul are "lower" and certain aspects are "higher." Each part of the soul is associated with a certain sphere of human life. From lower to higher, the

---

19. The *vav* may be viewed as a phallic symbol. The *yod* represents the male organ in a state of dormancy, whereas the *vav* represents the male organ in a state of activity. Incidentally, whereas the *yod* and the *vav* are similar but different, the two *heh*s look identical. Although there are two kinds of receptivity, there isn't the same dynamic as we find in the transition from potential to actual, as represented by the difference between the *vav* and the *yod*.

five aspects are *nefesh, ruach, neshamah, chayah,* and *yechidah.* The five aspects of the soul correspond to the four letters of the Name and the ten *sefirot* in the following way:

י   *Keter: yechidah*
    Chochmah: chayah
ה   *Binah: neshamah*
ו   *Chessed, Din, Rachamim, Netzach, Hod, Yesod: ruach*
ה   *Shekhinah: nefesh*

Nefesh is the aspect of the soul that is most closely associated with the body, and it is sometimes referred to as "the animal soul." *Ruach* is associated with the spirit, that is, the emotional aspect of the human. It is also associated with the capacity for speech. *Neshamah* is associated with the mind, that is, the power of intelligence or understanding. *Chayah* is associated with the capacity for wisdom, and *yechidah* is associated with the will or capacity for choice. *Chayah* and *yechidah* are closely related; they are sometimes regarded as one. They are both associated with the *yod,* but *yechidah* is associated with the upper tip, or *kotz,* of the *yod,* which represents the fact that *yechidah* is the very highest aspect of the soul. It is also important to note that *nefesh* and *neshamah* have a feminine character; *ruach, chayah,* and *yechidah* have a masculine character. The significance of this doctrine for the Jewish spiritual path will emerge in the coming chapters.

THE JEWISH SPIRITUAL PATH:
THE WAY OF THE NAME

JUDAISM TEACHES THAT THE TORAH is God's revelation to mankind, particularly to the children of Israel, but with consequences for all humanity. The word *Torah* is often mistranslated as *Law*. Although the Torah includes a teaching about a system of law for the people of Israel, the term Torah itself does not mean *law* but rather *teaching*, or *way*. Thus, the Torah itself may be referred to as the *Derech Hashem*, or the Way of God. What then is the spiritual journey according to Judaism? Stated simply, the Jewish spiritual journey is nothing other than the path toward *devekut*, which means "bonding" with God.[20] Yet, if God is not a physical being, what can it mean to bond with God?

In this book, our approach is to understand God's essence as Being itself, and the *sefirot* as the ways in which Being is manifest. On this approach, the spiritual journey involves an ever increasing appreciation and sensitivity and knowledge of Being, together with the process of becoming more "in tune" with Being, by living in accord with the *sefirot* or divine ways. The journey is *practical*, in that it involves physical or bodily actions; it is *emotional*, in that it involves the cultivation of certain feelings or passions; it is *intellectual*, in that it involves understanding certain teachings about God and about the Way. It should be emphasized that the Jewish spiritual path involves the body just as much as it involves the soul. Toward the culmination of this book, we shall

---

20. A classic formulation of this notion is in Ramchal, *Mesilat Yesharim: Beveur Chovat Ha-adam Beolamo*. The notion that *devekut* is the goal of Torah is prominent in Chassidic literature. See *Netivot Shalom* Volume 1: Essay 5; Vol. 2, p. 14. Every *mitzvah* is another way of reaching *devekut* with God. We shall have more to say about *devekut* in the final chapter of this book.

find that the spiritual path also involves a level of the human being that transcends action, emotion, and the intellect.

Kabbalah describes the Jewish spiritual path as a growth or maturity from spiritual infancy to spiritual adulthood. There are certain character traits and modes of thinking which are infantile and certain others that are mature. Using Kabbalistic terms, the spiritual journey involves growing from *katnut* (childhood) to *gadlut* (adulthood). In general, we shall find that the move toward maturity involves a move away from a narrow focus on oneself, toward a more objective or universal perspective. The more one can step outside of oneself, so to speak, and see oneself as part of a greater whole, the more one has matured or grown along the Jewish spiritual path. Naturally, this process is related to an increasing awareness of God or Being itself. The more one becomes aware of Being itself, the more one realizes that particular things or beings – including oneself – are only part of a much greater whole.

Using more common traditional terms, the Jewish spiritual path involves the cultivation of certain *middot*. This term requires explanation. Again, the *sefirot* are the ways in which God's essence is manifest or expressed in the world. The *sefirot* refer to divine qualities. In both Kabbalistic and non-Kabbalistic Jewish literature the term *middot* (singular: *middah*) is often used to refer to the character traits of a human being. The Jewish spiritual path involves the cultivation of good *middot*, or virtues, and the avoidance of bad *middot*, or vices. The four-lettered Name serves as a "roadmap" for the spiritual path. The lowest stage of spiritual growth is symbolized by the *last* letter of the Name, and the highest stage is symbolized by the *first* letter of the Name. Each stage involves the cultivation of certain good *middot*, or virtues, that correspond to the divine *sefirot* associated with each of the four letters of God's Name. Hence, the Jewish spiritual path – and the subtitle of this book – is *The Way of the Name.*[21]

---

21. As mentioned earlier, *Derech Hashem* (usually translated *The Way of God*) is the name of a classic work by Ramchal. That book is mainly a theological work, but it also addresses the Jewish spiritual path, especially toward the end. Ramchal does not explicitly connect the title of his book to the four aspects of the Name as taught by Kabbalah. However, perhaps it is no accident that Ramchal divided his book into four parts, which may be seen as corresponding to the four letters of the Name. See below, Chapter 4, footnote 59.

THE FOUR-FOLD STRUCTURE
OF THE MORNING SERVICE
(*SHACHARIT*)

THE WAY OF THE NAME infuses all Jewish spiritual practice. However, there is a particularly strong connection between the Way of the Name and the Morning Service, or *Shacharit*.[22] Anyone who is familiar with *Shacharit* will probably know that it has four main parts, which are, the Morning Blessings (*Birchot Hashachar* and *Korbanot*), Verses of Praise (*Pesukei D'Zimrah*), the reading of the *Shema* and its Blessings (*Kriyat Shema u-virchoteha*), and the Standing Prayer (*Amidah*). What is less widely known is that Kabbalah teaches that these four parts of the *Shacharit* correspond to the four letters of the Name, in the following way:

י The Standing Prayer (*Amidah*)
ה Reading of the *Shema* and its Blessings (*Kriyat Shema u-virchoteha*)
ו Verses of Praise (*Pesukei D'Zimra*)
ה Morning Blessings and the Sacrifices (*Birchot Hashachar, Korbanot*)

The proper way to read the above chart is *from the bottom toward the top*. A person who goes through *Shacharit* starts at the lowest stage

---

22. See *Derech Hashem*, toward the end. Ramchal writes that *Shacharit* has four parts, and that there is a correspondence between the letters of the Name and the sections of the *Shacharit*. He also says that there are four *olamot*, or realms, and that they correspond to the parts of the prayer. He alludes to the notion of prayer as a ladder, with the *Amidah* as the highest point. The material after the *Amidah*, including *Tachanun, Ashrei, U-va Letzion,* and *Alenu,* are supplementary prayers and do not constitute an additional part. To some degree, they represent a descent from the ladder of the spiritual encounter, back to the reality of everyday life. We shall touch upon some aspects of these prayers in the final chapter of this book.

and works one's way up to the highest stage. Accordingly, the *Shacharit* has been called a "divine ladder" by which a person may ascend toward higher spiritual levels.[23] The ladder has four rungs; each rung is one stage of *Shacharit*. Indeed, we shall find that to some extent there is a progression within each stage as well.

In this book, we shall have much to say about both the structure and content of *Shacharit*. Our purpose is to illuminate how the Morning Service, in form, content, and style, helps us cultivate the *middot*. Here and there we will note certain halachic points about the liturgy that help us cultivate the *middot*. Many things that seem arbitrary about *Shacharit* take on deep significance if understood in light of the Way of the Name. Just to take one example, at certain places one is supposed to sit and at others, one is supposed to stand. Another example has to do with the frequency of certain words or terms in certain sections rather than others. For example, *kedushah* is mentioned in *Yishtabach* but not once in *Baruch She'amar*. Such matters will be explained in this book. If a person goes through *Shacharit* with an appreciation of the four-fold structure, and with an understanding of the *middot* that are related to each stage of the service, the *Shacharit* is transformed from a routine ritual into a powerful vehicle for spiritual growth.

A clarification is necessary. In saying that there is a correspondence between the four stages of *Shacharit* and the four levels of spiritual growth, we do not mean that each stage of *Shacharit* exclusively relates to *one level only*. Rather, each stage of *Shacharit focuses* on certain *middot* – but not to the utter exclusion of the other *middot*. (Recall the point made earlier regarding the *sefirot*. Each letter is associated with specific *sefirot*, but all of the *sefirot* are interconnected.) A related point is that a person who follows the Jewish spiritual path repeatedly goes through the four stages. There is a constant cycle of advance from lower to higher levels, then refinement of the lower levels, and then advance again. We shall revisit this theme toward the end of the book.

Each of the following chapters is devoted to one letter of the Name, starting with the last or "lowest" letter and advancing to the first or "highest" letter. Hence, the structure of this book itself mimics the pattern of the Name. Each chapter has three major goals: first, to explain the divine *sefirah* or *sefirot* associated with that letter; second, to explain

---

23. *Zohar* (1:149b) refers to prayer as a ladder. Maimonides (*Guide to the Perplexed* II:10) quotes a *midrash* which says that the ladder which Jacob saw in his dream (Genesis 28:12) had four rungs.

the corresponding *middot,* or virtues, associated with that letter; third, to explain how the relevant section of *Shacharit* helps cultivate those *middot.* To study and reflect on these matters is to study the Way of the Name. More importantly, to implement these lessons in one's life is to follow or walk along the Way of the Name.

ה

LOWER *HEH*

DIVINE PRESENCE (*SHEKHINAH*)

THE LAST LETTER OF THE NAME, or the "lower" *heh*, represents the *sefirah* of *Shekhinah*. *Shekhinah* stems from the Hebrew word *shakhen* which means dwell, reside, or be present. So, *Shekhinah* is often translated as the *indwelling* or *presence* of God.

One might tend to think of *Shekhinah* as an independent entity created by God. In that case, the *Shekhinah* is a spirit-like substance or entity that hovers in certain places and is perhaps visible on certain occasions. Such a view suggests that God and the divine presence are two separate things, and this implies a duality in God. Instead, here we follow our guiding notion that the essence of God, or *ein sof*, is Being itself, and the *sefirot* have to do with the ways in which Being is manifest or expressed. Still, if *Shekhinah* is not an entity, what does it mean to talk about the indwelling or presence of God?

Firstly, *Shekhinah* represents the sheer fact that *everything that exists is an expression or manifestation of Being*. As stated earlier, God's essence, or Being itself, is *ein sof*, or infinite. It can never be totally manifest. God's essence is *transcendent*, that is, above and beyond all description and definition, and therefore all expression. Nevertheless, it is an undeniable fact that everything that exists manifests or expresses Being in some way. Even the lowliest of things, such as earth, sand, rocks, toads, cockroaches, etc., exhibit or express Being. On this approach, to speak about *Shekhinah* is not to speak about some entity, but rather to speak about the fact that everything is an expression or manifestation of Being, from the tiny pebble to the brilliant blazing star, from the cockroach to the human being.

It follows that *Shekhinah* is related to the concept of *omnipresence*, or the notion that "God is everywhere." The notion of God's *omnipres-*

ence is related to the tremendous variety or plurality that we find in the world. Being is manifest in an infinite number of possible things and in an infinite number of ways. Occasionally, Kabbalists represent this notion by speaking of God's lowliness (*shiflut*) or humility (*anvatanut*). God is depicted as "lowering" himself to be present in all things. We may understand this "lowering" as a metaphorical way of speaking about the fact that Being is expressed even in such things as cockroaches, vermin, lice, etc. It is true that there is more beauty, power, intelligence, and grace expressed in some creatures than in others. Certain creatures (such as a thoroughbred horse or a great whale) exhibit great physical strength or speed, other creatures (such as a seahorse or a butterfly) exhibit finesse and delicacy, and some creatures seem to exhibit no great esthetic qualities at all (such as lice or vermin – yet surely, even these have some remarkable features as well). As mentioned above, there is something special about the way in which Being is manifest in the human being. However, in some respect, all creatures exhibit *Shekhinah* equally, for they are all manifestations or expressions of Being.

Shekhinah represents the most obvious or "outward" (*chitzoni*) aspect of God or Being itself. It is in virtue of this aspect that God is "available" or *immanent* (as opposed to *transcendent*). *Shekhinah* is always with us, wherever we are, wherever we go. More than that: Judaism teaches that God is in some way *influenced* by what we do. (Perhaps God is influenced only because He *chooses* to be influenced; but He is influenced nonetheless.) In this way, God is characterized as *receptive*; this is, so to speak, the "feminine" side of God. For example, the Talmud says that when the people of Israel go into exile, the *Shekhinah* goes with them; indeed, when the people of Israel suffer, the *Shekhinah* suffers.[1] Even in the depths of sorrow and trouble, and even in the depths of sin, God is still available and in some sense approachable. This too is associated with *Shekhinah*. God is always approachable only because God is always everywhere.

Receptivity is a feature of reality that is found throughout the natural world. Indeed, almost anything in the natural world can be acted upon. There is a kind of *pliancy* and indeed, *vulnerability* in nature. Yet, some things seem more pliant and vulnerable than others. The earth is receptive in that it receives seeds and rain. Craters and vessels are receptive. Clay, wood, and even stone can be carved, but clay and wood are more

---

1. On the idea that God goes into exile with Israel, See Genesis 46:1-4; *Tractate Megillah 29a*. On the idea that God suffers with Israel, see Psalms 91:15; *Mishnah Sanhedrin 6:5*; *Yalkut Kurdistan* quoted in *Torah Shelemah*, on Exodus 1:10, no. 99.

pliant than stone or steel. Women are biologically receptive in that they receive seed from men. Even the fact that a woman can carry a child is a sign of her receptivity. In any case, the pliancy of things is another way of talking about *Shekhinah*. It is a plain fact that this is a feature of reality.

Kabbalah explains that it is partly for this reason that *Shekhinah* is symbolized by the letter ה, which is an "open" letter. Again, the ה is open on the bottom and also open on the top. For the Kabbalist, the openness of the letter *heh* symbolizes the receptive nature of reality, which is associated with *Shekhinah*. [2]

The opposite of softness or receptivity is rigidity and activity, which are associated in Kabbalah with the next letter in the divine name, the *vav*. While the *heh* represents the receptivity of a blank tablet or empty parchment, the vav represents the instrument or stylus that does the carving or writing. Again, whereas the *heh* is a feminine letter, the *vav* is masculine. This relates back to the points made earlier (in the Introduction) regarding Hebrew grammar. The *heh* is a feminine ending whereas the *vav* is a masculine ending. Due to the feminine nature of this *sefirah*, Kabbalists occasionally refer to *Shekhinah* as "daughter" or sometimes "wife."

Another concept associated with *Shekhinah* is *malchut,* or kingship. The lowest *sefirah* is called *malchut* or Kingship because it represents the fact that God is *involved* with the mundane affairs of the world.[3] While the creative, intellectual, and moral character traits of God are associated with higher *sefirot*, it is the *sefirah* of *malchut* that represents God's involvement, so to speak, in every corner of the physical world. If not for that involvement, none of the higher aspects of the divine would be present or effective at all. Hence, this lower *sefirah* is designated as *malchut,* or Kingship. Combining the notion of Kingship with the feminine aspect of this *sefirah*, the Kabbalists occasionally refer to *Shekhinah* as Queen or Matron.

---

2. God's compassion, or *rachamim*, is indicative of a higher *middah* that we shall discuss in the next chapter. The point here is that in order to be compassionate, God must be present and receptive. The same thing is true in the case of the human being. In order to be compassionate, one must be present and receptive.

3. See Ramchal's comments on *malchut* in *Derech Hashem* 4:4:2. In fact, there are different aspects of God's kingship; some are loftier than others. We shall find that some aspect of *malchut*, or kingship, is relevant to each of the four letters of the divine name. The highest *sefirah* is *keter* which means Crown, and that too is associated with the notion of royalty. The paradoxical nature of *malchut* (as both the lowest and in some sense the highest aspect of God) is a major theme in much Kabbalistic literature. See below, Chapter 3, note 9.

In a sense, *Shekhinah* is the most fundamental *sefirah*. Although there are loftier *sefirot*, such as will, wisdom, benevolence, justice, etc. – and there are good reasons for why they are considered lofty – there is something so basic about *Shekhinah* that, in a certain respect, it is the most important *sefirah* of all. An analogy may help explain this point. Suppose a composer produces a great work of music. In his music, the artist displays many of his talents, such as, creativity, intelligence, sensitivity, passion, orchestral ability, etc. However, the most basic thing which the artist displays is his *ability to express himself at all*. If he could not express himself, then he surely could not display any of those qualities just mentioned. Similarly, *Shekhinah* represents the very fact that God, or Being, is manifest or expressed in beings and things. The other *sefirot* have to do with the *particular ways* in which Being is expressed, such as, the orderliness and beauty in the world. Yet, without that very manifestation itself, nothing would be exhibited at all. The Kabbalists occasionally express this point by saying that all of the higher *sefirot* "act through" the lower *sefirah* of *malchut*.

As mentioned, Kabbalah teaches that the various *sefirot* correspond to various elements of the human body. Occasionally, the Kabbalists say that *Shekhinah* corresponds to the female sexual cavity. This brings to mind the notions of receptivity and vulnerability discussed above. Occasionally, the Kabbalists will say that *Shekhinah* corresponds to the feet. Feet are where a human being touches the ground. The feet are in some sense the lowest and least important part of the human, yet without feet we cannot stand; the entire body rests on the feet. Furthermore, it is with our feet that we move from place to place, and that we can be present in one place and then another. Thus, Kabbalah uses the expression "God's feet" to refer metaphorically to *Shekhinah,* or divine presence.

Earlier we alluded to the Kabbalistic teaching that certain names of God are associated with specific divine attributes or aspects. The name associated specifically with the lower *heh* or *Shekhinah* is *Adonai.* The term *Adonai* comes from *Adon* which means Lord or Master, but it also calls to mind the word *aden* which means a socket or a receptacle. This term occurs in Scripture where the description of the *mishkan,* or tabernacle, occurs. The *mishkan* is God's dwelling place. The *adanim* are the sockets into which the beams were inserted that formed the walls of the *mishkan,* or tabernacle. Normally, one doesn't think of sockets as the most important part of a building. But, the truth is that without the sockets, the walls cannot stand, and without the walls, there is no building. What the sockets, or *adanim,* are to the tabernacle, the *Shekhinah* is to the other divine attributes. Hence the name *Adonai* is associated with *Shekhinah*.

Like God, the human being has certain lofty aspects and certain less lofty aspects. Our creative and cognitive abilities and our emotional character traits are loftier or more "inner" (*pnimi*) than our gross physical abilities or powers. Thus, the Kabbalists speak of different aspects of the human soul. The more elevated aspects of God correspond to the higher aspects of the soul. The lowest part of the soul is the *nefesh*, and it corresponds to *Shekhinah*. In Scripture, *nefesh* is associated closely with *dam*, or blood.[4] The blood courses through the veins, delivering sustenance to the body. This aspect of the human soul is most like the soul one would find in an animal. In Scripture, animals also have a *nefesh*. So, in some way this is our least important aspect. Yet, as the Sages teach, *im ein kemach ein torah*; if there is no flour (for bread), there is no Torah.[5] In other words, if we did not have the ability to move, eat, drink, digest, etc., we would be dead, and what good would our intelligence and grace be then? If our body is not functioning, none of our other more elevated qualities can be expressed. Hence, just as the *adanim* are the most basic part of the *mishkan*, so too the *nefesh* is the most basic aspect of the soul.

As everything in the world is an expression of Being, it follows that colors too are expressions of being. Hence, Kabbalah teaches that different colors reflect or symbolize different aspects of Being. Consequently, different colors correspond to different *sefirot*, and to different letters of God's Name. The lower *heh* may be represented by the color red. Red (*adom*) is the color of blood (*dam*) and the color of the earth or soil (*adamah*). The Torah says that man's body was created from the clay or soil, and that is why the human being is called *Adam* (earthling). In its original meaning, the term *adam* connotes the physical matter from which the human being is made. Thus, the color red is associated with the earthly nature of the human, and thereby with the lower *heh*.[6]

In summary, so far, to speak of *Shekhinah* is to acknowledge that everything that exists is an expression of Being itself, and that reality

---

4. See Deuteronomy 12:23.

5. *Mishnah Avot* 3:17.

6. In Kabbalah, the correspondence between colors and *sefirot* is not rigid or fixed. See Ramak, *Pardes Rimonim*, chapter 10. In different contexts, the same color may represent one *sefirah* one way, yet in another way represent a different *sefirah*. For example, red is associated with *malchut* but it is also associated with *gevurah*. Sometimes, white is associated with *malchut*, and sometimes with *keter*. Something similar is true of divine names. The same divine name may refer to one *sefirah* in one context, and a different *sefirah* in another context.

has a receptive and pliant quality. From this perspective, the belief in *Shekhinah* is rationally based on ordinary experience. One does not need to rely on revelation or on the *mesorah* (tradition) to realize that reality has this character. However, as we shall see later, reliance on the *mesorah* is required when it comes to more specific teachings about the manner in which Being is manifest or expressed in the world. We turn next to the *middot*, or virtues, that are associated with the first level of the spiritual journey.

RECEPTIVITY (*KABBALAH*)

THE SPIRITUAL JOURNEY INVOLVES a deepening of one's relationship with God. There are simple and basic ways of relating to God, and then, there are more complex and advanced ways of doing so. The first and lowest stage of the spiritual journey corresponds to the lower *heh*. We have seen that the lower *heh* is associated with the receptive aspect that we find in reality. Similarly, the first stage of the spiritual journey begins with the *middah* of receptivity, that is, *an acknowledgement and acceptance of certain very basic facts about reality, and in particular, about oneself.* A receptive person is someone who takes things in, who absorbs things, who acknowledges that which is given to her. A receptive person is sensitive and mindful; she takes stock, so to speak, of who she is, what she is, and what are the conditions of her immediate circumstances. These include but are not limited to certain basic facts about oneself, such as, that one is a bodily creature with a psyche or consciousness of some sort; that one lives and breathes, eats and drinks, ingests and excretes; that one experiences pleasure and pain; that one sees, hears, walks, talks, etc. A receptive person takes note of these things and pays attention to them.

In Hebrew, the term for receiving or reception is *kabbalah*. Perhaps it is no accident that this term is also one of the names for the Jewish tradition, which is "received" by each generation from its predecessors. Although it has become common to use the term Kabbalah to refer specifically to the esoteric or hidden teachings within the Jewish tradition, the fact is that in rabbinic literature the term is used to refer to the Jewish tradition as a whole. It is easy to see that receptivity is a basic *middah*, and that it corresponds to the lower *heh*. Receptivity is a kind of *openness*. In order to grow spiritually, one has to be *open*; one has to

47

pay attention and *accept* certain basic and obvious facts about oneself. This is the feminine *middah* of receptivity, or *kabbalah*, and, this is the beginning of the spiritual journey.

Now, immediately a question could be raised, for it seems that *naturally* we are receivers. By nature, I am a creature who takes in all sorts of things. Physically, I eat and drink. I am a creature that *takes in* or experiences sights, sounds, tastes, smells, textures; I experience pleasure and I can suffer pain. Precisely because I am a bodily creature, I undergo things that happen to me. What then is meant by the *virtue* of receptivity? If we have it naturally, how can it be a *middah*, or a virtue?

Our question leads us to a better understanding of receptivity *as a virtue*. There is a difference between *receptivity* and *passivity*. Consider the situation of an infant. An infant is a rather passive creature. Yet the infant is in some sense radically *unaware* of his status as passive. Hence, while he is *passive*, he is not genuinely *receptive*. To be receptive, a person must be *aware* of himself as a receiver. Differently stated, a person becomes a receiver only once he recognizes himself as a receiver. This means not only recognizing but accepting, acknowledging, and also *receiving* one's own receptivity (!). It involves *embracing* this aspect of our nature with all of its implications. If I do not recognize myself as a receiver, then, while I may indeed *undergo* pleasures and other experiences, I cannot genuinely *receive* them.

Hence, it is entirely possible and in a way rather tempting to pretend that one is *not* a receiver. It is tempting to pretend one is not a receiver, for as we shall see soon, the fact that we are receivers is connected with the fact that we are dependent and fragile; sometimes, it is hard to admit that one is dependent and fragile. Whether we like it or not, the fact that we are receivers is a crucial aspect of our nature as beings in this world. One who has not faced and acknowledged this fact has not even reached first base, so to speak, on the spiritual journey.

We have noticed that there is something reflexive about receptivity, for it involves a *turning in* on oneself, a reception of our own receptivity. A related point is that receptivity involves taking an *objective standpoint* with respect to oneself. In order to recognize that one is a receiver, a person has to be able to "step outside of oneself" and see that he or she is a part of a greater whole. The infant cannot cultivate receptivity precisely because he is not yet able to make a conscious distinction between himself and the outside world. As a person grows, he becomes more able to see how he relates to that which is external to oneself. Kabbalists might describe this as an advance from *katnut* to *gadlut*. Indeed, as we shall see in the course of this book, spiritual growth generally involves some *advance in objectivity*, that is, some advance in realizing that one is part of a greater world *outside* of oneself.

It turns out, then, that receptivity involves some *action* or *activity* on one's part. The action in question is the action of *receiving*. It is not a completely passive *middah* – indeed, no *middah* is completely passive. Nevertheless, Kabbalah characterizes receptivity as a "feminine" *middah*, because it focuses more on *taking something in* rather than on *giving something out*. As we go forward in this book, we shall find that, relatively speaking, certain *middot* involve more *receptivity* and certain other *middot* involve more *activity*. Still, receptivity itself is the quintessential feminine *middah*. And, in a way, all of the other *middot* are built upon receptivity as a foundation.

One of the issues to be explored in this book is to what extent the Jewish spiritual path requires belief in specific Jewish doctrines, such as the belief in divine providence or the belief in the divine revelation of the Torah. It seems that receptivity is a *middah* that does *not* depend on any special Jewish doctrines. One does not need to believe in divine providence or revelation to realize that receptivity is a quality that is worth cultivating. Even an agnostic (someone who does not believe in God or doubts the reality of God) can cultivate receptivity. Nevertheless, we shall see later that this receptivity of basic things about oneself is the first step toward a more advanced kind of receptivity associated with the upper *heh*. The advanced kind of receptivity *does* involve an acknowledgement of divine providence and divine revelation. Hence, we shall find that it is not possible for an agnostic to cultivate the receptivity associated with the upper *heh* – unless, of course, he gives up his agnosticism.

In sum, receptivity involves taking stock of certain very obvious and basic things about oneself and one's immediate surroundings. These things are so obvious that we tend to take them for granted, but they are really quite astonishing. As we shall see later, much of Jewish liturgy especially in the first stage of *Shacharit* is designed to train ourselves to focus attention on certain facts about ourselves. When we take stock of these facts, we are naturally lead to two further character traits, or *middot*, namely, gratitude (*hoda'ah*) and humility (*anavah*). We now turn our attention to these *middot*.

GRATITUDE (*HODA'AH*)

WHEN I TAKE STOCK OF MYSELF, the most basic thing that I realize about myself is that I am, I exist. But, not only do I *exist*, I also *live*, as a human animal. Kabbalistically speaking, I am aware of myself as having a *nefesh*. I can breathe. My body functions. I can open my eyes and see. I can get up, I can sit down. I can move my limbs, I can walk, I can talk, I can put on clothes, I can tie my shoes, and so forth. In other words, when I take stock of myself I realize that I have certain *gifts* or good things, and this includes not only my body, but also such necessities as food, water, air, clothes, and so on. After *receiving* these things, the next step is to *appreciate* them. In Hebrew this is called *hakarat ha-tov*, or recognition of the good. The phrase *hakarat ha-tov*, or *recognition of the good,* has a fruitful ambiguity. It can mean recognition of the goodness *in particular things or states of affairs*, such as, the fact that I can see or hear. However, it can also mean recognition of *the good* or *goodness itself.* As we shall see later, the recognition of the goodness of particular things is a stepping-stone toward the recognition of that which is truly good, namely, God.[7]

Let us take this point one step further. It is not only the case that I have certain things that are basic such as the body, air, water, etc. I also find within the world certain *esthetic* qualities. For example, it is not only the case that the sun which is necessary for my existence comes up every day, but that the sunrise is awesome and on occasion, beautiful. Not only do I have food to eat, but there is an incredible variety of foods and drinks, and food can be quite tasty and delicious. Not only can I see to get around and fend for myself, but I see a world in which there are colors

---

7. This is a major theme in *Chovot Halevavot: Shaar Habechinah*.

and natural beauty. Not only do trees exist so I can use them for wood, but trees are beautiful. Not only can I hear what's going on around me so I can pursue my needs, but I can hear beautiful sounds and find music pleasing. Humor too is something that should not be taken for granted. While laughing and joking surely must have some survival value, the degree to which humans are capable of laughing and having an all-around good time seems to go well beyond what is necessary for subsistence or survival of the species. In other words, the world in which I find myself in is not merely one where I can subsist. It is also esthetically pleasing.

Moreover, the human body itself has a certain beauty to it. Of course, some humans are more exquisitely beautiful than others, just as some food and drink are tastier than others. Some sunrises are not so beautiful because it's cloudy. Some landscapes are not beautiful but rather ugly.[8] The relevant point is that the esthetic quality of our world is a dimension that we can receive, take note of, and appreciate. One should also take note of the fact that there are indeed many pleasures in life that are unnecessary for our survival. Just for example, sexual pleasure seems unnecessarily intense, beyond what is necessary for survival. One could have easily imagined that the reproduction of the species could take place without such intense pleasure. The fact that there are such intense pleasures in life is something one should take note of and appreciate.

We should note the dependence of *appreciativeness* on *receptivity*. It is only if I acknowledge myself as a receiver that I will not take things for granted. If I somehow avoid recognizing that I am a receiver, or if I delude myself into thinking I am not a receiver, I will think of everything I have as somehow automatically *mine* and I will not be appreciative. If I am not receptive, I can *undergo* pleasures or good experiences, but I will not be *reflective* about the fact that I have these good experiences, and so, I will not be appreciative.

Often we take the most basic things about ourselves for granted. But we should not do so. We should be amazed every time we wake up in the morning and reacquaint ourselves with who we are, and what we have. It is all too easy to fall into the habit of taking for granted our most basic yet most amazing bodily functions. That is why we need continually to renew our recognition of them. Unfortunately, sometimes it takes an illness to remind ourselves of how fortunate we are to have our health and

---

8. It is not our aim here to try to *define* what makes something esthetically pleasing or beautiful. Whether or not one could provide such a definition, the fact is that humans experience things as esthetically pleasing or enjoyable. It is therefore something to receive and appreciate.

our normal bodily functions. The fact is we get used to our natural gifts, and they cease to amaze us. At the very least, if we are not *amazed*, we should be *appreciative*. To be appreciative, we need to remind ourselves, and to receive them on a daily basis.

The sense of appreciativeness is one of the keys to happiness in one's life. If a child is taught from the earliest age to be appreciative of the "small" things, he will not be unhappy if he lacks luxuries, and he will not be "spoiled" if he has luxuries. Here is something odd about us: Most people would be elated if they woke up one morning to find that they had won the lottery and were to receive a million dollars. But, what good would winning the lottery be, if one could not breathe, eat, see, hear, smell, taste, touch, etc.? In truth, each day a person wakes up and just recognizes these "small" things, he ought to be even more elated than if he woke up to find that he had won the lottery! But we don't operate that way, because we fall into the habit of taking the "small" things for granted. Luckily, there is a cure for this: meditation and reflection and verbal acknowledgement of the "small" things – which reminds us they are not small after all! This is one of the main functions of the first stage of *Shacharit*, to which we shall turn later in this chapter.

So far, we have discussed appreciativeness for good things. Judaism teaches that the good things we have are not the result of any cosmic accident or blind mechanical forces of nature, but rather they are part of the providential design of the universe. Using *pashut*, or common, religious language to express this teaching, we would say there exists a God or a Supreme Being who intentionally causes us to have these gifts. We would add that it is not sufficient to appreciate the good things themselves; we should also appreciate that God is the cause of these gifts.[9] Once again, in this book we are not thinking of God as *a being*; rather we are thinking of God as *Being itself*. Instead of saying that God is an entity who causes good things, we may say that God or Being is manifest in just such a way that good things happen, and that creatures such as humans exist, who have the gifts described above. Differently stated, God is the "causal ground" of all things, including our natural gifts or abilities to live, breathe, walk, talk, and so on. Hence, it is not

---

9. On the *pashut* view, an epistemic gap must be faced. Namely, how do we know that there is a being, separate and apart from the good things, which is the cause of those things? Perhaps there is a good answer to this question. However, on the approach followed in this book, there is no gap at all. It is a plain fact that Being is manifest in just such a way that we experience good things. The issue that remains is whether this is happening intentionally or accidentally.

sufficient to appreciate these good things themselves; we should also appreciate the fact that God or Being is the causal ground of our gifts. The appreciation of one's natural gifts constitutes the first stage of an appreciation of God or Being itself, which will be developed more fully in the ensuing stages of the spiritual journey.

Going further still, Judaism teaches that one should not only *appreciate* one's gifts but also *verbally express* that appreciation. It is one thing to appreciate something or someone; it is another thing to verbalize that appreciation. Why is it so important to express it in words? One reason is that if we are not in the habit of expressing it, we inevitably lose our sense of appreciation for it. Another reason is that until and unless we express our appreciation in words, *there is something missing in the appreciation itself.* Any time we put our feelings or thoughts into words, they are stronger and more concrete. Finally, and most importantly, according to Jewish tradition, the expression of appreciation in words brings us closer to a good relationship with God. Since God is providential, and interactive with what goes on in the world, God responds not only to what we *do,* but also towhat we *say.* God reciprocates our effort to recognize Him as the source of all. In other words, Judaism teaches that the universe is constructed in just such a way that when we verbally express appreciation for our gifts, and for God as the source of our gifts – this has the effect of leading to even greater good in the future. In Jewish liturgy, this is one function of saying a blessing, or *brachah.* We shall return to this point later.

Moving beyond *appreciativeness,* a further step is the cultivation of *gratitude* or *thankfulness.* Gratitude involves a disposition to express not just appreciation but thanks, that is, an expression of appreciation that is *directed to the giver of some good.* One reason why it is important to express thanks is that if we don't get into the habit of saying thanks, we inevitably come to take those gifts for granted. Another reason is that if we receive a gift, we owe some kind of debt to the giver, and we discharge that debt by giving thanks. The giving of thanks is like a verbal token of payment for the gift. In Hebrew, the word for thanksgiving is *hoda'ah.* It is no accident that this word also means *consent* or *admission.* In the Talmud, the term is often used in the context of consent or admission to a debt.[10] The act of thanksgiving is in some way an attempt to acknowledge a debt. In this regard, the English expression "giving thanks" is instructive. The same thing is true in Hebrew. For example, we speak of *latet shevach vehodayah* (to give praise and thanks) to God. Why do we

---

10. See *Mishnah Shavuot* 6:1.

speak of *giving* thanks rather than *saying* thanks? After all, what really are we "giving" when we give thanks? The answer is that *giving thanks* is in a way an attempt to give something back – it is an attempt to repay a debt of sorts. We shall return to this point in the next chapter.

Our discussion helps to sharpen the difference between saying a blessing (*brachah*) and giving thanks (*hoda'ah*). These two things are commonly confused, but they are not identical. A *brachah* is an expression of recognition that God or Being is the source of something.[11] A *hoda'ah* goes a step further; it is an expression of thanks for something good. A *brachah* is in a sense more basic than a thanksgiving. One can't thank a person until and unless one first recognizes that he or she is the cause or source of some good. Thus, a *brachah* is more primary than a *hoda'ah*.

Appreciation and gratitude are not merely intellectual or cognitive virtues; they also involve an affective or emotional dimension. A person who recognizes her gifts should be happy or at least pleased in some way, and her expression of gratitude should be done with a certain amount of enthusiasm. However, a polite "thank you" can be executed without an excessive amount of enthusiasm. As long as one says "thank you," one has done the deed, even if it is done somewhat grudgingly. We shall see later that the cultivation of enthusiasm is more pertinent to the second stage of the spiritual journey.

Before leaving this section, let us consider whether the *middot* we have discussed can be plausibly cultivated by someone who does *not* believe in divine providence. Our aim in doing this is to see just how far one can go on the Jewish spiritual path without accepting or believing specific doctrines taught by Judaism.

First let us consider whether appreciativeness, or *hakarat ha-tov*, requires belief in divine providence. As we found in the case of receptivity, it seems that *hakarat ha-tov* does *not* require belief in traditional Jewish doctrines. If a person has cultivated receptivity, he can also cultivate *hakarat ha-tov*. An agnostic believes or suspects that the good things which he has are a result of some cosmic accident or the result of blind

---

11. One must also recognize that something bad or painful comes from God. This is the idea behind the Jewish teaching that "a person is obligated to bless on the bad, just as one blesses on the good." *Tractate Brachot* 54a. Thus, there is a blessing to be said upon hearing of the death of a close relative (*baruch dayan emet*). It does not make sense to *thank* God for bad things, and Judaism does not expect that we do this. But it does make sense to recognize that ultimately everything comes from God, including even bad things. This point underscores the difference between a *brachah* and a *hoda'ah*.

forces of nature that so happened to result in his having the good fortune to breathe, see, eat, think, etc. But still, surely he can *appreciate* these things. Perhaps he can one go step further. He can realize that the world is structured in just such a way that he is the recipient of good things. There is, in effect, at least a "natural providence" at work in the world, even if it is the result of blind forces or cosmic accident. And, if the agnostic can be appreciative, he can also cultivate the practice of *expressing* this appreciativeness in words or symbols.

However, the matter is different with respect to the *middah* of gratitude or thankfulness regarding one's natural gifts. Gratitude involves a disposition to express appreciation that is directed *to the giver*. It involves the acknowledgement of a debt that the recipient in some way owes the giver. Gratitude for our natural gifts makes sense only if one believes in God and divine providence. It makes sense only if one believes that one's natural gifts are provided *intentionally* by God, and only if "God listens" or hears our thanks. If God were the cause of the good, but did so by necessity or without intention, then God does not deserve our thanks. Alternatively, if God is deaf to our thanks, or hears but doesn't care whatsoever, there seems to be no reason to give thanks. Hence, gratitude for our natural gifts makes sense as a virtue only if one believes in God and in divine providence.

So far we have discussed the *middot* of receptivity and gratitude. We turn next to the final *middah* associated with the first stage of the spiritual journey, that of humility, or *anavah*.

HUMILITY (*ANAVAH*)

RECEPTIVITY TO ONE'S GIFTS is a double-edged sword in the following way. Suppose I recognize that I have the gift of sight, the gift of breathing, the gift of the functioning of my physical body. Suppose I marvel at the digestive system and the respiratory system and all the other marvelous workings of my body. At the same time, I must inevitably recognize how dependent I am on sight, breathing, and the functioning of the body, and how easily things could go wrong. What would happen if I could *not* see? What would happen if I could *not* breathe or my body did *not* function? Indeed there are literally billions of discrete events going on in my body that allow me to function and live. Yet, any one of those billions of things could easily malfunction! So, in taking stock of the self, one notices not only all the wondrous things about oneself, but also how dependent, indeed, how fragile, one is. Certainly, a receptive person recognizes not only how much he has to be thankful for, but also that he is limited, dependent, and subject to biological death.

The recognition of one's limitations is humility, or *anavah*. Humility is sometimes confused with the vice of *low self-esteem*. Proper self-esteem is a *recognition of one's genuine worth*; humility is a *recognition of one's genuine limitations*. These are not incompatible at all. Just because one has limitations (and obviously we all do) does not mean one has little or no genuine worth. Just because one has limitations or failings does not mean one should exaggerate them to the point of thinking or feeling that one has no good qualities at all, or that one is worthless. Moreover, we should not confuse humility with *modesty*, the latter having to to do with how one portrays oneself to others and how one speaks about one's gifts, accomplishments or worth. An immodest person is someone who flaunts the gifts that they actually have. There is a difference between recognizing one's gifts, which is a good thing, and flaunting them, which is bad. Thus, a person could be genuinely humble and still immodest in that he or she flaunts the virtues or good qualities which he actually happens to have. Conversely, a person could be modest in not flaunting his virtues to others, yet also lacking in humility insofar as he does not recognize his own limitations. Humility is a much deeper virtue than modesty.

Let us note once again the dependence of humility on receptivity. It is only if I acknowledge myself as a receiver that I can be humble. In fact, to be a receiver is to be *dependent*. Indeed, I can see, walk, talk, move, eat, drink, etc. Indeed, I have bodily functions that are remarkable. But I don't "own" any of these things in any permanent way. Any of these privileges can be taken away from me and if so, I will be at a loss. Life itself, my life, and my existence as I know it is rather tenuous. But I will come to grips with all of these things only if I am receptive. If I deceive myself into thinking that I am not a receiver, I will fail to cultivate humility.

Humility is a genuine recognition of and "facing up to" one's limitations. Humility is not merely paying lip service to the fact of one's limitations; it involves an affective aspect as well. Just as gratitude ideally involves some level of positive enthusiasm, humility involves more sober emotions. In fact, humility as we have defined it is linked with fear. If I face up to my limitations and realize how tenuous my existence is, I am naturally inclined to some measure of fear – that is, fear that my body could stop functioning, or that the conditions which enable my life to continue could easily stop. In short, humility is connected to fear of death.

In connection with receptivity, earlier we spoke of the notion of *openness*. Humility and openness have an obvious connection. If a person is humble, he is more likely to be open, in the sense of being receptive to criticism and to change. There is something arrogant about being closed-minded. A closed-minded person might be polite, but there will be inevitably something smug about such a person. Similarly, appreciativeness is connected with humility. If I appreciate what I have then I will be more likely to be humble. And, if I am humble, I am more likely to be appreciative. In this way, all of the *middot* associated with the lower *heh* are interconnected.

A general point about these *middot* (indeed, all *middot*) is that they are matters of degree. A person can be somewhat receptive, very receptive, and even still more receptive. The same applies to humility and gratitude. One can also grow in having a greater degree of these *middot* over time. Another point is that one might be receptive to, or thankful for, or humble about certain things in one's life but not others. One may turn a blind eye to certain things in one's life yet not to others. Perhaps there is always room for improvement. As one grows in the spiritual journey, one becomes more receptive, more thankful, and more humble.

Earlier we discussed whether a person might cultivate receptivity, appreciativeness, or gratitude without believing in divine providence or any other special doctrines of Judaism. Here let us consider whether a person who does not believe in divine providence can cultivate humility. It seems that one certainly may, and indeed, one *ought* to, cultivate humility *independently* of any belief in divine providence. Even the agnostic can recognize his dependency, his finitude, his limitations, and his puniness in the face of the universe. This kind of humility is appropriate, regardless of one's beliefs about divine providence or revelation.[12]

We can easily see how the *middah* of humility relates to the concept of *Shekhinah*. Earlier we discussed the concept of *shiflut* with regard to God. In Kabbalistic literature God is described as lowering himself to be expressed in physical things that are limited and mortal. We understood this to mean that Being itself is present or manifest even in the simple and "lowly" things of this world, including those things that are weak and dependent. Similarly, a person who cultivates humility recognizes and accepts the dependent nature of the self. It is through the *middah* of humility that one meets the *Shekhinah*.

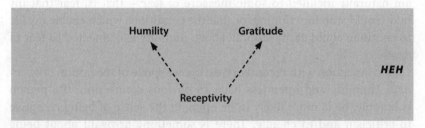

Earlier we noted that Kabbalah teaches that certain *sefirot* are on the right side while others are on the left side and still others are central. We can make a similar distinction for the *middot*. Gratitude is a "right side" virtue; humility is a "left side" virtue, and receptivity is a "central" virtue. Gratitude involves recognition of our gifts or blessings; it is something to be happy about. On the other hand, humility involves recognition of our flaws and limitations; its mood is solemn. Receptivity is in the

---

12. Later, in the chapter on the *yod*, we shall find that there is a more advanced type of humility that presupposes more developed beliefs about God. That higher kind of humility is not feasible for the agnostic.

middle; it is happy in one way and solemn in another way. I am happy about being a receiver, but it is also a solemn thing to realize that I am a receiver. Hence, receptivity is a "central" *middah*. Another reason it is central is that receptivity is the foundation and root of the other two *middot*. The chart below represents the relationship of these *middot*.

This concludes our discussion of the *middot* associated with the lower *heh*. In the next section, we shall see how the first stage of *Shacharit* helps us to cultivate these *middot*.

THE FIRST STAGE OF *SHACHARIT:* MORNING BLESSINGS AND THE SACRIFICES

KABBALAH TEACHES that *Shacharit* has four major stages, which correspond to the four-lettered name of God.[13] The first stage is made up of *Birchot Hashachar* and *Korbanot;* that is, the Morning Blessings and the recitation of the Scriptural passages that describe the Sacrifices. In this section, we shall see how the first stage corresponds to the lower *heh.* We shall also find that the theme of a four-fold structure recurs as a motif even *within* the first stage of *Shacharit.* This reinforces the significance of the four-fold pattern as the key to unlocking the secrets of the Jewish spiritual path.

The central purpose of the first stage of *Shacharit* is to awaken our awareness of *Shekhinah,* that is, to awaken our awareness of God as manifest even "in the lowest realms," and to arouse within us the *middot* of *kabbalah, hoda'ah,* and *anavah.* Much of the first stage of *Shacharit* draws our attention to our bodily functions, and leads us to recognize that (even) our body and its functions are an expression of God. Gratitude and humility are two natural outgrowths of this recognition. The recitation of the Sacrifices also fits in with these themes. If said with proper concentration and appreciation, the first stage of *Shacharit* constitutes the initial step along a deeply transforming and rewarding spiritual journey. Of course, one cannot cultivate the *middot* merely by

---

13. To follow this section, one should keep close at hand a traditional *siddur,* or prayer book. The discussion here follows the Ashkenazic *nusach,* or custom. However, nothing major hinges on which *nusach* one follows. Incidentally, it is taught that it is better to use a *siddur* that spells out the name י-ה-ו-ה rather than a *siddur* that uses an abbreviation (such as יי״). See *Piskei Tshuvot* on *SA:OC:* 5 (Vol. I: p. 65). This teaching reinforces the notion that during prayer one should continually visualize the Name, י-ה-ו-ה.

saying words. Rather, a person who goes through *Shacharit* with proper intent, or *kavannah*, sets the tone for the rest of the day, throughout which he or she strives to grow along the spiritual journey.

The very first thing a Jew does in the morning, when he or she regains consciousness – even before getting out of bed – is to say the *Modeh ani*. This is not a petitionary prayer but rather an expression of recognition and thanks. The word *modeh* is a form of the word *hoda'ah* discussed above, which means admission and thanks. The text reads as follows:

> *Modeh ani lefanechah, melech chai vekayam, shehechezarta bi nishmati bechemlah; rabbah emunatecha.*

In translation:

> I give thanks before you – living and permanent king! – for you have returned my soul within me with compassion; great is your faithfulness.

The notion that God has "returned" the soul is based on the traditional belief that during sleep a person loses part of his soul that is taken by God, and, when a person wakes or resumes consciousness, it is because God has returned that missing part of the soul. When a person sleeps, he temporarily loses a number of his usual waking capacities, and when he wakes, these capacities return to full force. The faithfulness referred to in the *Modeh ani* is the faithfulness that God keeps by restoring the soul to the sleeping individual. *Modeh ani* also hints at the traditional belief in the resurrection of the dead. In any case, the main point of *Modeh ani* is to express recognition and thanks that one is alive, and to recognize that God, who is the living and permanent king, is the source of one's life. It is surely no accident that the very first word that a Jew utters every morning is the Hebrew word for *thanks*. Just in this small formula alone, we see a simple but profound lesson: *from the very first moment of waking consciousness, a person should take stock of the fact that he or she is alive, appreciate it, and thank God for it.* If we think of the essence of God as Being itself, we can also think of our own individual existence and life as a small spark of God. The recognition and gratitude for our own life is the beginning of the spiritual journey, which ultimately involves a deeper and more mature relationship with God.

After *Modeh ani*, a person washes hands, uses the bathroom, and then says a few blessings. Earlier we described a blessing as an expression of recognition that some particular thing is a specific expression or manifestation of God or Being itself. Judaism teaches that we should be very careful about *particularizing* our blessings.[14] When we express recognition that God is the source of something, we tailor our blessing so that it recognizes that God is the source of that particular kind of thing.[15] As an analogy for understanding why this is so important, consider a thank-you note that one might write to a friend for a gift. A thank-you note is far more meaningful if it is tailored to the specific gift that is received, rather than if it is just a very general thank-you. The same point applies when we say blessings. We acknowledge not just that God is the source of everything generally, but that God is the source of very specific things as well. Each different kind of gift is a different expression or manifestation of God or Ultimate Being, and we want to recognize the unique character of each kind of gift.

Let us return to the main thread. After using the bathroom and washing hands, the following four-fold set of blessings are said in succession: (1) *Al netilat yadayim*, (2) *Asher yatzar*, (3) *Elokai neshamah*, (4) *Birchot hatorah*. These are (1) a blessing on the (rabbinic) commandment to wash our hands after waking, (2) a blessing on the wondrous internal bodily functions that allow us to live, (3) a blessing on having a living soul, (4) two related blessings on the Torah; one on the commandment to learn Torah, and one which recognizes that God chose the people of Israel and gave us the Torah. In this succession of blessings, we find a progression from lower to higher stages in the following way:

4. Blessing on the study of Torah
3. Blessing on having a vital soul
2. Blessing on bodily functions
1. Blessing on washing hands

The initial, lowest stage is listed on the bottom. Jewish tradition teaches that during the nighttime, a certain kind of ritual impurity, or *tumah*, falls upon the hands, and this *tumah* is washed away by the ritual hand washing. This too is associated with the fact that when we sleep, we are

---

14. There is a very general blessing that is said under certain circumstances; this is the responsive blessing, *Borchu et Hashem Hamevorach! Baruch Hashem Hamevorach leolam vaed!* ("Bless the Name that is blessed! Blessed is the Name that is Blessed forevermore!") We shall discuss this rather unique blessing in Chapter 3.

15. Hence the complicated laws of *brachot*, especially on food. For example, there is a different blessing for fruits of the trees as opposed to fruits of the ground. Also, certain food items have a special status, such as wine and bread; there is a specific blessing for each of these items.

in some way closer to death than when we are awake. Another explanation is that during the nighttime our hands come in contact with unclean parts of the body. Either way, the necessity for this hand washing is associated with our "lowest aspect" – that is, our corporeal and mortal nature. Moreover, we *do* things physically with our hands; hands are the main instrument of bodily action. When we wash our hands in the morning we are preparing and elevating our hands to do good and holy work. Ideally one should have this in mind while washing hands. Still, the hands are *external* limbs. Hence the washing of the hands and the relevant blessing pertain directly to our bodily nature.

Next comes the blessing which is said after using the bathroom. While the first blessing focused on our *external* limbs, i.e., the hands, this second blessing involves recognition of the *internal* wondrous bodily functions that allow us to live. At first glance, one might think it unseemly to concentrate so much attention on the fact that we excrete waste. But the sages emphasize the importance of saying this blessing with great focus and intent. When we say this blessing we should be thinking not only of the fact that we are able to excrete, but more generally that our biological functioning involves the mechanism of literally billions of channels and passageways in our bodies that need to work *just so* in order for us to live even for one moment. In saying this blessing, we express recognition of the wondrous working of our bodily functions, and that they have their source in God. Putting the point differently, in saying this blessing, a person recognizes that God or Being is manifest in just such a way that there are countless intricate mechanisms which allow a person to digest food and to excrete waste –in short, to live.

Thirdly, going one step higher, the blessing *Elokai neshamah* expresses recognition that one has not only a body but also an animating or vital soul. There are, after all, many organisms in the world with wondrous inner workings, such as plants, but they do not breathe or move from place to place. In this third blessing we recognize God as the source of our animal vitality. This blessing recalls a theme mentioned earlier in the *Modeh ani*, namely, that we thank God for restoring our soul, and here we allude explicitly to the traditional belief that God restores the souls of the dead. Whereas earlier in the *Modeh ani* we did not use God's name, here in *Elokai neshamah* we allude to God directly. Moreover, in this blessing we allude to a more spiritual aspect of the soul, as we say, "*tehorah hi*" (it is pure). In the *Modeh ani*, there is no reference to the purity of the soul.

Finally, going even one step higher, we say two blessings on the Torah. The first one expresses recognition that God is the source of our commandment to study Torah and that God is the "teacher of the Torah to his people Israel." The second blessing expresses our recognition that God chose the people of Israel to give them the Torah. Implicit in the first blessing is the recognition that God has a mind or intellect, and that by studying Torah we can participate in God's intellect. This will become a major theme in the third stage of *Shacharit*. Implicit in the second blessing is the recognition that God has the capacity for choice and that he has expressed that capacity in choosing the people of Israel for a special mission. In this way, these two final blessings refer first to divine intellect, and second to divine choice. In sum, in this succession of blessings, we find a four-fold progression from lower to higher aspects of both man and God.

The next section of the first stage involves putting on *tallit katan* (the small four cornered garment with *tzitzit*, or fringes), *tallit gadol* (large four cornered prayer shawl with *tzitzit*) and *tefillin* (phylacteries). The most obvious fact about *tallit* and *tefillin* is that they are *physical* or *bodily* garments. The deeper meanings and symbolisms of the *tefillin* and the *tallit* will emerge only later in the third stage of *Shacharit*, when we explicitly refer to them while reading the *Shema*. At this first stage, one's focus is not so much on what these ritual objects mean or symbolize, but rather on *the sheer physical action of putting them on.*

These activities relate to the central purpose of the first stage of *Shacharit* in the following way. *Shekhinah* represents that aspect of God that is most available to us; that aspect of Being which is manifest in the lowest realms, particularly, the body. In some sense, the *Shekhinah* is always present, for as we said above, God or Being is omnipresent. Yet, we can be more or less in tune with or consciously focused on God. When we engage in any spiritual act, especially prayer, we are consciously focusing on God. By putting on the *tallit katan,* *tallit gadol* and *tefillin,* a person engages one's body in this spiritual endeavor.[16] The *tallit katan* and the *tallit gadol* are garments which enclothe the body, and the *tefillin* are placed or tied on specific parts of the body. In putting on the *tefillin,* a person is compelled to focus attention on the specific areas where the *tefillin* must be placed, including one's bicep, forearm, hand, fingers, head, neck, and eyes. By putting on

---

16. It is worth noting that the *tallit katan* and *tallit gadol* are four cornered garments, and the *tefillin* contains within it four sections. The number four may allude to the four-lettered Name. Thus, by putting on these garments one connects one's body in a very literal way to the Name.

tallit and *tefillin*, one engages one's entire body in a relationship with God. Stating the same point using Kabbalistic language, by putting on *tallit* and *tefillin* we are physically accepting or receiving the divine presence, or *Shekhinah*.[17]

Once again, we find here a four-fold progression from lower to higher stages. One starts with the *tallit katan*, which is a small garment that is worn all day, usually under one's shirt. The *tallit katan* is worn even by young men or boys, and it is worn even in the bathroom. An adult continues by putting on the *tallit gadol*, which is worn only during prayer, and never in the bathroom. One continues by binding first the *tefillin* to the arm, and only then placing the *tefillin* on the head, as if it were a crown. The restrictions on when it is appropriate to wear the *tefillin* are even more stringent than the restrictions on when it is appropriate to wear a *tallit gadol*. Furthermore, whereas the *tallit gadol* is wrapped around the body loosely, the *tefillin* are literally tied to one's body. The *tallit gadol* does not have any words of scripture; the *tefillin* contain portions of the Torah. The four-fold progression from lower to higher stages here is obvious: by putting on the *tallit katan*, then the *tallit gadol*, then the *tefillin* of the arm, and then the *tefillin* of the head, one moves from more superficial or external (*chitzoni*) levels, to more advanced or internal (*pnimi*) levels.

The next section in the first stage is a litany of blessings known as *Birchot Hashachar*. Many if not most of these blessings express our recognition of God as the source of our various physical abilities, including our ability to wake up, to see, to stretch, to stand erect, to walk, to be refreshed by sleep. Other blessings focus on rather mundane things or "simple gifts" we are thankful for, such as, the crowing of the rooster in the early morning, the fact that we have clothes and shoes, even hats and belts. It is precisely these simple gifts which are so necessary for the flourishing of human life. In saying these blessings, we express recognition that these things are expressions of God or Being itself. By saying

---

17. In traditional Judaism, it is taught that *tallit* and *tefillin* are obligatory only for men. One reason is that positive commandments that are "time bound" are only obligatory on men; these practices only apply during the day, so women are exempt. But based on what has been said, a possible Kabbalistic explanation is the following: The purpose of these practices is to *prepare the body to engage the Shekhinah*. Since women are by nature more receptive than men, there is no need for these accoutrements. By nature, women have a closer identification with *Shekhinah*, since it is the feminine aspect of God. If this is correct, women do not put on *tefillin* or *tallit katan* because they can reach the same level of connection with *Shekhinah without* putting on the *tallit* or *tefillin*.

the blessings, we heighten our awareness of *Shekhinah*, that is, God or Being as manifest or expressed in the physical realm.

We have seen how the first stage of *Shacharit* provides the opportunity for a person to cultivate the *middot* of receptivity and gratitude. It also provides the opportunity to cultivate the *middah* of humility. As mentioned earlier, the recognition of one's physical capacities is a double edged sword. In recognizing that my life is returned to me upon waking up from sleep, I should be appreciative and thankful for such a wonderful gift. Yet at the same time, this very recognition makes me realize how *frail* and *dependent* I am. There is nothing that I do myself to restore my consciousness within me (except perhaps for setting an alarm clock). My waking is a natural phenomenon which I do not myself bring about; it just happens. I am also quite vulnerable when I am sleeping. Furthermore, in recognizing that my biological functioning depends on millions of things working properly in my body, I implicitly recognize how frail and dependent I am. As we say in the text of the blessing after using the bathroom, ". . . if one of those apertures were to close, or one of those closed valves were to open, it would not be possible to survive. . . ." Similarly, the morning blessings prompt a person to think about what condition he would be in if he could not see or hear, or if he did not have clothes or shoes to wear. Surely, one would not survive for very long! In this way, the recitation of *Birchot Hashachar* cultivates not only appreciativeness and gratitude, but also humility.

The last blessing in *Birchot Hashachar* is worth examining in some detail. This blessing begins by recognizing that God is the source for removing sleep from our eyes, and drowsiness from our eyelids. We go on to petition God to help us walk in the way of his Torah and his commandments, to keep us from sin, and to not allow our evil inclination to control us. It makes good sense that this should be one of the first blessings or prayers of the day. For as we start the day we want God's help in getting us to do good and avoid evil. This blessing also grows naturally out of a focus on one's biological nature. When I reflect on myself as a biological creature, I realize not only that I am frail and dependent, but also that I have cravings and lusts. Some of my cravings and lusts may be for things that are wrong or evil. Now, we do *not* pray that God should *abolish* our evil inclination, or *yetzer hara*, for then we would no longer be human. But we *do* pray that God should not allow our evil inclination to dominate us. In any case, the recognition of our capacity for sin ties in closely with humility. In this blessing, I recognize and admit that not only am I limited, frail, and dependent, but also that I am capable of sin. This is perhaps the most important aspect of humility, which involves recognizing not only one's limits but also one's potential for failure.

The theme of humility is developed further in the next section of the first stage, namely, the recitation of the Biblical portion of the *Akedah,* or Binding of Isaac, and the portions describing the *Korbanot,* or Sacrifices. The sacrifices are commandments which involve the body, in fact, literally, the bodies of animals. This fits in with the general theme of this stage of the *Shacharit,* which corresponds to the body or most outward aspect of the human. The sacrifices are among the more "bodily" of all the commandments. Furthermore, one classic explanation given for sacrifices has to do with the notion that through sacrificing an animal, a person vicariously represents his willingness to sacrifice one's own body for the sake of achieving atonement before God.[18] This ties back to the episode of the Binding of Isaac, wherein Abraham expressed his willingness to sacrifice his beloved son, Isaac. Although we ourselves cannot perform the sacrifices, the sages say that by reading and studying these passages, it is as if we have performed them. Thus, through reciting and studying these passages, we serve God in a physical or bodily manner. Even the passages regarding the more refined activities of lighting of the Menorah and offering of the incense involve physical actions.[19]

In connection with humility, note the numerous references to *dam* (blood) in this first stage of *Shacharit.* While the term *dam* occurs not even once in any of the other three stages, it occurs numerous times in this section. Also, the term *adam* (earthling) occurs several times in this section and very few times in any other section of *Shacharit.* Indeed, death is mentioned in this section several times as well. These persistent references to *dam, adam,* and death reinforce the link between this stage of *Shacharit* and the *nefesh,* the lowest part of the soul which is most animal-like and is intimately associated with the body. By reminding us of our mortality, these sobering allusions reinforce the virtue of humility.

Earlier we noted a four-fold progression within the morning blessings themselves. In the recitation of the Sacrifices, we find yet another four-fold progression. The table below (read from bottom to top) exhibits this

---

18. See Ramban's commentary to Leviticus 1:9.

19. On the more elevated significance of the incense offering, see below, Chapter 4, p. 235.

progression (listed on the left-hand side) and its parallel to the earlier progression (listed on the right-hand side):

4. The 13 rules by which Torah is   ➡ 4. Blessing on the study of Torah
   interpreted
3. The passage on the *Tamid*   ➡ 3. Blessing on having a vital soul
   (Daily Sacrifice)
2. The passage on the Removal of   ➡ 2. Blessing on excretion of waste
   Ashes
1. The passage on the use of the   ➡ 1. Blessing on washing hands
   Wash Basin

First, we read the section involving the *kiyor*, or wash basin. The wash basin was used by the priests before they did their service in the Temple. This corresponds to the hand washing and its blessing.[20] Next, we read a section involving the removal of the ashes, or "waste" from the previous day's sacrifice. This corresponds to the using of the bathroom and its blessing. Next we read the section involving the *Tamid*, or daily sacrifice. This corresponds to the *Elokai neshama*, the prayer which thanks God for restoring the soul. Our very life comes from God, and the daily sacrifice is a formal recognition that life depends on God. Finally, after all the sections involving the services in the Temple are recited, we conclude the first stage of the *Shacharit* with a teaching of Rabbi Yishmael on the thirteen ways in which the Torah is interpreted. This corresponds to the blessings on the Torah.

There is yet another four-fold progression within the first stage itself, starting with the passage, *Le'olam yehe adam*, through the recitation of the *Tamid*. In fact, all four stages of the entire *Shacharit* are encapsulated in miniscule within the first stage. The following table (read from bottom to top) shows this progression.

4. The Morning Sacrifice, or *Tamid*   ➡ 4. The *Amidah*
3. The "little" *Shema*   ➡ 3. The main reading of *Shema*
2. The obligation to praise God   ➡ 2. The verses of Praise, or
                                          Pesukei D'zmira
1. The frailty of the human being   ➡ 1. The Morning Blessings

---

20. One reason given for the washing of the hands in the morning is that it mimics the hand washing of the priests before doing service in the Temple. See *Mishnah Berurah* on SA:OC: 4:1.

We start the passage of *Le'olam yehe adam* with a reflection on our frailty and limitations. This corresponds to the first stage of *Shacharit*. Next, we describe our fortunate lot in that we are in the position of having both the opportunity and the obligation to praise God. This corresponds to the second stage of *Shacharit*, which consists in verses of praise. Next, we say the first sentence of *Shema*, which corresponds to the third stage of *Shacharit*, namely, *Kriyat Shema*. This is sometimes known as "the little *Shema*" to distinguish it from the main recitation of *Shema*, which is in the third stage of *Shacharit*.[21] Immediately thereafter, a small passage serves as a bridge between the *Shema* and the recitation of the sacrifices. This passage contains the theme of *geulah*, or redemption, and it mimics the passage later on in *Shacharit* after the *Shema* which leads up to the *Amidah*. The morning sacrifice, or *Tamid*, signifies worship of God, which corresponds to the *Amidah*, the fourth section of *Shacharit*.[22] Thus, within the first stage itself we find in miniature a four-fold progression that mimics the overall four-fold structure of the entire *Shacharit*.

Finally, note the sheer variety of the first stage of *Shacharit*. Of all the four stages, this one has the greatest variety in content, style, and literary sources. Here we find poems, blessings, praises, petitionary prayers, passages from Scripture and rabbinic literature. Remarkably, we find at least one passage from every single book of the first five books of the Torah; selections from the Prophets, and also the Holy Writings (including even the somewhat obscure *Kohelet*). We find a wide selection of passages from almost every genre of Rabbinic writing, including selections from the Mishnah, Talmud Bavli, Talmud Yerushalmi, Midrash Halacha, and even a Kabbalistic prayer in the form of a poem (*Ana bekoach*). This contrasts sharply with the other three sections of *Shacharit*, each of which contains only one or two genres of text. A related point is that the appropriate tone of voice that is suitable for each of these different kinds of texts differs as well. The *Modeh ani* would normally be said, upon waking, in a whisper. Most of the morning blessings would be recited aloud, but without any particular tune. The poems might be sung in a tuneful voice. The scriptural passages might best be chanted

---

21. It is taught that the entire portion of the "little *Shema*" was not originally part of the first stage of *Shacharit*. It was introduced during a time of oppression, when the regular *Shema* could not be said in public or at its proper time during the service. See *Shibboleh Haleket* 6.

22. Rabbi Yehoshua ben Levi teaches that the *Amidah* was instituted to correspond to and in some way stand in for the *korban tamid* (daily sacrifice). *Tractate Brachot* 26b. This will be a major theme below in Chapter 4.

with the cantillation notes (*trop*). The rabbinic passages might be read in tone suitable for study. We shall find that in the other three sections the appropriate tone of voice or mode of speech is more focused or restricted.[23] The wide variety of content and texts found in the first section is not accidental. Again, the lower *heh* corresponds to the outward manifestation of God or Being, which is to say, *Shekhinah*. It is also related to the notion of omnipresence. God or Being is everywhere. The variety of texts and modes of speech with are found in the first stage of *Shacharit* expresses the notion that God or Ultimate Being is manifest in a multiplicity of different ways.

A related point concerns the variety of appropriate bodily poses or physical positions that a person is supposed to assume during the first stage of *Shacharit*, especially when compared with the more specific poses in the other three stages. To explain this point, a few preliminary remarks regarding the significance of one's posture are necessary. The connection between posture and spirituality should not be taken lightly. In many spiritual traditions, one's posture plays a crucial role in developing certain meditative states. Jewish liturgy pays much attention to posture. Certain prayers are supposed to be said standing, and others are said sitting. In fact, the fourth stage of *Shacharit* is called the *Amidah*, i.e., the standing prayer, precisely because it is supposed to be said standing. This shows the significance given by the Rabbis to one's pose or physical position during prayer. Indeed, there is a Kabbalistic explanation that underlies the importance of sitting versus standing: sitting represents *kabbalah*, or reception, whereas standing represents action or doing. When we are taking something in or absorbing something, we are supposed to be sitting. But, when we are trying to accomplish or do something, we are supposed to be standing. Thus for example when we learn Torah, it is appropriate to sit; in fact a study hall or seminary is called a "*yeshivah*" – place of sitting.[24] This is because learning involves taking things in. It is also taught that one should sit while eating. On the other hand, when we petition God or pray, generally we stand, for stand-

---

23. The second section (*Pesukei D'zimrah*) consists almost exclusively of verses of praise which one would *sing* (*zemer*). The third section (*Kriyat Shema*) contains some rabbinic material, and some Scriptural passages which ideally should be *chanted* with cantillation (*kriyah* with *trop*). The fourth section is the *Amidah*, which is made up of rabbinic blessings, and is said entirely in a *whisper* (*belachash*).

24. The standing at Mount Sinai to receive the Torah is an exceptional case, due to the unusual nature of that event. That was not merely a case of learning but a case of divine revelation. We shall discuss this more in Chapter 4.

ing represents action, and prayer is an attempt to change something in the world. We shall return to this theme throughout the book.

Now, let us return to the first stage of *Shacharit*. A unique thing about this stage when contrasted with the other stages is that it is in the first part where the widest variety of appropriate postures is found. *Modeh ani* is said while still reclining in bed. Many of the morning blessings should be said standing, but some can be said while sitting. Originally, the blessing of *matir asurim* ("He releases the bound") was said upon sitting up in bed; *zokef kefufim* ("He straightens the bent") was said upon rising and stretching one's limbs. Upon entering the synagogue and reciting *Mah Tovu*, it is appropriate to bow slightly while saying *eshtachaveh* (*I shall bow*).[25] The "little Shema" is best said while sitting; some hold that the passages describing the sacrifices should be said while standing; the rabbinic passages from the Mishnah and Talmud are best said while sitting. As we shall see later, no other stage of the four stages exhibits this variety. Like the variety of texts and modes of speech, the variety of postures in the first stage of *Shacharit* expresses the notion that God or Ultimate Being is manifest in a multiplicity of ways – and that we must relate to God in a multiplicity of ways.

In summary, the first stage of *Shacharit* corresponds to the lower *heh*, the *Shekhinah*. In this stage, a person cultivates an awareness of *Shekhinah*, that is, an awareness of God as manifest in a multiplicity of ways, and especially in the most mundane or earthly ways. By reciting the morning blessings and the portions describing the sacrifices, one cultivates the *middot* of receptivity, gratitude, and humility. Just as the sockets, or *adanim*, constituted the basis for the *mishkan*, or resting place, for God's presence, these *middot* constitute the foundation of the Jewish spiritual journey.

---

25. This teaching is found in the *Zohar* (I:11a).

וֹ

VAV

THE HOLY, BLESSED IS HE
(*HAKADOSH, BARUCH HU*)

WE HAVE SEEN that the lower *heh* represents *Shekhinah*, or divine presence, that is, the very fact that God's essence or Being is manifest in the world. In this chapter, we delve into the Kabbalistic teaching that the *vav* in God's Name represents the *characteristic ways* in which God is manifest or expressed. These characteristic ways constitute God's *personality* or the *divine character traits*. Just as a human person may be known by the way he acts, so too, God is known to some degree by the way he acts. In the philosophical tradition, these are referred to as the divine "active attributes" or "attributes of action." The recognition of these divine character traits forms the basis of the second stage in the Jewish spiritual path.

Occasionally, Kabbalists refer to the divine personality as *Hakadosh Baruch Hu*, or *the Holy, Blessed is He*.[1] The term "holy," or *kadosh*, indicates separateness or apartness.[2] God is in some way separate or different from all else. The divine essence is never fully manifest in any particular thing or set of things. If we understand God's essence as Being itself, we may say that *Being itself* is distinguishable from particu-

---

1. The phrase *Hakadosh Baruch Hu* is often translated as "The Holy One, Blessed be He." However, the word "One" does not occur in the original Hebrew phrase. The phrase *Baruch Hu* may be understood as a performative statement, to wit, "Blessed *be* He" or "*may* He be blessed." It may also be understood as a descriptive statement that the Holy (being) *is* blessed.

2. See Maharal, *Gevurot Hashem*, Second Introduction. See also *Tanya* 46. We shall delve more into *kedushah*, or holiness, in the next chapter. As we shall see, the concept of *kedushah* pertains more aptly to the upper *heh* than the *vav*. In the phrase "*Hakadosh Baruch Hu*," what is more relevant to the *vav* is the "*Baruch Hu*" part, rather than the "*kadosh*" part.

lar *beings*. *Being* is infinite, indefinite, and in some sense indescribable; *beings* are finite and describable. On the other hand, the term "blessed" connotes the fact that every being is an expression or manifestation of Being. Furthermore, there are certain characteristic ways in which Being is manifest in things; these characteristic ways constitute God's personality. Thus the phrase *Hakadosh Baruch Hu* represents something of a paradox. On the one hand, God is separate or transcendent; on the other hand, God is the source of that which is manifest and expressed within the universe. Moreover, while *Shekhinah* represents the more receptive aspects of Being and is therefore characterized as feminine, *Hakadosh Baruch Hu* represents the more active aspects of Being, and is therefore characterized as masculine. As mentioned earlier, in Hebrew grammar, the *vav* plays the role of a masculine indicator, and, even the shape of the *vav* hints at the masculine aspect of reality.

Kabbalah teaches that there are six main divine character traits or active attributes. The *gematria,* or numerical value, of the letter *vav* is six, and it is taught that the *vav* hints at these six attributes, or *sefirot.* The number six may seem arbitrary at first glance but, as we shall see, Kabbalah offers an explanation of why there are exactly six. There are three main ones and three subsidiary ones. The three main ones are *benevolence (chessed)*, *restraint (gevurah)*, and *compassion (rachamim)*. These are sometimes referred to as God's "moral attributes." As noted earlier,[3] these *sefirot* correspond respectively to the right arm, the left arm, and the chest. The three subsidiary ones are *victory (netzach)*, *majesty (hod)*, and *foundation (yesod)*. These correspond respectively to the right thigh, the left thigh, and the reproductive organs (both male and female). The latter three are regarded as offshoots of the first three. Kabbalah also teaches that the six *sefirot* correspond to the six directions: up, down, right, left, forward, and backward. Hence, they are sometimes referred to as the "six directions," or *shesh ktzavot.* Like the six directions, all the *sefirot* are interrelated, and they cannot be defined or explained independently of one another.

The purpose of the next several sections is to describe and explain the six *sefirot*, to the extent necessary for our main purpose, namely, to illuminate the Jewish spiritual path. Along the way, we shall address the question, to what extent the belief in the six *sefirot* is based on ordinary experience, and to what extent this belief is based on tradition (*mesorah*).

---

3. See above, Introduction, footnote 16.

Benevolence (*Chessed*)

In this book, we understand the *sefirot* not as entities that exist, but rather as ways in which Being, or *ein sof,* is manifest or expressed. We have already spoken briefly about the *sefirah* of *chessed. Chessed,* or benevolence, connotes the free outpouring or sharing of Being, whether it is deserved or undeserved, and whether it is needed or not needed. In a certain respect, it is the most significant of the six *sefirot* symbolized by the *vav.* Anything that exists, from an atom to a galaxy, from a pebble to a planet, exhibits this sharing or outpouring to some degree. The fact that certain things grow and flourish is a further expression of divine *chessed.* Crops grow, animals and humans are nourished. Humans live, work, love, and reproduce. Indeed, in one organism alone, there occur literally billions of discrete acts of *chessed.* Divine *chessed* is expressed in infinite and endless ways throughout the universe. This aspect is symbolically represented as "the right hand of God" that gives generously and with favor.

It is worth noting the subtle but crucial difference between *chessed* and *shekhinah.* Like all the *sefirot,* they are related and interdependent, but they are not identical. *Shekhinah* is the manifestation or expression of Being; *chessed* is the sharing or outpouring of Being. Some analogies may be helpful to explain this difference. A footprint that is left in someone's front lawn is a manifestation or expression of one's presence. On the other hand, a gift left on the front porch is not only a manifestation of one's presence, but an act of sharing or benevolence. The footprint corresponds to *shekhinah;* the gift corresponds to *chessed.* Another analogy is as follows: In creating a work of art, an artist reveals or expresses himself in that artwork. This corresponds to *shekhinah.* But, in creating a work of art, an artist shares something of himself in his work. The skill and energy of the artist are, as it were, poured into the artwork. This act of sharing is a matter of *chessed.* Finally, when a generous man gives charity to the poor, he reveals something of himself, or his nature, in that act of giving. At the same time, he shares something of himself as well. Sharing and revealing are related, but they are not identical. In fact, one can also reveal oneself by *taking something away* or *punishing someone,* and that certainly does not count as an act of pure *chessed.* We shall return to this point later.

Before moving on to the next *sefirah,* let us consider the following question. Shall we say that the belief in divine *chessed* is rationally based on ordinary experience? Or rather, is it based on *mesorah*? In some sense, it is undeniably true that Being is manifest or expressed in countless good ways and in countless things. It does not take any special act of reliance on tradition or dogma to recognize that Being is shared in the universe. To this extent, belief in divine *chessed* is a rational belief that is based on ordinary experience.

However, two questions remain. The first is whether the manifestation and expression of Being is, as it were, just a matter of luck or good fortune (or a matter of "natural necessity"). Judaism teaches that *chessed* is a part of an intentional divine plan; but one might conceivably regard the apparent *chessed* in the world as merely fortuitous. An agnostic might agree that Being is manifest and expressed in countless things and in countless ways; yet he does not regard this as an intentional phenomenon. Either there is no explanation for it at all, or there is a naturalistic explanation for it. (A naturalistic explanation is one that does not appeal to divine intentions.) We shall return to this issue later in this book, when we discuss the nature of divine intention, that is, when we discuss the three highest *sefirot*. The point here is that based on ordinary experience alone, one might come to the conclusion that *chessed* is not a result of divine intention.

A second question is whether the outpouring of Being that we find in the universe is as complete or as full it could be. On the surface, it surely seems that there could be greater *chessed* expressed in the world than in fact there is. Some plots of land are wastelands. Numerous planets are barren. Sometimes crops don't grow; some people are not able to have children, and in some cases disease and illness occur. It seems that one could easily imagine a world in which there would be more joy, happiness, bliss, etc., than there is now. Indeed, Judaism teaches that ultimately there *will be* a more complete and full expression of God's *chessed*, in the Messianic era and in the next world. However, it seems that this belief is based on revelation and accepted as a matter of traditional teaching. Based on ordinary experience, it is not readily evident that there will come such a time. We shall return to this issue later.[4]

Restraint (*Gevurah*)

While *chessed* connotes the outpouring or sharing of Being, *gevurah* connotes a *limitation* or *restraint* of that outpouring or sharing.[5] The

---

4. See the discussion in Chapter 3 below.

5. The connection between *gevurah* and restraint is hinted at in the teaching in *Mishnah Avot* 4:1. *Ayzeh hu gibor? – Hakovesh et yitzro.* Translation: Who is a *gibor* (mighty person)? The one who (*kovesh*) restrains his inclinations.

Kabbalistic term for limitation or constraint is *tzimtzum*. There are a number of ways in which the sharing or outpouring of Being is limited or constrained.

First, anything that exists exhibits some limitation or constraint. For example, any given physical thing must have a specific shape and size. That means that it does *not* have a different shape or size than it does. Furthermore, any given thing has certain properties but not others. It also does certain things but not others. A rock or a stone is an expression of Being, and it has certain properties, but it doesn't do much. A tree is an expression of Being, but it is limited in certain ways; it does not walk or think. On the other hand, humans walk and think, but they do not have wings or grow flowers. Even the entire universe, taken as a whole, is limited or defined in certain ways. In the physical world, there are certain physical constants and certain natural laws in accord with which the world generally operates (the law of gravity, other laws of physics, etc.). The universe that we inhabit is the way it is, and so it thereby exhibits limitation in the sense that it is *not* the way it isn't. Hence, anything that exists expresses both *chessed* and *gevurah*. If there were no such principle as *gevurah*, nothing in particular would or could exist at all.[6]

Let us go back to *chessed* for a moment. We can make distinctions among different expressions of *chessed*, depending on how "complete," or *gamur*, the *chessed* is. An act of *chessed gamur* involves a *free gift* that is totally unearned and undeserved. For example, the existence of the universe itself is an exhibition of *chessed gamur*; the universe did not deserve to be created. But, once the universe exists, there are some things that exist and some events that happen in the world that are *earned* or *deserved*. When these things happen, this is not *chessed gamur*; this is an expression of *gevurah*. For example, if a farmer works hard to plant and nurture apple seeds, he ultimately reaps a harvest of apples. This is partly an expression of *chessed* because the apples, like anything else

---

6. Compare this notion with the rabbinical teaching (*Tractate Chagigah* 13a) regarding the divine name, *Shaddai – sheamar le-olamo dai* (The name *Shaddai* is an acronym for "He who said "enough" to his world.") In creating the world, God had to place limits on the world; otherwise, there could not be a world. It turns out that *gevurah* itself is a type of *chessed*. This point is made in *Sha'ar Hayichud Ve-ha'emunah*, chapter 6. As we shall see later, a similar point applies to the spiritual virtue, or *middah*, of *chessed*, or benevolence, as a human trait. Every act of giving requires some restraint or limitation. Whether one gives a dollar or a hundred dollars to a poor man, the gift has some limit. In addition, giving without restraint will backfire. Examples include spoiling a child or giving an alcoholic a drink. Genuine benevolence always requires some restriction.

that exists, are expressions of Being. But it is also an expression of *gevurah* because in this case, what the person receives is *earned* by his work. The harvest was not a totally free gift; the farmer earned it by hard work. This reflects *restraint* or *limitation* in the following way. The harvest is tailored or limited in a certain way to match the work that the person did. He does not reap a harvest of melons or peaches, nor does he reap an infinite amount of apples. Similarly, the world operates in just such a way that not only are there free gifts, but also, people (and to some degree, animals) may earn at least some of what they have. Kabbalah views this as an expression of divine *gevurah*.

Furthermore, Judaism teaches that aside from "hard work" there is yet another way in which we can earn or rather *deserve* certain things, and that is, by doing good deeds and/or fulfilling the *mitzvot,* or divine commandments. The universe is designed in just such a way that the righteous are rewarded and the wicked are punished, in this world and/ or the next world. Now, a reward is an expression of *chessed*, but it is also an expression of divine *gevurah*, since the reward is not a totally free gift. Similarly, the punishment of the wicked is an expression of divine *gevurah*. Indeed, most punishments involve a *deprivation* of some sort or other (especially, death, and especially, "death" in the next world). So, both reward and punishment are not cases of pure benevolence, or *chessed gamur,* but rather *gevurah*. In this context, *gevurah* is translated as severity or justice. (The more common Hebrew term for justice is *din.* Hence, sometimes the *sefirah* itself is referred to as *din* rather than *gevurah*.)

Earlier we noted that *chessed* is symbolized by the "right hand of God." *Gevurah* is represented as the "left hand of God." The left hand is generally weaker than the right hand, and this weakness reflects the restraint or withholding which is exhibited in *gevurah*. Kabbalists also refer to this aspect as "God's left hand" to signify that divine *chessed,* or benevolence, is in some way more powerful and primary than divine justice. The outpouring or sharing is the main thing; the restriction or tailoring is secondary. Moreover, even when there is punishment, the ultimate purpose is to advance divine *chessed* in the long run.

Let us consider whether it is evident to ordinary human experience that the universe operates in accord with the principle of *gevurah*. The alternative is that it is believed on the basis of revelation and/or the *mesorah*. Surely, it is obvious that beings that exist in the world exhibit limitation. But one could argue that this is not a result of any divine intention but simply an inevitable fact that would be true in any possible universe. Second, it is certainly true that many people earn what they get in this world by hard work. In general, the old saying "you reap what you sow" is very true. For the most part, people get what they deserve in life. Yet, it is surely not obvious that *gevurah* is complete or perfect. It seems that not everybody gets what they deserve. A man can work very hard, but circumstances don't fall into place, and he doesn't get what he worked for. From a strictly rational point of view, without reliance on revelation, it seems that in some sense, *gevurah* is not fully operational. Finally, without reliance on revelation or tradition, would we think that *justice* is part of the very fabric of our universe? Again, if we think of *perfect justice*, this is surely not evident based on ordinary experience. While often the wicked and the righteous get what they deserve in this world, it seems not always to be the case. The belief that divine *gevurah* is fully operational is not based solely on ordinary experience. It is a teaching based on revelation, and it involves reliance on the *mesorah*. It seems to involve the belief in the Messianic era and the next world. We shall return to this issue later.[7]

Compassion (*Rachamim*)

The third *sefirah* is *rachamim*, which is usually translated as compassion or mercy. In our world, certain things happen that are neither earned nor deserved, but are *needed*. Creatures have needs, and when they are filled, that is called an act of *rachamim*, or compassion. Indeed, all creatures have many needs that are constantly being fulfilled from moment to moment. Humans are constantly in need of air to breathe; thus at every moment that any human is given air to breathe, that is an act of divine *rachamim*. Every cell in our body needs oxygen; the delivery via the blood is an act of divine *rachamim*. Indeed, there are literally trillions of discrete acts of divine compassion transpiring at every moment, within each living creature alone.

Another example of this is the supplying of food to the hungry. When animals or humans are hungry, they do not necessarily *deserve* to be provided with food. However, if a creature is hungry, he is in need. Thus, the feeding of the hungry is an act of compassion by one who is able to do so. Similarly, the healing of the sick is an act of *rachamim*. A sick person may not *deserve* to be healed. However, someone who heals him would be thereby fulfilling his need. Thus, the fact that the hungry are fed and the sick are healed is said to be an expression of divine *rachamim*. In our world, there are literally billions of cases of hungry creatures being

---

7. See the discussion in Chapter 3 below.

fed and sick creatures being healed every day. This is an expression of divine *rachamim*. Indeed, Judaism teaches that God's revival of the dead (*techiyat hametim*) is considered the fulfilling of a dire need; so that is an act of great *rachamim*. As we say in the *Amidah*, "God revives the dead with *rachamim rabim* (abundant compassion)."

This way of understanding divine *rachamim*, or compassion, agrees with Moses Maimonides' approach to understanding divine emotions that are often ascribed to God in the Torah. Maimonides argues that even though the Torah often depicts God as a being who has emotions such as pity, love, anger, etc., this needs to be taken as a roundabout way of referring to God's *actions*.[8] According to Maimonides, God does not really undergo emotions in the way that humans do. Rather, we say that that God is compassionate because God causes certain actions (such as the feeding of the hungry, the curing of the sick, etc.) which are the kind of actions that a compassionate person does. The approach here is similar. To speak of divine *rachamim* is to speak about the fact that our universe is structured in just such a way that the hungry are fed, the sick are cured, and so forth.

Kabbalah teaches that *rachamim* constitutes a blend, or *mizug*, of *chessed* and *gevurah*. Hence, it is symbolized by the chest or torso, which represents a balance between "right" and "left." This may be explained as follows.[9] Earlier we said that an act of *chessed gamur* is one in which there is some giving that is unearned or underserved. We also said that one way in which *gevurah* is expressed is in the act of giving someone what he has earned or deserved. Now, another way in which an act of giving does not count as *chessed gamur* is if the act of giving fulfills a need, and, especially, a dire need. For example, if a poor man is starving, and I give him a meal, that does not count as *chessed gamur*. An act of *chessed gamur* is a totally undeserved or unneeded gift. An example of *chessed gamur* would be inviting a friend over for lunch, or giving someone a present. There is no obligation or duty to invite a friend over for lunch or to buy him a present. But, to ignore a need, especially a dire need, where one has the ability to fulfill that need, and where a person has no countervailing reason not to fulfill that need, is callous, even if it is not unjust. It is the proper or right thing to do, even if it is not obligatory or demanded by justice. Hence an act of *rachamim* is a *mizug*, or blend, of *chessed* and *gevurah*.

Again, we ask, is it evident to ordinary experience that the world op-

---

8. *Mishneh Torah: Hilchot Yesoday Hatorah* 1:11–12; *Guide to the Perplexed* I:54.
9. See Maharal, *Gevurot Hashem* 62.

erates in accord with the principle of *rachamim*? The same points made above hold true. It is evident that to some extent the world operates in accord with *rachamim*. Literally, billions and billions of creatures have their needs met every day. But it is not clear whether this is intentional, or a result of some kind of cosmic luck. Furthermore, based on ordinary experience it seems that *rachamim* in the world is not complete or fully operational. In the world as we experience it, not all needs are filled. All animals and all people die sooner or later. And, some die of disease or starvation. Many people get sick and do not get cured. At least on the surface, it seems that *rachamim* is not perfect or completely operational. Why this happens is a theological question. Traditional Judaism affirms that God is fully compassionate, but it is not clear that one would or should believe this without relying on the *mesorah,* or tradition. We shall return to this issue later.[10]

In summary so far, the three *sefirot* – *chessed*, *gevurah* and *rachamim* – represent God's "moral attributes." It is in virtue of these attributes that we say that God is "morally good." *Chessed* represents the sheer or free outpouring of being, and this is associated with the right hand. *Gevurah* represents the restraint and/or tailoring of that outpouring, and the giving of that which is earned or deserved; this is associated with the left hand. *Rachamim* represents the giving of that which is needed; it is a blend or balance of the other two *sefirot*. *Rachamim* is the central *middah* and it is associated with the chest or torso.

Victory and Majesty (*Netzach* and *Hod*)

Whereas *chessed*, *rachamim*, and *gevurah* involve God's *moral* aspects, *netzach* and *hod* involve God's *esthetic* aspects.[11] God is not only morally good, that is, benevolent, compassionate, and just; rather, God's essence is expressed in just such a way that certain things are pleasing or appealing to the human senses. God gives us not only what we need; God gives us "frills" or "extras." This can happen in two different ways. We find in our world certain things that are *beautiful* or *pretty*. This is symbolized by *netzach*. We also find certain things that are *awesome* or

---

10. See the discussion in Chapter 3 below.

11. This way of understanding *netzach* and *hod* is based on the Kabbalistic teaching that *hod* and *netzach* are the more outward (*chitzoni*) aspects of *chessed* and *gevurah*. *Netzach* and *hod* are said to be represented by *yachin* and *boaz*, the two grand columns that were in the Second Temple. (*Shaarei Orah,* chapter 3). These may be taken to symbolize the esthetic qualities of divine beauty and majesty, which were particularly evident in the Temple.

majestic. This is symbolized by *hod*. For example, the fact that there are trees that bear fruit for humans to eat is an expression of divine *chessed* and *rachamim*. Without food we could not survive. But the fact that trees are pretty to look at is not only an expression of *chessed* but of divine *netzach*. Similarly, the fact that the sun causes plants to grow is an expression of divine *chessed*; the fact that the sun is also a brilliant mass of energy is an expression of divine awesomeness, or *hod*.

Sometimes, beauty and awesomeness are found mixed together; sometimes not. We find beauty in a flower or a delicate creature such as a butterfly. We find awesomeness in the sea, the starry sky, or even something forbidding, like a tornado or volcano. A mountain range such as the Alps or a natural wonder such as the Grand Canyon might be viewed as an expression of a combination of both beauty and awesomeness. In any case, nature or reality is such that it exhibits beauty and majesty. The beauty or attractive quality of nature is an expression of *netzach*; the awesome aspect is an expression of *hod*. We can see why *netzach* is associated more with the "right" side and *hod* with the "left" side. The right side connotes the positive or "user friendly" side of reality; the left side connotes the more threatening or scary part of reality. The beauty of trees is not particularly scary or threatening; the awesomeness of a mountain range or a tornado does involve something scary or threatening.

The significance of esthetic appreciation is underemphasized in some Jewish circles. This is a grave mistake. The Rabbis held that it is religiously significant for us to recognize the beauty and awesomeness in God's world. They established blessings for many of these things, including a blessing on seeing or experiencing extraordinary natural wonders and even on seeing an extraordinarily beautiful person.[12] This shows that it is our religious duty to recognize not only God's benevolence and justice but also God's awesomeness and beauty. Nevertheless, whereas *chessed* and *rachamim* are said to correspond respectively to the right and left arms, *netzach* and *hod* are said to correspond to the right and left thighs. In a human body, the thighs support the chest and the head, not the other way around. This symbolizes the Judaic teaching that the esthetic dimension of reality is secondary when compared to the moral dimension. Everything that is beautiful or awesome is an expression of divine benevolence and divine restraint, but not everything that is an expression of benevolence and restraint is beautiful or awesome. Thus, God's moral aspects are in some way more important or fundamental

---

12. *SA:OC*: 225:10. See *Artscroll Siddur* p. 228.

than God's esthetic aspects. After all, the fact that God gives us what we need is more important than the fact that God gives us "extras" or frills that are not necessary for our existence. This has an important consequence for human behavior as well, as we shall see later when we discuss the *middot* associated with the *vav*.

Once again, let us consider whether it is evident to ordinary experience that the world operates in accord with the principles of *netzach* and *hod*. Again, the same points made above hold true. There is no question that Being is manifest in ways that are awesome and beautiful. Still, one may question whether this is intentional or a result of blind chance. Also, it does not seem that these principles are fully operational. There are ugly and boring things in this world; at least, so it seems. Not every sunset is beautiful; not every landscape is majestic. Again, there may be some theological explanation for why this is so. We shall return to this issue later.

Foundation (*Yesod*)

As we have seen so far, all the *sefirot* have to do with various ways in which God's essence or Being is manifest or expressed in the world. Next, Kabbalah teaches that in some sense, God is "reproduced" within the world. The *sefirah* of *yesod* alludes to this feature of our world. In saying this, of course we do not mean that the world is literally a *duplication* of God. That would be impossible. Rather, the world is a *creative representation* of God. This requires explanation.

What does it mean to say that the world is a creative representation of God? How is this different from *Shekhinah*, which signifies that God's essence or Being is manifest in the world? An analogy may help clarify this notion. When a man makes an invention or craftwork, he manifests himself in that work and expresses some or even all of his abilities. However, when a man *has a son*, he thereby in some way *re-presents* himself in his son. (The hyphenated term "re-presents" connotes the idea that the father *presents himself anew* in the son.) Of course, that is not to say that he literally reproduces a facsimile or exact copy of himself. Rather, the son is in some way a "re-presentation" of the entire man, in a way that a craftwork would not be. It is also possible for a man to replicate or re-present himself in a creative work, such as a book or some work of art. This would happen only if the artwork somehow reflected the totality of its author. Similarly, Kabbalah teaches that God is in some way *replicated* in the world. How to understand this in detail is not so simple. The basic idea is that there is something about the world *as a whole* which matches or corresponds to God *as a whole*.[13]

Kabbalah teaches that human beings play a significant role in this "replication." The Torah teaches that God created the human "in his image." The human being has a special affinity or kinship with God that all other things lack. We have already said that the various divine ways correspond to the various limbs of the human being. An extension of the same point is that the sum total of the divine ways corresponds to the human being as a whole. Of course, humans are only humans in the context of a world that has other elements as well, including earth, sky, sea, plants, animals, and so forth. Hence, the creative representation of God is not the human being in isolation, but rather the human being as *a creature that lives in a world of a certain sort*. Still, the key element in the re-presentation of God within the world is the human being.

Furthermore, Judaism teaches that there is something special about the Israelite that mimics the divine nature. In the Talmud and Zohar, the Israelite is referred to as the human *par excellence*.[14] It must be remembered that Judaism teaches that *any human being can become an Israelite by adopting the way of life prescribed by the Torah*. Therefore, this is not a doctrine of racial superiority. It is rather the notion that if a human being commits to living a certain way of life, as outlined by the Torah, then he or she can become more divine in some way. Indeed, the Torah itself is also a creative expression of God, in which God represents himself, as an artist might represent himself in an artwork. Hence, many passages in Scripture, Talmud, and liturgy refer to God as the father of the Israelites, or the Israelites as the children of God.[15] Thus, the people of Israel play an especially significant role in the "representation" or "reproduction" of God within the world. They do so only when they walk in the way of Torah.

Not surprisingly, and as noted above, *yesod* corresponds to the reproductive organs. The reproductive organs initiate the reproduction of offspring. Symbolically, the reproductive organs represent the reproduction or re-presentation of God within the world. It is not accidental that when the Torah describes the creation of the human being in God's image, it explicitly says, "male and female he created them." The

---

13. Thus a Kabbalistic code word for the *sefirah* of *yesod* is the Hebrew word "*kol*" which means "all" or "everything."

14. *Tractate Bava Metzia* 114b; *Zohar* 2:25b.

15. One example is Exodus 4:22. In the liturgy, see the blessing of *Ahavah Rabbah* (discussed below in Chapter 3).

reproductive capacity of the human being is itself part of God's "re-presentation" of himself within the world. Of course, God does not have physical apparatus or reproductive organs. The point is that the physical apparatus of the human being mimics or represents a certain aspect of our universe, namely, that Being is in some sense replicated or represented in our universe.

Once again, let us pose the question whether it is evident based on ordinary experience that such a principle is operative in the universe. Again, the answer is to some extent yes, and to some extent, no. Obviously, the phenomenon of reproduction is found in our world. We tend to take this feature of our world for granted, but we should not. It is also obvious that Being is exhibited or present in the world, and so in some sense it is true that Being is "re-presented." However, it is not obvious that this process is intentional or purposive. One might perhaps plausibly believe that the existence of things in the universe is some kind of cosmic accident. Nor is it evident that God is "reproduced" in this world in the fullest way possible. Judaism teaches that the day will come when God will be re-presented more completely. Still, this belief about the future is based on revelation and accepted as part of the *mesorah*. We shall return to this issue later.[16]

In general, the *vav* is associated with the masculine rather than feminine aspect of God. Again, the feminine aspect is associated with God's *receptive* attributes; the masculine aspect is associated with God's *active* attributes. Hence, the Zohar occasionally refers to the six *sefirot* of the *vav* as the "son" and sometimes as the "husband." It is also taught that *yesod* corresponds specifically to the lower tip of the *vav*, which also hints specifically at the male reproductive organ. Kabbalah teaches that *yesod* is not an independent attribute on the order of the previous five. *Yesod* is the divine aspect that "collects" from all the other divine attributes and then blends them all together into something that contains them all. This is similar to what the male sexual organ does. It manufactures a "seed" which in some way encodes an entire re-production of the whole man, which it then shares with the female to a make a new whole which mimics the original whole. Similarly, it is by virtue of the combination of God's masculine and feminine aspects, the *vav* and the *heh*, that the world has the structure and character that it has.

As noted in the previous chapter, the divine name that corresponds to the lower *heh*, or *Shekhinah*, is *Adonai*. The name associated with the

---

16. As we shall see in Chapter 4, *keter* involves the notion of *maximal* divine self-expression. Hence, there is a strong link between *yesod* and *keter*.

vav and the six *sefirot* is the Name, י-ה-ו-ה. On the surface, this seems puzzling. As explained earlier, the Name signifies the entire array of *sefirot*. However, in Kabbalah, the Name has a broad use and a more narrow use. In its broad use, it refers to the whole array of *sefirot*. In its narrow use, it refers specifically to God's *rachamim,* or compassion. Thus in rabbinic literature one finds the contrast made between י-ה-ו-ה and the name *elohim*. It is taught that י-ה-ו-ה symbolizes compassion whereas *elohim* symbolizes *gevurah,* or justice. Since God's *rachamim* overwhelms God's *gevurah,* and since *rachamim* is the central *sefirah* of the six *sefirot* of the *vav,* the name י-ה-ו-ה is sometimes used to designate all of the *sefirot* of the *vav.*

Another explanation for why the Name is associated specifically with the *vav* is as follows. The *sefirot* of the *vav* have a special status, in that the *vav* connects the upper *sefirot* (*keter, chochmah, binah*) with the lower *sefirah* (*shekhinah*). The Kabbalists associate this connective aspect of the *vav* with the role played by the *vav* in ordinary Hebrew grammar. The *vav* plays the role of "and" in English; it constitutes a grammatical connective. The *vav* is compared to the trunk of a tree that connects the top of the tree with its roots. Since the *sefirot* of the *vav* play this central connective role, the Name is associated in particular with the *vav.* Since *rachamim* is the central *sefirah* of the central pole, it plays a special role in holding all the *sefirot* together. Hence, sometimes the Name is associated specifically with the *vav,* for it is the symbol of connectivity.

In the previous chapter, we noted that the lower *heh* corresponds to the *nefesh* or lowest part of the human soul, sometimes called the animal soul. Kabbalah teaches that the *vav* corresponds to the next highest part of the soul, often referred to as *ruach* – sometimes translated as *spirit, breath,* or *wind.*[17] Whereas *nefesh* is associated with the blood that courses through the veins delivering sustenance to the body, *ruach* is associated with the breath or breathing. In general, the blood flow is not something one can consciously control. On the other hand, breathing is something one can control, at least to some degree. This relates to the fact that whereas *nefesh* represents a passive aspect of the human, *ruach* represents a more active aspect. Furthermore, *ruach* is associated with the power of speech[18] and with our character traits, including our capac-

---

17. Animals that breathe are considered higher in the order of things than creatures that do not breathe. Thus in Judaism an animal that breathes must be ritually slaughtered before consumption; the same thing is not true for fish.

18. Note the phrase used by *Targum Onkelos* on Genesis 2:7: "*ruach memallelah*" (a spirit that speaks).

ity for compassion, benevolence, and justice – as well as their opposites. It is with our breath that we speak or express ourselves verbally. It is with our breath that we can sing and exclaim with jubilation, or wail, or give forth a sigh. Thus, *ruach* is associated with our emotional life. The term for one's emotional state in Modern Hebrew is *matzav ruach* – literally, the condition of one's spirit.

There is also a connection between the *vav* and *divine* speech. As explained above, the *vav* is associated with the active attributes. But, the Torah teaches that God acts *through speech*. Thus for example much of the creation story in the Torah involves God's speech (as in, "Let there be light," "Let the earth give forth . . ." etc.). Indeed, the Talmud says that God created the world *ba'assarah maamarot*, that is, with ten utterances or speech acts. What exactly that means is not so simple. After all, God doesn't have physical lips or a mouth. So, what does it mean to say that *God speaks*? Moreover, if we understand God's essence as Being itself, what can it mean to speak of divine speech? A full answer is not possible at this stage, but we can say the following. When humans speak, they *reveal* their thoughts and intentions. Similarly, divine speech is a *revelation* of divine thought and intent. All that God needs to do to act is to *reveal* his thought and intent, and the deed is done. Of course, one can press the question, what is divine thought and intention? We must postpone that discussion until we reach later stages in the book, since the divine mind and will are associated with the upper *heh* and the *yod*. The main point here is that the *vav* symbolizes not only God's active attributes, but also divine speech, that is, the revealing of divine will and thought.

Earlier we mentioned the Kabbalistic teaching that different colors represent different manifestations or expressions of Being and so different colors correspond to different letters of the Name. Recall that the lower *heh* may be symbolized by the color red. Again, red is the color of blood (*dam* in Hebrew) and also the color of the soil or earth (*adamah*) from which man was created, and thus it is the basis of the name for the human or earthling (*Adam*). Here we may add that the *vav* is symbolized by the color green,[19] the color of grass and vegetation. Whereas the soil, or *adamah*, is the basis of life, the greenery that grows from the soil represent living things. Green is a universal symbol of life. Green is the color of lush meadows, leafy trees, oases in the desert. Also, trees release oxygen which allows us to breathe. Thus there is a biological connection

---

19. Ramak writes that green is the color of *tifferet*, which is the central *sefirah* of the *vav*. See *Pardes Rimonim* 4:4; also 10:1.

between green things and breath, or *ruach*. Generally, red is considered an austere or forbidding color, and green is considered a more pleasant and "user friendly" color. Perhaps it is not an accident that red is the universal color for "stop" whereas green is the universal color for "go." Thus it makes sense that green is associated with the *vav*, which represents the active attributes.

One more note on the *vav* is necessary. In the previous chapter, we discussed the notion of kingship in connection with the lower *heh*. Recall that the lower *heh* signifies that God is *omnipresent* in the world; this is one aspect of God's kingship. Like a king, the realm of God reaches everywhere. Kabbalists refer to this aspect of God as the Queen, or *Matrona*. Here we may add that, in a different sense, kingship is associated with the *vav*. The *vav* signifies that God is the benevolent, and compassionate, judge of the world, and this may be summed up symbolically by saying that "God is the King" in the sense that God is the providential guide and overseer of the world. In speaking of this aspect of God, the Kabbalists would not use the term *Shekhina* or *Matrona*, but rather the masculine phrase, *ha-Melech,* or the King.[20]

This concludes our exposition of the six *sefirot,* or divine attributes, associated with the *vav*. We shall soon turn to the *middot,* or virtues, that are associated with the *vav*. First we must address some general points regarding the transition from lower to higher stages of the spiritual journey.

---

20. See Ramak, *Pardes Rimonim: Erchei Hakinuyim. Hamelech* refers to *tifferet,* which is the central *middah* of the *vav*. On the other hand, *malka* and *malchut* are associated with the lower *heh*. We also find the phrase in rabbinic literature (e.g. in *Alenu*): *Melech, malchei hamlachim, Hakadosh Baruch Hu.* As stated earlier, in Kabbalah, *kudsha brich hu* is associated with the *vav*. In the next chapter, we shall see that *Hamelech* is associated also with the upper *heh.*

GROWING FROM STAGE TO STAGE

IN ORDER TO UNDERSTAND and follow the Jewish spiritual path, we must consider not only each of its four stages, but also how one makes the transition from one stage to the next. Indeed, the transition from one stage to the next is often the most challenging aspect of the journey. Consider the metaphor of the "ladder" once again. If each rung represents one stage, the transition between each rung is represented by an empty space between the rungs. While standing on a rung, one stands on something solid. In between each stage, there is nothing solid to stand on. Yet, in order to get to the next level, one must take one's foot off the current rung in order to place it on the next rung. Precisely at that juncture, there is a danger of slipping or falling. The same thing is true of the spiritual journey. At the point of transition, there is a difficulty, and to some degree a danger of falling. In fact, some degree of "falling" or at least insecurity may be inevitable.[21]

How does one get from one rung or stage to the next? Before answering this question, one must bear in mind that Judaism teaches that the spiritual journey is not something that the seeker does completely on one's own; it is also involves divine activity. If a person strives to go higher, divine activity occurs which helps the person reach the next level.[22] Kabbalists speak of an *itaruta di-le-tata* ("awakening from below") and an *itaruta di-le-ela* ("awakening from above").[23] The awakening

---

21. *Shaar Hayichud Ve-ha'emunah* (Introduction).
22. See *Tractate Shabbat* 104a: One who comes to purify himself is aided (from on high). Also, *Tractate Yoma* 39a: If a person sanctifies himself a little from below (i.e., on his own), he is sanctified much from on high (i.e., by God).
23. *Zohar* 1:88a.

from below occurs when a person strives to reach God. The awakening from above is when God strives, as it were, to reach the person. In other words, going up the spiritual ladder is a *two way* process. The seeker goes up, but also, God, as it were, comes down. Prayer and meditation work to advance the spiritual journey not only because of the affect one induces on oneself by praying. Rather, prayer and meditation work because *God responds* to prayer. It is also taught that this faith (or knowledge) – that God helps us along the way – is crucial to counter-acting the insecurity or danger of "falling" mentioned in the previous paragraph.[24]

It is also important to recognize the role of education and upbringing in the spiritual journey. One way that we grow spiritually is simply by being taught, encouraged, habituated, cajoled or even forced to some degree along the path, by parents, teachers, and Rabbis. Our parents teach *middot* to us, and we teach *middot* to our children in all sorts of ways – by example, by providing incentives, by preaching, by habituation, by discipline, and sometimes by sheer force. There is no spiritual tradition that emphasizes teaching and discipline more than does Judaism. The spiritual path is *teachable*, at least to some degree. Indeed, this book itself is an exercise in the attempt to "teach" the Jewish spiritual path. Still, our focus in what follows is more on how a person may be inspired or motivated of his own accord to grow spiritually. Eventually, a person has to grow spiritually on his own, otherwise he remains in a state of *katnut*, or spiritual immaturity.

The spiritual journey then, involves working on oneself. God does not do all the work for us; nor do our teachers. We have to do some work too. How then do we get from a lower stage to a higher stage? What, in the first place, brings us to move from a lower to a higher stage? Let us go back to our starting point. *The spiritual journey is nothing other than a quest for a deeper and deeper relationship with God.* In some way, then, the lower stages involve a comparatively *superficial* relationship with God, while the higher stages involve a *deeper* relationship. It follows that the first step to transition is the recognition of a certain *inadequacy* within one's current level. This recognition leads to a realization that one needs to move to a new and higher level. Each stage has a good quality, but at some point, a person realizes that *remaining at that level is inadequate or unsatisfactory in some way.* This is one reason why all spiritual growth – indeed, all emotional and psychological growth – is usually somewhat painful or difficult.[25] It is painful and distressing to

---

24. *Shaar Hayichud Ve-ha'emunah* (Introduction).
25. See the notion of *merirut* in *Tanya*, chapter 31.

realize that one's current level is deficient. And, the greater the growth, the greater the pain. It is also worth noting that the more one recognizes this and is prepared for it, the easier it is to deal with the pain. A spiritual novice might be surprised and upset to find that growth is not always easy. A more mature spiritual person comes to expect that growth is not always so easy, and so is more prepared for challenges that inevitably lie ahead. He still experiences pain or difficulty, but because he's used to it, it doesn't hurt so much!

Another key idea is that if a person delves deeper into his current level, he sees not only its inadequacy but also that the level that he is at contains within it the very seeds that can lead him to a higher level. The situation may be likened to that of a child who plays with dolls or action figures – only to develop later to write creative fiction in which imaginary women and men are the main characters. Playing with dolls and action figures has its virtues, yet it also has its limits; writing an imaginative story with fictive characters may be seen as a development of that very capacity for imagination that is at work in playing with dolls. Similarly, the key to spiritual growth involves recognizing that one's current level is incomplete or deficient, yet also at the same time realizing the great potential that lies within one's current level.

We shall find that the recognition of both the inadequacy and the potential for growth is something that develops integrally within each stage, as one matures within that stage. Again, a danger lurks here, for one might come to sense the inadequacy of one's current stage, and then fall into despair, without moving to the next stage. It is well known in many spiritual traditions that at certain phases of spiritual growth, one may experience a "dark night of the soul." At that point one might even fall from one's current level, or worse still, fall completely off the path. The key is to bear in mind that although one's current stage is indeed inadequate, it bears within itself the very seeds of the next and higher stage. One must also bear in mind the point made above about divine help in the process. Still, it will always take some hard work to get to the next stage.

So far, we have said that spiritual growth is motivated by a desire to escape some inadequacy in one's current level. The same thing can be said in a more positive way. Spiritual growth is motivated by a natural human drive toward a deeper and deeper relationship with God.[26] In

---

26. Maharal writes that there is a natural drive for the *alul* (effect) to turn back toward its *ilah* (cause or source). See *Netivot Olam: Netiv Ha-avodah* 3. The notion that the soul seeks to "come home" to its source in God is found in many spiritual traditions.

truth, the flight from inadequacy and the drive toward a deeper relationship with God are really two sides of the same coin. An analogy may be helpful here. I might find myself bored and therefore decide to take up some hobby such as playing the piano. In this case, I am taking up a hobby to avoid boredom. However, I wouldn't take up that hobby unless I thought it would be fun or interesting to do so. In taking up that hobby, I am fleeing something negative as well as embracing something positive. Another analogy is as follows. A single man might feel that he is lonely, and to escape that loneliness he seeks companionship with a woman. At the same time, he would not seek companionship with a woman if he did not believe that it would add something positive to his life. Similarly, the advance in one's spiritual journey is not only motivated by a flight from something negative. It is also motivated by a positive desire toward a deeper and more profound relationship with God.

Finally, another aspect of spiritual growth or maturity is the process of taking a more and more *objective perspective* towards one's self and one's place in reality. To take an "objective perspective" is to look at one's self and one's situation from an external point of view, so to speak. In a sense, it is impossible to be completely objective about one's self, for one cannot ever literally step outside oneself to see one's self. Still, as a person grows, he sees himself more and more as a part of a greater and greater whole. An infant does not even make a distinction between itself and other objects or persons outside of itself. The infant does not even realize that he is only a part of a greater whole. (That is why we often refer to an infant as an "it" rather than a "he.") As the infant begins to develop into a child, he begins to realize that he is only a part of the world, and that there are other things and other persons in the world. Still, his concerns and interests may remain largely ego-centric. As a person matures further, he begins to learn to care about the interests of others outside of himself. The more one grows in one's awareness of the sheer magnitude and grandeur of the world outside oneself, the more one realizes how puny one is. The irony is that the more advanced you are, the more you realize how little you are in the grand scheme of things. Yet, since the scheme is grand indeed, that heightens your own importance as well.

The spiritual journey involves a continual process of increasing one's objective stance about one's self and one's place in reality. This is related to the Socratic teaching that the wiser you become, the more you recognize how little you know. It is also related to the Torah's teaching that the greatest prophet, Moshe, was the most humble of all men. With these general points in mind, let us now focus specifically on the transition from the lower *heh* to the *vav*.

EXISTENTIAL SHAME
(*NEHAMA DEKISUFA*)

IN THE FIRST STAGE – the level of the lower *heh* – a person cultivates the *middot* of receptivity, gratitude, and humility. These virtues are the crucial foundation and starting point for everything that follows in the spiritual journey. Nevertheless, with some reflection, a person comes to realize that there is something deeply unsatisfying about remaining at that level. In more positive terms, a person comes to realize that there is a deeper way of engaging with God – a way that goes beyond the *middot* of the lower *heh*. This realization propels a person toward the *middot* of the *vav*.

To begin with, in the *heh* level, a person focuses primarily on *oneself*. In this level, a person receives and appreciates one's *own* gifts, and recognizes one's *own* limitations. True, one must look outward in order to sense one's limitations relative to things outside oneself. But the limitations that one must recognize and come to grips with are *one's own*. As a person grows in intelligence and maturity, he cultivates an awareness and appreciation of the things in the world *outside* of oneself. Much as I may marvel at those natural gifts which I have and enjoy, I come to realize there is a "great big world out there" which includes so much more than myself. There are all sorts of creatures in the world, including not only other humans but countless species of animals, fish, plants, not to mention the sun, the stars and the planets. In fact, what I am capable of *receiving* is but only a miniscule portion of what is out there in the world.

I also come to recognize that I am not the only receiver in the universe. I come to recognize and appreciate the fact that *there are other receivers outside myself*. This is the cultivation of *empathy*, that is, the ability to recognize and appreciate *someone else's* experiences. We may view empathy as a more advanced version of receptivity. Instead of just

95

being receptive regarding my own gifts, I now receive (i.e. take stock) of the fact that *others* exist, and *others* have gifts as well. Indeed, if a person really appreciates something that he has, he should be able to appreciate that same thing *in someone else*. For example, if I marvel at the fact that I have sight, I should also marvel at the fact that others have sight. If I genuinely appreciate what it is for myself to be nourished, I can also appreciate what it means for others to be nourished. There is a progression from a) *being* nourished, to b) *appreciating* that one is being nourished, to c) appreciating that *someone else* is being nourished. These are all steps forward in "objectivity" – the ability to step outside oneself and reflect on one's situation from an external point of view.

Empathy, then, is the ability to recognize and appreciate that there are others outside myself who undergo experiences and have pains, pleasures, and so forth. But theoretically, I could appreciate that other creatures have similar experiences to mine, and yet still not be motivated to *do* anything for anyone else, or do anything at all, for that matter. To explain the transition, we may draw upon a powerful Kabbalistic idea, namely, *nehama dekisufa*, or "bread of shame."[27] Kabbalists use this phrase to describe the bread that is given as a free gift to a poor man. The poor man sorely needs the bread, and indeed he takes it and eats it, *but he doesn't fully enjoy the bread, precisely because he did not earn or deserve it*. Hence, the phrase "bread of shame." The terminology itself is instructive. Why is this phenomenon called "the bread of shame?" A more apt phrase might have been *the shame of not earning one's bread*. The explanation is as follows. It's *not* that the poor man enjoys the bread, and also coincidentally feels shame. The problem is worse. It is rather that the shame affects *the very bread itself*. The bread itself doesn't taste so good, because he has not earned it. Hence, it is called the "bread of shame."

The concept of *nehamah dekisufah* expresses a deep truth about the human condition. We may use the phrase "existential shame" to describe this phenomenon.[28] Surely, there is nothing wrong with receiving a gift

---

27. This notion is found in *Maggid Mesharim* 2:8. It is used as explanation for why the soul is willing to come down into this world, namely, to earn its place in heaven through good deeds. The same notion is expressed in different terms by Ramchal, who quotes a phrase from *Talmud Yerushalmi, Tractate Orlah* 1:3: "One who eats from that which is not his own, is embarrassed to look in the face (of the giver)." See *Derech Hashem*, chapter 2; *Da'at Tevunot* p. 26.

28. The phrase "existential shame" is used by different writers in different ways. For example, some might use the term to connote our reaction to the fact that we are lowly or disgusting creatures, who defecate, get sick, and die. This is a different sense

every now and then. But, there is something deeply unsettling about being constantly on the receiving end, especially of things that one desperately needs in order to live. At the level of the lower *heh*, I recognize and appreciate that I am the beneficiary of a world that exhibits design, beauty, pleasure, and so forth. Reflecting on just my own body alone, I realize that my biological functioning is itself an incredible gift. But eventually I realize something that is extremely unsettling, namely, *that I deserve none of this!* So, I begin to wonder, can I in some way *deserve* what I have? Can I somehow become *worthy* of having the natural gifts that I have? This triggers the development of the *middot* associated with the *vav*, which involve *doing* certain things which will enable me to *deserve* or be *worthy* of having what I have.[29]

In fact, we may distinguish two separate aspects of existential shame. The first and sorest aspect is that I receive many specific things that I don't deserve; these include my natural gifts and capabilities, as well as such necessities as food, water, air, clothing, and so on. To escape or alleviate this aspect of existential shame, I seek to merit or earn those things that I have. A second aspect lies in the very fact that I am a receiver. Because I am a receiver, I am dependent on that which is outside me. This too causes existential shame. To relieve this aspect of existential shame, I must do something to counterbalance or alleviate the very fact that I am a receiver. As we shall see, this is not an easy task.

Before going further, there is something implicit in what was just stated that must be uncovered. In order to start feeling existential shame, I have to perceive something about myself, namely, that in addition to being a *receiver*, I am also an *agent*, an *actor*. I am not a stone, or a plant. If I were not *capable of action*, I would not experience existential shame. A person feels existential shame only because deep down he realizes there is something he *could* be doing that he is not doing. The experience of existential shame is a bitter one, but within it are the very seeds of its cure. As explained earlier, this is a general truth about the spiritual path: the very sensing of one's inadequacies is itself a sign that the inadequacies can be overcome.

---

than the use of that phrase here. Also, as used here, existential shame should not be confused with humility, or *anavah*. There is no shame in *anavah*. *Anavah* involves recognizing one's true limitations. In the sense used here, shame occurs when we recognize something inadequate about ourselves *that can in some way be fixed, at least to some degree.*

29. A cautionary note: we shall see later that one cannot *completely* escape existential shame via the *middot* of the *vav*. The recognition of our inability to do so will inspire us to move on to the *middot* of the next level, the upper *heh*.

We have said that the negative experience of existential shame inspires a person to move beyond the *middot* of the *heh* level. The same thing can be said in a more positive way. Again, the *heh* level involves primarily *receptivity*; it does not involve much *activity*. A person comes to realize that insofar as he remains merely a receiver, he is a rather *passive creature*, that is, a being that is *acted upon* by things outside oneself. While it is true that one way of relating with God or Being is by *receiving*, a more robust and involved way of engaging in a relationship with God is by *acting*. This too is a fundamental truth about human nature: people want to *accomplish* and *achieve* things – whatever those things may be. We get bored sitting around doing nothing. The fact is that we are *beings*, and we have a natural drive *to be*, and that includes the drive to *do*, to *accomplish*, and to *achieve*. The drive *to act* is not just a matter of evading existential shame. Quite apart from a desire to "earn one's keep" or be worthy of what one has, a human being is motivated to be not just a passive recipient but a *doer* as well. This too leads to the *middot* associated with the *vav*.

MORAL, ESTHETIC, AND CREATIVE VIRTUES

THE *MIDDOT* OF THE *VAV* include the moral, esthetic, and creative virtues, which correspond to the six *sefirot* discussed above. Before delving into their details, a brief overview of all six will be helpful. The moral *middot* are *chessed* (benevolence), *rachamim* (compassion), and *gevurah* (justice). Just as God manifests Himself through the *sefirot*, or principles, of *chessed*, *rachamim*, and *gevurah*, so too, humans can and should cultivate these *middot*. The esthetic *middot* involve doing things that are beautiful or awesome.[30] These *middot* correspond to the *sefirot* of *netzach* and *hod*. Just as God manifests Himself in ways that are beautiful and awesome, so too it is fitting for humans to engage in actions that are beautiful or awesome. As we shall see, there are many ways in which ordinary humans can do beautiful or awesome things. Finally, the *middah* of creativity corresponds to the *sefirah* of *yesod*. It involves utilizing one's natural gifts for constructive purposes and not wasting them. Just as God is "replicated" within the world, so too, the human being can and should make a positive lasting mark or imprint upon the world.

Of course, humans cannot have these *middot* in the exact same way that God has them. Rather, there is something about the *sefirot* that humans are able to imitate. Alternatively, we may say that when humans cultivate these *middot*, the divine processes play out through human activity. In other words, humans can participate in the divine processes

---

30. To some readers this may come as a surprise. Many traditional Jews do not tend to think of esthetic sensibility or esthetic behavior as a *middah* that belongs in a *musar* book. This is a mistake. However, as we shall see, Judaism does teach that the moral *middot* are *more important* than the esthetic *middot*.

to some degree. It is worth noting that one can do an action that represents a combination of all or some of the six *middot*. For example, one can do an action that is both benevolent and beautiful; one can do an action that is both compassionate and awesome; and so forth. Still, the *middot* themselves are distinguishable from one another. As we shall see, Judaism teaches that of all of these *middot*, the moral *middot* are the most important ones. The esthetic and creative *middot* are, or should be, subordinate to the moral *middot*. The explanation for this will emerge below.

We have said that the *middot* of the *vav* are motivated by the desire to escape existential shame. At first glance, one might think that one can alleviate existential shame by *working for a living*. Indeed, we tend to think of "industriousness" or "diligence" as a virtue of sorts, and surely it is. If I work for a living, then to some extent I am earning what I have. However, the problem is that I cannot possibly merit my *natural gifts* that way. I could not work if I did not breathe, have arms, a brain, etc. By working, I might be able to earn my daily bread, but no work I could ever do would somehow merit my having my natural gifts. My life, my biological functioning is a priceless gift; no amount of work I do will ever "pay" for this gift. And, without my natural gifts, I would not have the wherewithal to earn a wage. Furthermore, while I may till the soil and work the land to produce crops, nothing that I do can be responsible for those natural conditions that make it possible for the land to produce crops. I don't have anything to do with making the rain come, nor with making it the case that seeds, when planted, bear fruit. Hence, it is impossible to alleviate existential shame by working for a living.

Unfortunately, some people fall into the delusion of thinking that because they work to make a living, they thereby overcome existential shame. Many such people are also under the delusion that they are somehow fully responsible for their material success. The truth is that while many people who are materially successful do work very hard, most of what they are able to achieve is actually not due to their own diligence, but rather to luck or circumstances for which they are not responsible. It is no accident that some of these people tend to have little or no interest in the spiritual journey. They feel quite existentially adequate as wage earners or producers of wealth. Some of these people realize deep down this doesn't work, even though they won't openly admit it. This in turn can create a "workaholic" syndrome, which goes something like this: On the surface, I feel that if I work, I am alleviating existential shame. Yet, deep down, I know this doesn't really help. So I work even harder and longer, thinking that if I do so, it will alleviate existential shame. But it still doesn't help. Thus I work even harder and longer still, but to no avail.

Let us turn then to the moral *middot*. We shall find that they do alleviate existential shame, at least to some degree. There are two ways to explain this: a simple way, and a more complex way. The simple way is as follows. If I live a moral life, then, my life is *morally worthwhile*. If my life is morally worthwhile, I shall feel that I am putting my natural gifts to good use. Thus I shall feel less shame about my natural gifts. In fact, I may even feel proud of myself and feel that I deserve having those gifts, because I have put my gifts to "good use."

The complex way involves understanding in detail the mechanics of *how* living a moral life alleviates existential shame. We said above that there are two aspects of existential shame. The first and sorest aspect is that I have certain specific things that I need, but do not deserve. So, I wish to *merit* or *earn* the specific things that I have. How can I possibly do that? Here we may draw upon another Kabbalistic notion, namely, that there is a difference between *receiving just for oneself* and *receiving not only for oneself, but also to share*.[31] If I receive *only* for myself, I am stuck with existential shame. But if I *share* what I have received, to help others *in need*, that will alleviate my shame. Similarly, if I use my natural gifts to help others in need, that will alleviate my existential shame. Consider once again the poor man who receives a gift of bread and experiences shame. Suppose that he takes the bread, eats some, but also *shares some of it with another poor man*. Even better: suppose that when he takes the bread, he takes it *with the intention* of sharing some of it with another needy person. This will alleviate his feeling of shame as he eats the bread. In this way, a person can alleviate existential shame by *sharing his natural gifts*, that is, by using them to help others who are needy. This is the *middah* of compassion, or *rachamim – helping others in need*.

The second aspect of existential shame mentioned earlier is that one experiences shame at the very fact that one is a receiver. The way to counteract that is to become a *giver*. This is the *middah* of generosity, or *chessed*. This *middah* is not restricted to giving to needy people specifically. Generosity, or *chessed*, involves *being a giver*, even to those who are not needy. Thus, typical acts of *chessed* include hosting guests for a meal, welcoming strangers, or doing favors for others. This counts as *chessed gamur* (pure benevolence) because the recipients have no claim

---

31. See R. Yehduah Ashlag. *Introduction to the Zohar* 11. See also Maharal, *Netivot Olam*, on *Chessed*.

on the host or benefactor.[32] By being a giver, I alleviate the existential shame of being merely a receiver.

Summarizing our discussion so far, we may say that the movement from the *heh* to the *vav* is similar to the development of a child who gradually realizes that instead of just being a sponge for his parents' generosity, he genuinely *wants* to contribute something to the family by (for example) helping with chores around the house. Now, this can happen only when the child really "gets" his situation, i.e., when he sees it for what it truly is. The child must a) receive (realize, accept, take stock of) not only the fact that he is a receiver, *but that others are receivers as well,* b) appreciate what he has, *but also appreciate what others have, or might have,* and, c) cultivate humility; that is, recognize how limited and insignificant he is, *especially in light of the fact that there are other receivers aside from himself.* These are the three virtues of *receptivity, appreciativeness,* and *humility,* taken to a more advanced level. Incidentally, this is another way of seeing that one cannot reach the *middot* of the *vav,* unless one has first cultivated the *middot* of the lower *heh.*

We have seen how existential shame gives rise to *rachamim* and *chessed.* It gives rise to *gevurah,* or justice, in the following way. If I am already advanced enough to experience existential shame at having gifts that I do not deserve, then I would, or at least, I should, experience something even worse if I were to *take away* things that are not my own, from others who already have them, or from those who have somehow managed to earn or deserve those things. Instead of calling that feeling *shame,* we may call it *guilt.* In order to avoid guilt, I must restrain myself from taking what is not mine, and from taking what others have earned. This self-restraint is *gevurah.* *Gevurah* goes further than this. It is not merely a passive self-restraint from doing certain things; it also involves *giving people their due.* For example, if someone has worked for me, I ought to pay him what I owe. If I borrow from someone, I ought to pay him back. In both of these cases, *not* doing so would be depriving someone of what they are due. It is not an act of *rachamim* or *chessed* to pay a worker or pay back a loan; it is a matter of *gevurah,* which in this context would be called *din,* or justice.

---

32. In *Netivot Olam,* Maharal argues that it is in the nature of a material being that it is a *mekabel* or receiver, and, it is in the nature of a spiritual being that it is a *mashpia,* or giver. A person who does *chessed* transforms himself from a mere receiver to a giver, and thereby elevates himself from the status of a mere material being to a spiritual being. Maharal uses this to explain why the first patriarch was called *Av-ram* (elevated father). This had to do with his being a man of *chessed.*

Putting the same point in other terms, if I wish to avoid existential shame by earning or deserving what I have, I must perforce accept the notion that others, too, can earn or deserve what they have. In other words, if there is a way for me to be worthy of my gifts, there must be a way that others can also be worthy of their gifts. And, if I expect others to respect and acknowledge that I am worthy of having certain things, I must respect and acknowledge that others can be worthy of having certain things. Hence, in order to escape or alleviate existential shame, I must cultivate the *middah* of *gevurah*, or justice.

In the previous chapter, we represented the fact that receptivity gives rise to gratitude and humility in the form of a table or chart. As the chart below indicates, compassion is an advanced form of receptivity. Moreover, compassion forms the basis of benevolence and justice. Like receptivity, compassion is a central virtue. Like gratitude, benevolence is a right-sided virtue. Finally, like humility, justice is a left-sided virtue. In the next chapter, we shall see how the *middot* of the *vav* blossom further into the *middot* of the upper *heh*.

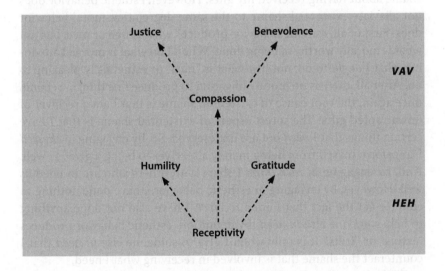

So far, we have discussed the moral *middot*. Let us move on to the esthetic *middot*, which involve doing beautiful or awesome things. The very idea of esthetic *middot* may raise some questions in the mind of the reader. Can ordinary people really be expected to do beautiful and awesome things? On the surface, this sounds overly demanding. Second, is it really true that the Jewish spiritual path involves doing beautiful and/or awesome things?

First, it is important to note that there are *degrees* of beauty and awesomeness in human activity. An example of extraordinary beauty might be something like a piano concerto by Mozart or a painting by Rembrandt. An example of an action that is extraordinarily awesome is traveling to the moon or winning a world championship sporting competition. Great artists and great athletes engage in extraordinarily beautiful and awesome actions. But if I dress nicely, or sing nice songs, or do nice landscaping, or gracefully decorate my house, I am also producing or doing something that is beautiful. Similarly, if I hike to the top of a mountain, or make an overseas voyage, or shoot a three point shot on a basketball court, that too is awesome. The term "awesome" here should be taken in the broad sense of "impressive." One doesn't have to be famous to do beautiful or awesome actions. Indeed, ordinary people do beautiful and awesome things all the time.

Now let us consider to what extent esthetic behavior alleviates existential shame. If I engage in beautiful or awesome actions, I shall feel that my natural gifts have been put to fine use. This makes me feel less shame about having received my gifts. However, esthetic behavior does not alleviate existential shame to the same degree that moral behavior does. First of all, esthetic behavior produces what is fine or nice, but not what is morally worthy of being done. When I do what is moral, I am doing what I *ought* to do, not just what is "nice" or esthetically pleasing to do. After all, there is no moral obligation to produce fine things. Second, once again, the root cause of existential shame is that I am a receiver of unwarranted gifts. The sorest aspect of existential shame is that I have certain things that I *need* but are undeserved. So, by engaging in *chessed* I transform myself from being merely a receiver to being a giver as well. And, by engaging in *rachamim* I share with others who are in need as well. However, by engaging in esthetic behavior, I have done nothing to counter-act the fact that I am a *receiver*. I have also not done anything to help someone else *in need*. By definition, esthetic behavior produces "extras" or "frills." It is only when I give to someone else *in need* that I counteract the shame that is involved in receiving what I need.

With these thoughts in mind, we may now clarify what is the role of esthetic behavior in the Jewish spiritual path. Earlier we noted that Judaism teaches that God's moral attributes, or *sefirot*, are in some sense more fundamental or important that God's esthetic *sefirot*. Similarly, Judaism teaches that, for humans as well, the esthetic *middot* should be subordinate to the moral *middot*. It is more important to be generous, compassionate, and just, than to do beautiful or awesome actions. It is never proper to do a beautiful or awesome action at the cost of doing something unjust or cruel. Also, as mentioned earlier, one can *combine* esthetic behavior with moral behavior. For example, one can create artistic works and share them with others. One can cheer someone up by singing them a song. One can "bring home" a championship victory as a gift to one's home town. In this way, one heightens the importance of esthetic behavior and elevates it to the level of moral behavior. More often than not, esthetic behavior is connected with benevolent behavior toward others. However, that still does not take away from the fact that even purely esthetic actions are, in themselves, fine or appropriate ones to do.

Finally, we turn to the *middah* of creativity, which corresponds to the divine *sefirah* of *yesod*. This *middah* has both a positive aspect and a negative aspect. The positive aspect involves *engaging in creative and/ or productive acts*. This can take various forms, including, but not only, having children, having a career, writing a book, exploring the world, coming up with a new invention, and so on. It involves leaving an "imprint" of oneself on the world in some way, that is, by accomplishing something. It does not necessarily mean doing something that makes a person famous. Even if I simply have a job, and I perform my task well, I am productive in some sense. In particular, if I do something in the world that *only I could have done*, that is even better. Thus, for example, the child that I bear would be uniquely my own product. But there are many things that only I can do in the world. It might be something like keeping a garden that no one else would have kept had I not done so. Anything that is "productive" is a creative act. The more the product is unique to me, the better. For, if it is unique to me, I shall have put my talents and gifts to a special use, which only I could have done.

On the negative side, the *middah* corresponding to *yesod* is restraint or control of the creative powers, that is, *not* using one's creative powers in vain or wasting them. Kabbalists connect the *middah* of *yesod* with sexual restraint, or *shmirat ha-brit*; that is, not using the creative organ improperly. The creative impulse should not be used in vain – creative desire should not be wasted but rather used for a constructive purpose. We are not talking merely about avoiding sexual impropriety, but rather the more general issue of using one's creative energies for a constructive purpose. For example, one can seek to "make a mark" upon the world by doing destructive things and unjust things and cruel things. One can also engage in silly or futile behavior as a way of "expressing oneself." This is like being promiscuous or spilling seed in vain.[33] The *middah* of *yesod* involves avoiding such behavior.

---

33. The *Zohar* treats spilling seed in vain as a serious wrongdoing. This appears

Through creative activity, one can alleviate existential shame to some degree. If I produce something, especially something that only I could have produced, I shall have made good use of my natural gifts. Hence, I shall feel less existential shame about having those gifts. Yet, like esthetic behavior, and for similar reasons, it does not alleviate existential shame to the same degree that moral behavior does. First, there is no moral obligation to be creative. By engaging in creative behavior, I am doing something constructive, but not (necessarily) what I *ought* to do. Therefore, it does not make me *morally worthy* of being alive. Second, when one engages in creative behavior, one does not (necessarily) become a giver, nor does one help someone else in need. Therefore, creative behavior does nothing to counteract the existential shame involved in receiving what one needs. Of course, as suggested earlier, one could *combine* creative behavior with moral behavior. For example, if a person invents a new cure for a disease, one is both creative and compassionate at the same time. Similarly, if one cooks a fine gourmet meal for another, one has engaged in creative and benevolent behavior. Through such actions, one may indeed alleviate existential shame. But then, the alleviation would stem from the fact that one is engaging in compassionate or benevolent behavior, which happens also to be creative. In sum, the moral *middot* alleviate existential shame more than do the creative and esthetic *middot*.

We have seen how the experience of existential shame motivates the cultivation of the six *middot* associated with the *vav*. The *middot* are also motivated by the natural human drive to *do, accomplish*, or *achieve*. The world we live in is a world that is bursting with activity, and by nature, we are not only receivers but doers. This inclines us to be creative in one way or another, to give and to share, to explore the world, to invent new things, to have children, to build empires. It also inclines us to esthetic activity.

Let us consider briefly the question as to what extent can these *middot* be cultivated by an agnostic. It seems clear that an agnostic could cultivate all of these *middot*, at least to some degree. Much of what has been said here could apply to an agnostic, including the experience of existential shame and the consequent inspiration to cultivate the moral, esthetic, and creative virtues. He too is motivated by a drive to do, to accomplish, and to achieve. Surely, an agnostic may cultivate benevo-

---

to be linked with the belief that spilling seed creates or unleashes negative spiritual forces in the universe. In light of the presentation here, one may understand "spilling seed" as representing the general notion of wasting one's creative abilities.

lence, compassion, and justice, as well as esthetic sensibility and creativity. However, whereas the spiritual seeker understands these *middot* as a way of deepening his relationship with God, an agnostic would not think of these *middot* in that way. In the next section, we shall see how the second stage of *Shacharit* serves as a vehicle to help us cultivate the *middot* of the *vav*, and thereby to engage in a relationship with God that advances beyond the *middot* of the lower *heh*.

THE SECOND STAGE OF *SHACHARIT*: VERSES OF SONGFUL PRAISE

IN THE FIRST CHAPTER, we saw how the first stage of *Shacharit* corresponds to the lower *heh* of the divine Name. By reciting the Morning Blessings and the portions of the Sacrifices, a person focuses on the Divine Presence, or *Shekhinah*, that is, God's essence or Being insofar as She is manifest in the physical world, and particularly in the natural gifts of one's own body. In doing so, a person cultivates the *middot* of receptivity, gratitude, and humility. We now advance to the second stage of *Shacharit*. The purpose of this stage is to express recognition and praise of God insofar as He manifests himself through the six active *sefirot*, and thereby to arouse within oneself the *middot* associated with the *vav*, namely, the creative, esthetic, and moral virtues.

The second stage of *Shacharit* is *Pesukei d'Zimrah* (hereafter abbreviated, *PZ*), often translated as, "Verses of Praise."[34] These are Scriptural verses drawn mostly from the book of *Tehillim*, or Psalms. In fact, the term *zimrah* connotes song or music; the more appropriate term for praise is *tehillah*, or *shevach*. Nearly all of *PZ* is in a poetic or songlike form. A better translation for *PZ* might be "Verses of Song" or perhaps, "Verses of Songful Praise." Indeed, the sages teach that one should recite *PZ* in a patient and unhurried manner.[35] This requirement should not be

---

34. The discussion here follows the Ashkenazic *nusach*, or custom. Nothing major hinges on which *nusach* one follows. The vexed issue of where exactly is the borderline between the first two stages, including the different customs about where to put the collection of verses beginning with *Hodu*, exemplifies that the border between these two stages is not so sharp. The situation is different with the other two stages. In those cases, it is universally agreed where one stage ends and another begins.

35. *SA:OC*: 51:8–9. *Mishna Berurah* (ad loc.) writes that one should enunciate

taken lightly. A person who hurries through or mumbles the verses is not fulfilling this portion of *Shacharit* in the best possible way, or perhaps, not fulfilling it at all. As we shall see, the singing of *PZ* plays a crucial role in helping a person advance from the first to the second stage of the Jewish spiritual path.

The advance to a higher and more mature stage in the liturgy is reflected in the increased stringency regarding the laws regarding verbal *hafsakot*, or interruptions, during the prayer.[36] In the first stage of *Shacharit*, all interruptions are permitted, unless one is the middle of a blessing. This indicates that the first stage is a relatively relaxed stage of prayer. In that first stage, one has just woken up from sleep, and so a certain lack of rigor is fitting. However, once a person begins *PZ*, one may not engage in idle conversation. Certain congregational responses are permitted, such as answering *amen* to another blessing. The increased stringency regarding interruptions is related to the fact that *PZ* constitutes one unit, which begins with a blessing and ends with a blessing. It also reflects the fact that in comparison to the first section of *Shacharit*, the second section demands a higher level of concentration.

Before *PZ*, there is a brief transitional phase between the end of the first stage and the beginning of the second stage. This is made up of the Rabbi's *Kaddish* (known as *Kaddish derabbanan*) which is said immediately after the study of the passage from Rabbi Yishmael. This is followed by Psalm 30, which is then followed in turn by the Mourner's *Kaddish* (*Kaddish Yatom*). The recitation of these *Kaddishim* is not a mandatory part of the order of the prayer, and if there is no mourner present these *Kaddishim* may be omitted. The *Kaddish* itself is a fascinating piece of liturgy, which we shall discuss in more detail in the next chapter. Basically, the *Kaddish* is an exultant affirmation of the greatness and holiness of the Name of God, and the declaration that his great name be blessed, exalted and extolled in any way possible, beyond anything and everything that can be said.

In general, the *Kaddish* serves as a *conclusion marker* at the end of a stage of prayer. Thus there is a (Mourner's) *Kaddish* at the end of the first stage, a mandatory *Kaddish* at the end of the second stage, and another mandatory *Kaddish* at the end of the fourth stage of the *Shacharit*. The *Kaddish* draws our attention to the Name of God. Given the Kabbalistic teaching that each stage of *Shacharit* corresponds to one letter of God's

---

each word "as if one is counting coins." *Piskei Tshuvot* (ad loc., p. 433) emphasizes the appropriateness of singing *PZ*.

36. *SA:OC:* 51:5. For a convenient summary, see *Artscroll Siddur* p. 59.

name, it makes good sense that after each stage of the prayer, we pause to recognize and exalt God's name. An important exception is that that there is no *Kaddish* between the third and fourth stages. As we shall see later, this exception bears important lessons regarding the transition between the upper *heh* and the *yod*, both in terms of the liturgy and in terms of the *middot* that are associated with these higher two stages. We shall return to this point in the next chapter.

Psalm 30 is a preparation for *PZ*. Until this point in *Shacharit*, no mention of any form of the term *zemer* (song or praise) has yet occurred. Here, the Psalmist exalts God for having "lifted my soul (*nafshi*) up from the grave," that is, for having saved his life, *so that he can praise God.* God is to be praised for allowing me to live, and for turning my "eulogy" into *machol*, or "dance." The major theme of this psalm is that life is worth living even if only to praise God. If I live life merely as an animal, my life shall have been lived in vain. But if I praise God with spiritedness, my life takes on higher meaning. In Kabbalistic terms, this psalm may be taken to represent a transformation from the level of *nefesh* to the level of *ruach*. Again, *nefesh* is the animal level of the soul; *ruach* connotes the more human level. Thus, Psalm 30 serves as a fitting prelude to *PZ*.

The Verses of Songful Praise are introduced by the blessing, *Baruch Sheamar*, and concluded with the blessing, *Yishtabach*. In saying the first blessing, we perform the very self-conscious act of focusing on what we are about to do, that is, sing the praises of God. In saying the concluding blessing, we again perform the very self-conscious act of expressing the significance of what we have just done. Later we shall note some of the points of difference between these two blessings.[37] The main point here is that by saying these blessings, we indicate that we are not reciting verses just for the sake of reading, nor even for the sake of pious study (*talmud torah*). Rather, our intention is to sing these verses *in order to praise God.* We also affirm that God is blessed even just insofar as he is worthy of praise.[38]

In many prayer books, *Baruch Sheamar* is preceded by a brief

---

37. See next chapter, pages 164ff.

38. It is instructive that the Rabbis did not establish a *birchat mitzvah* (blessing for a commandment) but rather a *birchat shevach* (blessing of praise) for saying *PZ*. See Ba"ch on *Tur* 51; he discusses the issue of whether this blessing is obligatory. This contrasts sharply with the blessing that precedes *Hallel* (on those festive days when we say *Hallel*). The praise of *PZ* is one that would be appropriate, even if there were no such thing as divine commandments. The same is not true of *Hallel*, which is linked with the notion of commandments.

Kabbalistic meditation involving the Name.[39] Like the *Kaddish*, this meditation brings our mind to focus on God's Name and in particular on the unification of the two aspects of God corresponding to the lower *heh* (*Shekhinah*) and the *vav* (*kudsha brich hu*). In simple terms, the "unification" of the two aspects of God represents the harmonization of the active and receptive aspects of God. Our goal is that the masculine and feminine aspects should work together in harmony, both in God, and in us. It is no accident that this meditation on the aspects of God's name occurs in this transitional stage between the phases of *Shacharit* that correspond to the feminine lower *heh* and the masculine *vav*. For those wearing *tzitzit* (ritual fringes), it is customary to hold the two front *tzitzit* while saying *Baruch Sheamar*. This custom is also based on Kabbalah.[40] A simple explanation is that the two front *tzitzit* correspond to the two lower letters of the Name, that is, the lower *heh* and the *vav*. (Later, during the third stage we will hold all four *tzitzit* together, symbolizing the unification of all four letters of the divine name.) All of this highlights the connection between the first two stages of *Shacharit* and the last two letters of the divine name.

The basic content of *Baruch Sheamar* is that God is worthy of exultant praise insofar as God is the source and benefactor of the natural world in all of its glory. God is the actor behind the scenes of everyday life; God is compassionate on all living creatures (*merachem al ha-aretz, merachem al habriyot*) and God is just (*meshalem sachar tov leyerav*). God is "*yachid, chay haolamim*" – the unique one who is the very life of all worlds (or realms of reality), and therefore God is "*melech mehulal batishbachot*" – the King who is exalted through praises. The blessing does refer to "those who fear him" and "those who are his devout ones." However, there is no explicit reference in this blessing to the patriarchs, nor to Israel, the exodus, the revelation at Sinai, etc.[41] Clearly, the main

---

39. The text of the meditation beginning with the phrase "*leshem yichud*" runs as follows: *For the sake of unifying the Holy Blessed is He and His Divine Presence, with reverence and love, to unify the yod-heh with vav-heh, with complete unity, in the name of all Israel, behold I prepare my mouth to give thanks and to praise my creator!*

40. See *Piskei Tshuvot* on 51. The Ari's explanation for this custom is more complex but what is offered here may be seen as a simpler version of what he says.

41. The only reference to a particular individual occurs when we say that we will praise God with *shirei David*, that is, the poems of David. An oblique reference to Israel does occur in the phrase, *hamehulal be-feh amo* (the one who is exalted by the mouth of *his nation*). Yet, even here, the name Israel is not mentioned. It is also absent from *Yishtabach*. The absence of the name Israel from these blessings is conspicuous. As we shall see later, this sharply differentiates the second stage of *Shacharit* from the third and fourth stages.

theme of this blessing is to express exultant praise for God insofar as
He manifests himself *in the world generally*, through the attributes of
generosity, compassion, and justice. As explained above, these are God's
moral qualities – the main *sefirot* associated with the *vav* in God's holy
name.[42]

This initial blessing highlights the notion that God *speaks*.[43] The very
first words of the blessing are *Baruch Sheamar, vehaya ha-olam* (Blessed
is He *who spoke*, and the world came to be). As noted earlier, it is through
speech that God acts. Throughout the entire blessing of *Baruch Sheamar*
there is an emphasis on speech and different types of speech-acts. Thus
for example we say, *baruch omer ve-oseh . . . baruch gozer vekayam*
(blessed is the one *who says* and does. . . . blessed is the one who *de-
crees* and fulfills). This blessing also highlights *our* ability to speak. After
all, praise is a form of speech. There is even an explicit reference to the
"mouth" of God's people, and the "tongue" or language of his devoted
servants. The conclusion of the blessing is "*Baruch atoh Hashem, melech
mehulal batishbachot* (Blessed is Hashem, the King who is exalted with
praises.) One might have imagined that the conclusion should have been
something like, *Baruch atoh Hashem, melech gadol umefoar* (Blessed
is Hashem, great and wondrous king). If we are praising God, why not
praise him for being a great King? It seems odd and almost tautologous
to praise God *for being exalted with praises*. However, the emphasis on
both divine and human speech in this blessing is not accidental.[44] This
second stage of *Shacharit* corresponds to that aspect of the soul known
as *ruach*, which represents the capacity for speech.

It is also no accident that in the blessing *Baruch Sheamar* we repeat
the word *baruch*, or *blessed*. This word occurs no less than thirteen times
in this blessing. There is no other blessing like this in the entire Jewish
liturgy. The phrase *Baruch Hu*, (blessed is He) occurs in this blessing.[45]

---

42. Some form of *rachamim* is mentioned three distinct times in this blessing.
(*Baruch merachem al ha-aretz . . . baruch merachem al habriyot . . . ha-el, ha-av,
harachaman.*) A Kabbalistic explanation for this might be that the attribute of *rachamim* is the central *sefirah* associated with the *vav*.

43. There are exactly 87 words in this blessing. 87 is the *gematria*, or numerical
value of the Hebrew letters, *Peh* and *Zayin*. It is taught in the name of the Ari (*Sha'ar
Hakavanot* p. 78) that the number 87 stands for the Hebrew word, *be-feh*, which
also has a value of 87 and means, "with the mouth." This reinforces the connection
between *PZ* and speech.

44. Even before the blessing itself, the meditative prayer "*leshem yichud*" mentions "the mouth." See above, note 39.

45. References to God's name (*shem*) also occur in this blessing. We say *baruch
hu, u-varuch shmo* – "blessed is he, and blessed is his name," and toward the end, we

On the surface, this phrase seems unnecessary. All of this underscores the fact that *PZ* corresponds to the *vav*, that is, the aspect of the divine known as *Hakadaosh, Baruch Hu.*

After the initial blessing, *PZ* consists of a long section of verses beginning with "*Hodu*," followed by *Mizmor Le'todah* (Psalm 100) and then a collection of verses beginning with *Yehi Chvod.* The central and most important part of *PZ* consists of Psalms 145–150, which are the last six chapters of the book of Psalms.[46] These psalms are known as *Ashrei* and the five *Halleluyahs.* The main theme of *PZ* is that of *blessing and praising God for his benevolence, compassion, and justice as displayed in the beautiful and awesome workings of nature.* As explained earlier, a "blessing" is an expression of recognition that God is the source of something. Every blade of grass, every drop of water, every ray of sunshine is an expression of Being. Every motion that every creature makes, every breath that every living thing takes, is an expression of divine benevolence, compassion, and restraint or justice. As discussed earlier, even within one creature organism alone, there are literally billions of discrete events that are happening in just such a way that that creature can function and live. Also, each particular creature expresses divine restraint, insofar as it is precisely what it is, and not something else. The fine detail in the universe is utterly astonishing. Countless creatures are constantly supplied with their needs, until the moment they die or are extinguished. When one contemplates the world, the sea and all its contents, the planets, the cosmos . . . this not only boggles the mind but moves the heart.

While God's special relationship with Israel is mentioned periodically throughout *PZ*, the main emphasis of *PZ* is actually *not* on God's special relationship with Israel. In the (halachically) most important Psalm 145, no mention whatsoever is made of the people of Israel[47] or the Torah. As in *Baruch Sheamar*, the only hint of personalization is in the opening phrase, *Tehillah Le-David* – "A psalm of David." The main function of

---

declare that we will praise God *adey ad shmo hagadol*, or "to the extent of his great Name."

46. Halachically, this is the essential part of *PZ* (aside from the two blessings at the start and finish). Thus, if one is unable to say all of *PZ*, one should at least say Psalms 145–150; of these Psalms, the most important one is Psalm 145. See *SA:OC*: 52:1. Incidentally, a remarkable correspondence may be seen between the five Halleluyahs and the five aspects of the soul. See the Appendix, Meditation 6.

47. The introductory phrases beginning with the word "*Ashrei*" (Fortunate are those who dwell in your house . . . Fortunate is the nation who has this relationship with Him . . .) are *not* part of Psalm 145.

PZ is precisely to sing God's praises insofar as God is manifest in the everyday workings of the natural world, in all of its glory and beauty.[48] Indeed, Psalm 145 emphasizes God's providential guidance over the *entire* universe and *all* mankind. One verse underscores this by saying that the Psalmist's purpose here is *Lehodia livnei ha-adam gevurosav,* "to make known *to mankind* his awesome deeds." The universal message also comes through in the fact that in this Psalm the word *kol,* or "all," occurs seventeen times! The last verse sums it up: "May *all* flesh (*kol basar*) bless his holy Name."

Indeed, throughout *PZ,* there is not a single mention of God's love (*ahavah*) for the people of Israel. This contrasts with all the other three stages of *Shacharit,* where God's love for Israel is mentioned and in fact plays a crucial role (especially in the third and fourth stages of *Shacharit*). In fact, the Hebrew word for love (*ahavah*) is almost entirely absent from *PZ.* No form of this word occurs in *Baruch Sheamar,* and it occurs only once in the entire *PZ,* namely, in Psalm 145, where the Psalmist writes that "God watches over *those who love him.*" Even here, this verse is not talking about God's love for Israel, but rather those who love God. Again, the point of *PZ* is that all humanity, indeed, all creation should praise God. While it is true that Israel has additional reasons to thank and praise God – this is not the central theme of *PZ.*

In *PZ,* we also find an expression of *esthetic* appreciation of the beauty and awesomeness inherent in the natural world. We express praise not only for the goodness (*tov*) in nature; we also express praise for the beauty (*chen*) in nature. As the Psalmist exults, "*yismachu hashamyim ve-tagel haaretz, yiram hayam u-mlo-oh*" which translates as, "*Let the heavens rejoice and the earth celebrate; let the sea and all its contents thunder forth!*" Every element of the natural world should praise God, even *etz pri v-chol arazim,* "the fruit trees and all the cedars" (Psalm 148). Indeed, *PZ* includes a number of references to fields, grass, and trees. No doubt, *PZ* is the most "green" of all the four stages of *Shacharit.* This also constitutes a link between *PZ* and the *vav,* which as we saw earlier is represented by the color green. We include praise for God insofar as the cold and freezing weather is sometimes unbearable (*lifney karato*

---

48. *PZ* includes *Shirat Hayam,* that is, the Song that the Israelites sang after the miraculous splitting of the sea. However, this was not included in the original text of *PZ.* It is not mentioned as part of the required order of prayer by Maimonides (*Hilchot Tefillah: Seder Hatefillah*) nor by *Shulchan Aruch.* Interestingly, Maimonides does mention a custom (apparently no longer in vogue) of saying the Song of the Sea *after Yishtabach.* See *Hilchot Tefillah* 7:13. This fits well with points made later in Chapter 3. See note 88.

mi yaamod, "who can bear the freezing cold?"). If a person does not react with awe and wonder in recognizing the workings of the natural word – there is something sorely lacking in that recognition. This is one reason why *PZ* should be *sung,* not read dispassionately. We shall return to this point shortly.

Another theme of *PZ* is the exultant recognition of God as King, or *Melech.* While the theme of *malchut* had already emerged in the first stage of *Shacharit,* it is even more prominent in the second stage. The theme of *malchut* is mentioned numerous times, both in *Baruch Sheamar* and *Yishtabach.* It is also mentioned in *Yehi Chavod* and in *Ashrei.* Whereas in the first stage of *Shacharit,* we recognize God as King in the sense of the omnipresent *Shekhinah* who is found in all places, in this second stage we express recognition of God as King in the sense that God is the benevolent provider and guide of the world, in all of its natural wonder. One does not recognize a King with mere words; one recognizes a King with fanfare, trumpets and song. This emerges especially in Psalm 150, the last of the five *Halleluyahs.*

Another aspect of *PZ* is that of *magnifying* or *aggrandizing* God's Name. This is mentioned in *Baruch Sheamar* (*negadlah shmecha*) and in *Ashrei* (*gadol Hashem umehullal meod*). By expressing praises of God, we "aggrandize" His name, which has to do with *making public* the recognition of God insofar as He is manifest in the wondrous workings of the cosmos. Indeed, even the mentioning of God's name is part of the process (as we say in *Baruch Sheamar, nazkir shimcha*). Related to this is the concept of *hillul,* which is related to *Hallelu-yah.* One might wonder how is *hallel* different from *shevach? Shevach* connotes praise too, but *hallel* specifically means to *make some noise* – in this context, noise that is made in praise. Thus we say, *Halleluhu benevel ve-chinor* (with flute and harp). Although it is not prevalent Jewish custom to do so, it would seem that playing musical instruments during the Halleluyahs would, in theory, be very appropriate. The purpose of *PZ* is to aggrandize God's Name with praise; this requires noisemaking. It should not be said in a whisper!

After *Ashrei* and the *Halleluyahs, PZ* continues with a passage from *Chronicles* (1:29) that runs as follows: "*And David blessed Hashem. . . . and he said, blessed are you Hashem, the God of Israel, Our Father from time immemorial. Unto you Hashem is the greatness, the might, the balance, the victory and the majesty; for all in the heaven and earth is under your kingship. . . .*" This phrase is understood by the Kabbalists as a reference to the six *sefirot* associated with the *vav.*[49] It is no accident that

---

49. The phrase in Hebrew: "*Lecha Hashem hagedulah vehagevurah vehatifferet*

the only place in the entire *Shacharit* where we allude directly to the six attributes by their Kabbalistic names is here in *PZ*, the stage that corresponds to the *vav*. Just a few lines later we cite a passage from *Nehemiah* (9) that mentions the *brit* (covenant) that God made with *Avram*, which was sealed or symbolized by the change of his name to *Avraham* and by his circumcision. Kabbalistically, this may be taken as an allusion to *yesod*. Earlier we noted that *yesod* has to do with reproduction; the main "reproduction" or "re-presentation" of God in the world is the human being. How fitting then is it that this passage begins by referring to God here as *elokai yisrael, Avinu*, "the God of Israel, our father."[50] The allusion to God as "our father" implies that we are reproductions of the divine.

Let us dwell briefly on the passage regarding *Avraham* in this passage. What exactly is the function of this section here? Surely it is a form of praise, for here we praise God for having established a covenantal relationship with our patriarch Avraham. But there is a deeper message. Avraham was the first person with whom God made a *brit* in which his name was changed and his body was changed. Avram made a true mark on the world. He was Avram and he then became Avraham. The name change is symbolic of his making a mark, *making a difference* in human history. From the beginning of Adam and onward, perhaps with the exception of Noah, no human being had made such a profound influence on world history until Avraham. He made a mark by participating in a covenantal relationship with God, which then set the destiny of the Jewish people and indeed world history on its course. Hence, Avraham serves as a model for all individual humans that follow, to make a positive mark in human history. His "mark" was symbolized by a physical mark, namely the circumcision which is on the reproductive organ and which symbolizes *yesod*. We shall return to this point shortly.

As the main function of *PZ* is to express *praise* rather than mere *thanks*, it is worth discussing some important differences between them.

---

vehanetzach vehahod, ki kol. . . ." Kabbalistically, *gedulah* is a code word for *chessed*; the word *kol* is a code word for *yesod*. (See note 13 above.) The other *sefirot* are mentioned by their more commonly known names.

50. The phrase is more commonly read as "the God of Israel our father." On this latter reading, the term "father" is a modifier of our patriarch Israel, not God. But see the Kabbalistic commentary on Chronicles by Moshe David Valli (a student of Ramchal) who takes the term "father" to refer to God. Interestingly, we first refer to God as "the father" in *Baruch Sheamar*, but in the actual verses of *PZ*, this is the first occasion. Even here it is ambiguous. We refer explicitly to God as our father later in the blessing of *Ahava Rabbah* and then in the *Amidah* as well. This dovetails with points made later in Chapter 3 (p. 176).

When a person gives thanks, he gives thanks for some good or benefit that he has received from the person whom he thanks. On the other hand, a person may praise someone for some good thing that someone has done – *whether it is to himself or to someone else*. In fact, one may praise someone for doing something noble or admirable, *even if that thing was not particularly intended to benefit anyone else at all*. For example, we can praise an artist or an athlete for creating a work of art or achieving some remarkable feat, even if his accomplishment was not intended to benefit anyone. Moreover, thanks are given for some benefit that we receive. Hence, I can give thanks only for something that I can grasp or comprehend. For example, I can thank someone for giving me a fine meal. I may not know how the chef prepared the meal, but when I give thanks, I give thanks *for that benefit which I have received*. However, I can *praise* someone for doing something that I cannot fully grasp or comprehend. Thus I can praise the same chef for his culinary skills, even if I myself do not understand the precise nature of those skills. Similarly, I can praise Einstein for inventing the theory of relativity, even if I myself do not understand the theory very well. In other words, thanksgiving is limited to what I can comprehend; praise is not limited by my own comprehension.

Another difference between thanks and praise is that whereas thanks are directed primarily to the giver, praise involves a third party. As explained earlier, the main point of giving thanks is for the receiver to acknowledge and in some way pay back a debt *to the giver*. While certainly one may choose to thank someone publicly, one can thank someone quite adequately in private. On the other hand, the point of praise is not to pay back a debt, but rather to express admiration. This expression can be made in the presence of the person himself, but it doesn't count as praise unless it is in the presence of others. We praise someone properly by *letting others* know of how much we admire him for what he has done or accomplished. The more public is the praise, the greater the praise it is.

Precisely because *PZ* is praise rather than mere thanks, it is crucial that we *sing PZ* rather than merely *recite* it. To give thanks, or even to bless, one needs only a very rudimentary form of speech. There is no need to be poetic in order to give thanks. Even a mumbled or whispered word of thanks or blessing constitutes an act of recognition that God is the source of something. However, a mumbled word cannot constitute an act of praise. In an act of praise, the *form* or *manner* of expression is just as important, if not more important, than the *content* of what is being said. Indeed, the best way to praise someone is with poetry and song.

This last point helps explain something that is otherwise rather puzzling. Much of the content of *PZ* is repetitive. Several verses are repeated word for word in their entirety.[51] Of all the four stages of *Shacharit*, *PZ* is the longest and most repetitive. The explanation lies in the fact that it is in the very nature of praise and song to be repetitive. The basic construction of any song is a beat or tempo of some sort, which is by nature, repetitive; a beat is established only by a repeated tapping or drumming at the exact same interval. Moreover, almost any song or piece of music that one can find involves the "statement" of a melody and then a repetition of that melody over and again, sometimes in different ways, sometimes in exactly the same way. Generally, one does not enjoy hearing the same sentence repeatedly recited. However, if a song is esthetically pleasing, one can sustain hearing it repeatedly – up to a point. In a poem or song, the *form* or manner of expression is no less important than its verbal content. Indeed, the repetitive nature of a song indicates that content is in some ways *less* important than the form. In a paradoxical way, repetition indicates that the verbal content is not the main point. If the content were the main point, there would be no need for repetition![52]

The themes of repetition and song are related to another aspect of *PZ* discussed above, namely that of *magnifying* or *aggrandizing* God's Name. By repeatedly expressing praises of God, we thereby "aggrandize" His name, which has to do specifically with *making public* the recognition of God insofar as He is manifest in the wondrous workings of the cosmos. This is yet another reason why *PZ* should be sung, and sung aloud and preferably in public. A song that is silent is simply not a song. In fact, it is not only appropriate to sing *PZ*, but also to physically move or sway (Yiddish: *shuckle*) during *PZ*. One's whole body should be moved, literally, in the praise of God. In fact, in *PZ* there are two explicit

---

51. Examples of repeated verses are *Kol haneshama, etc.*; *Hashem Yimloch le-olam vaed*; *Hashem hoshea hamelech yaanenu beyom korenu*; *Ve-hu rachum, etc.* In general, the book of Psalms is highly repetitive (relative to other biblical books).

52. There is a strong parallel between *PZ* and the *maggid* section of the *Passover Haggadah*. The telling of the story of the exodus is a form of praise, or *shevach*, and that is why the *maggid* section is the longest and most repetitive part of the *Haggadah*. See also *Netivot Shalom, Pesach, Maamar* 7 (Vol. 2, p. 249). The author discusses the power of speech that is connected with the word *Peh-sach* (the mouth that speaks). Because it is a from of praise, the *sippur* (telling) the story of the exodus involves not merely remembering it but *haggadah*, i.e., expatiating on the story. Hence, the sages say, *kol hamarbeh lesaper be-yetzias mitzrayim, harei zeh meshubach* – "anyone who expatiates on the story, is praiseworthy." Here, verbosity is a virtue!

references to praising God with *dance*.[53] Although it is not customary to dance during *PZ*, the motion of one's body in the praise of God is certainly appropriate.

While *PZ* should be said in a songful manner, the same is not true of any other stage of *Shacharit*. As mentioned in the previous chapter, each stage of the Prayer has its own distinctive mode of expression. The first stage includes a number of diverse kinds of texts which are ideally recited in different manners. Hence, the distinctive mode of expression for the first part is precisely that it is extremely diverse. The third stage includes a portion of the Torah which ideally should be *chanted*, but not *sung*. (We shall discuss the difference between chanting and singing later.) Finally, the fourth section is supposed to be said silently. At each stage, the form of expression for each of the four sections reflects the role that is played by each of these stages in the Jewish Spiritual path. We shall discuss the unique qualities of the third and fourth stage in subsequent chapters. At the moment, the important point is that the enthusiastic singing of *PZ* is crucial to its function.

Kabbalistically speaking, the part of the soul that is most engaged in *PZ* is the *ruach*. Again, *ruach* is associated with the power of speech and with spirit, in the sense of "spiritedness," that is, liveliness and enthusiasm. In *PZ*, emotions are supposed to be stirred. The very word, *emotion*, is related etymologically to *motion*. (The root of emotion is *emouvoir*, to stir up.) *PZ* should be said with great emotion; it should move us, and we should move, when we say it. Emotions are not completely rational; they are stirred by rhetoric and poetry. That is precisely why *PZ* reads more like a repetitive sermon than a concise lecture. As we shall see in subsequent chapters, this contrasts sharply with the third and fourth stages of *Shacharit*, which are more cerebral and concise than *PZ*.

As we saw earlier in this chapter, the key to advancing from the lower *heh* to the *vav* is to step outside of oneself and see the larger world. The singing of *PZ* is a vehicle for arousing the virtues associated with the *vav*. In this stage of *Shacharit*, we go beyond the receptive qualities of thanksgiving and humility associated with the lower *heh*, and we advance to praise for God insofar as he is manifest through the *sefirot* associated with the *vav*. In doing so, we ignite within ourselves the corresponding *middot* associated with the *vav*, namely, the moral virtues of *chessed*, *rachamim*, and *gevurah* as well as the esthetic and creative

---

53. See the last two of the five Halleluyahs, which refer to praising God with "*machol*," or dance. We have already noted a reference to the same term for dance above in Psalm 30.

virtues that correspond to *netzach*, *hod* and *yesod*.[54] The point of singing
God's praises is not merely to sing God's praises for its own sake, but also
to kindle within ourselves a passionate desire to participate in the divine
ways of benevolence, compassion, and justice. Furthermore, in singing
PZ we awaken within ourselves our esthetic sensibility to the beauty and
awesomeness that we find in nature. The singing of *PZ* itself constitutes
an esthetic activity of sorts. The world is filled with beauty and grace,
but it is all too easy to forget this. What better way to remind ourselves
of this, and be inspired by this, than by starting our day with exultant
praise for God insofar as He is manifest in the beautiful and awesome
wonders of nature?[55]

The notion that *PZ* is supposed to inspire us to action emerges clearly
in the well-established custom of setting aside money for charity during
PZ.[56] It is no accident that this custom takes place toward the end, or
climax, of *PZ*, and not during any other stage of the *Shacharit*. It is no
accident that the custom to give charity occurs almost immediately after
mentioning the Kabbalistic names of the six *sefirot*. In the very same
breath that we recognize and praise God for his generosity, we ourselves
engage in an act of generosity by giving charity. Of course, the idea is not
merely to execute one good deed for the day and get it over. On the contrary, the idea is to cultivate within ourselves a spirit of generosity that
begins in that moment of charity and will last the entire day and beyond.

---

54. The Kabbalists teach that the *Zemirot*, or songs of praise, are also a way of
preparing for the *tefillah* (fourth stage of *Shacharit*) by "pruning" (from the word
mezamer, pruning) i.e., getting rid of bad thoughts or inappropriate intentions that
one might have in prayer. (*Shaarei Orah*, chapter 1, 6–7.) By praising God in *PZ*, one
seeks to ensure that when one comes to the *Amidah*, or Standing Prayer, one will
pray with the right intentions, i.e., God-directed ones, rather than selfish ones. The
point of *PZ* is to draw one's focus away from self-absorption, and to break outside of
oneself to see oneself as part of a greater whole.

55. See Ramchal, *Mesilat Yesharim*, chapter 21 on *Acquiring Chassidut*. One
of the ways to cultivate *chassidut* is by reading Psalms. When Ramchal speaks of
chassidut, he is talking about a more advanced *middah* than what we are discussing
here (i.e., *chessed*). However, the basic point is the same. Reading Psalms can inspire
us to advance beyond our present level.

56. *Bava Batra* 10a. *SA:OC*: 92:10; *Mishnah Berurah* ad loc. The practice of giving charity is preparatory to the petitionary prayer of the fourth stage. On a simple
level, we are saying to God that he should listen to our prayer in light of the merit
that we have given charity. A deeper way of looking at this is as follows. During the
tefillah, we aim to achieve a bond (*devekut*) with God. (See the discussion in Chapter
4 of *devekut*.) In order to reach that stage, one must first engage in the imitation of
God's ways, by doing acts of *chessed*. For it is only if one follows in God's ways that
one can bond with God.

As explained earlier, *standing* connotes activity whereas *sitting* connotes receiving. Most of *PZ* is said while sitting. In expressing our appreciation of the wondrous workings of the natural world, we are operating more as *receivers* than as *doers* or *givers*. Yet, it is customary to stand during the recitation of *Vayevarech David*. Here we express our recognition that the purpose of *PZ* is not just to recognize God's greatness passively, but also to inspire us to act in God's ways. It is not surprising that the custom of giving charity occurs in that section where we stand. It is said that the Ari would make a point of standing during this giving of charity. Furthermore, the recapitulation of Avraham's unique role in Jewish history, and the description of his name change from Avram to Avraham is meant not only as a praise of God, but also as an inspiration for each of us to live up to his legacy, by actively making our own unique contribution. Just as he made a mark on the world, so too can we, in our own modest way, make a mark on the world. In doing so, we cultivate the *middah* of *yesod*.

In this chapter, we have seen how the second stage of *Shacharit* corresponds to the *vav*. In this stage, we express praise for God insofar as He is manifest through the divine active attributes. We arouse within ourselves the moral, esthetic, and creative virtues. Of course, one cannot cultivate these *middot* simply by praying in the morning. A person who sings *PZ* with proper intent and understanding sets the tone for the rest of the day, throughout which he strives to develop these *middot*. *PZ* should be sung with enthusiasm and spirit. Some swaying or *shukling* is a good thing too. The singing of *PZ* should be an exhilarating and inspiring experience that literally moves us beyond the receptive attributes associated with the lower *heh* and toward the active attributes associated with the *vav*. Yet, as wonderful as it is, we shall soon see the inadequacy of remaining at the level of the *vav*. This brings us to the next chapter.

ה

UPPER *HEH*

INTELLIGENCE (*BINAH*)

SO FAR, WE HAVE SEEN that the lower *heh* of God's Name represents the *Shekhinah* or divine presence, and that the *vav* represents *Hakadosh Baruch Hu*. We now move on to the upper *heh*. Kabbalah teaches that the upper *heh* is associated with the *sefirah* of *binah* or divine intelligence. It is partially in virtue of *binah* that God is regarded as a *person*.[1] Of course, this does not mean that God is a human being. Rather, it means that God is a *rational agent*. God has intentions and designs. He communicates with humans in words, and he comprehends what humans are saying. In virtue of his ability to communicate, he engages in revelation (*giluy*), prophecy (*nevuah*), and he gives commandments (*mitzvot*). Insofar as God is a person, he can and does enter into interpersonal relationships with humans. The notion that God is in some sense a person is a crucial aspect of Judaism and indeed any form of monotheism.

On the common or *pashut* conception, God is conceived as an entity or a being. On this view, to say that God is intelligent is to say that God is a being who thinks, and that God knows what's going on in the universe. God is a non-physical entity who has a mental life. The notion that God is an entity who has a mind raises some interesting questions and puzzles. On this conception, God has a consciousness or a mind, but no body. His consciousness is sort of like ours, but it is vaster and grander. He is a non-physical being who is thinking of all true facts at once, including all past, present, and future facts. It is hard for us to imagine what that

---

1. In fact, it is not only in virtue of *intelligence*, but also in virtue of *will* and *wisdom* that God is a person. Divine will and wisdom are associated with the *yod*, which is the subject of the next and final chapter.

might be like, or even how it could be possible. Also, one might wonder how God can know what colors, textures, smells, pains, pleasures, etc. feel like without having the bodily apparatus to know what those things actually feel like to those who have sense organs. This conception also seems to imply change in God; for, as the world changes, it seems that the contents of God's mind would also change.[2] Despite such issues, one may hold fast to this way of thinking about God. However, in this book, we aim to think of God, and God's intelligence, in a different way – but in a way that preserves the notions of revelation, prophecy, and commandments.

Once again, let us think of God's essence as Being itself. On this conception, God is not an entity, and the divine attributes (including intelligence) are not properties or qualities that inhere in some entity. What then can it mean to speak of divine intelligence or *binah*? We have already addressed this briefly in the Introduction.[3] Here we shall delve into the matter more deeply. To speak of divine *binah* is to say that Being is expressed or manifest in just such a way that the universe has a structure and a plan in accord with which it operates. On this view, *binah* is not an entity, nor is it a quality that inheres in some entity. While on the surface, the Torah speaks as if God is a being who has a mind like ours, we may understand this is as a metaphor or roundabout way of saying that the world has a certain kind of order and structure, such that we can relate to God as we would toward a rational agent. On this view, God doesn't have a mind or consciousness in the way that we do. This way of thinking about God escapes the puzzles mentioned above in connection with the *pashut* conception. Still, our next step is to delve more deeply into what in particular is that order or structure, and what it is about that structure that makes it reasonable to speak of God as a "person."

Judaism teaches there are two ways in which the universe has a structure or order. One is that, as the ancient Greeks put it, the universe is a *cosmos*; it has an order or structure that is quite evident to us. The universe is not simply a random collection of things and events. There are certain governing principles, and all things happen in accord with these principles. Most obviously, there are regularities in nature, sometimes called scientific laws, or laws of nature. This may be termed *divine providence* in a sense. Precisely because the world is a cosmos, it is intelligible to us. We can make reasonable predictions based on experience, and

---

2. The medieval Jewish philosophers struggled to resolve such problems. For example, see Maimonides, *Guide to the Perplexed* I:68.

3. See p. 27.

we can plan our actions accordingly. This fact is plainly obvious, and does not require revelation to be believed. However, it is often taken for granted. It is *remarkable*, that is, something worthy of being remarked on. For the Kabbalist, recognition of the natural order of the universe is part of what is involved in recognizing divine *binah*.

In addition to the regularities of nature, Judaism teaches that there is another way in which the universe is ordered. Namely, there is a *cosmic goal* toward which things are heading.[4] There are governing principles that have to do with this end. Indeed, the lower six *sefirot* or active attributes are the governing principles. The fact that the world operates in accord with *chessed, rachamim, gevurah*, and the other *sefirot* is not accidental. These principles are part of an intentional plan. This also may be termed divine providence but in a more full-fledged way. It's not simply that there is an order; rather, the order is such that there is an end or goal. There is a certain *cosmic process* going on, such that the divine plan is being played out. Things are happening in just such a way that there is a goal for world history, and especially human history.

Another way of stating the doctrine that there are two kinds of regularities is to say that there is a "lower order" and a "higher order." This doctrine is found in Maharal and Ramchal. The lower order is known as *derech ha-teva* (the way of nature). This is what seems operative most of the time: *olam keminhago noheg* (the world runs according to its usual custom). The higher order is *olam hanivdal* (the world that stands apart). The higher order can "supervene" or override the lower

---

4. Using philosophical terms, Judaism teaches that world history is "teleological." In other words, human history is heading toward an end, or *telos*. The notion that history is teleological is espoused by many religions and by many philosophers. Of course, different philosophers and religions espouse different doctrines about what exactly is the goal. Judaism teaches a very particular doctrine about what the goal is and how we will get there. Such a view is implicit in much of the Bible, but it is explicit in the Maharal (*Gevurot Hashem*) and in the Ramchal (*Derech Hashem*). One could view much of Kabbalistic teaching in this light as well. Kabbalah teaches that there are certain metaphysical rules or laws in accord with which the world runs; we can explain historical events in light of these rules and in light of the ultimate goal. To be clear, the view that history is directional is also held by those who hold fast to the *pashut* view of God as an entity. The point here is that one does not *need* to conceive of God as an entity in order to believe in the directionality of cosmic and human history. To believe in divine intelligence *just is* to believe that the universe operates in a certain way; it does not *require* the belief in a non-physical entity who is directing the world toward its end. Thus, the view espoused here is more "ontologically parsimonious" than the *pashut* view. On that notion, see above, Introduction, note 10.

order. Thus miracles sometimes occur. A "miracle" may be defined as an unusual intervention in the ordinary workings of nature in order to advance the divine plan. Such suspensions of the natural course of events are not haphazard or without explanation; they may be explained by appealing to a higher set of principles that override the lower, natural regularities.

Miracles are often associated in Kabbalah with the upper *heh*. On the common, or *pashut*, view, a miracle occurs when the entity, God, intervenes in nature and causes some event to happen that is irregular, but which advances God's plan in some crucial way. On the present view, a miracle is an irregular event that advances the divine plan, and it is explained by the fact that the universe has a certain orderly structure that is designed in just such a way as to lead to the ultimate goal.

So far, we have said that if we understand God's essence as Being itself, we may understand divine *binah* in terms of the doctrine that the universe has a structure such that it is headed toward a great cosmic goal. In the next section, we shall begin to articulate what the cosmic goal is. However, we need first to discuss the key notions of revelation, prophecy, and commandments. If God is not understood as an entity, what can it mean to say that God reveals himself, that he hears prayer, that he speaks, or that he gives commandments?

First, let us consider divine revelation (*giluy*). As noted earlier, anything and everything that exists is *already* a manifestation or expression of God's essence or Being. In some sense, anything and everything that exists is a divine revelation. However, here we are using the term revelation in a more restricted sense. In this context, a revelation of God is an *unusual* event that in some way demonstrates certain features of God or Being that are not knowable through ordinary experience. It might be an event that demonstrates to human beings the very fact that divine providence supervenes on the natural order. For example, the smiting of the first born during the night of Passover is regarded as a "revelation" of God.[5] In experiencing this event, the people of Israel came to know in a palpable way that God is providentially involved in human history, that God carries out justice, and that God has a special relationship with the people of Israel. Another example is the experience of the people of Israel at Sinai, which is regarded by Judaism as the most important divine revelation that has ever occurred. An unusual series of events took place at Sinai, wherein it was made known to the people of Israel

---

5. *Sifrei Devarim* 301:21. This is also quoted in the *Haggadah*.

that the forces of nature are subject to divine control, and also that the people of Israel have a divinely ordained mission.[6]

Next, what is prophecy (*nevuah*)? More generally, what does it mean to say that God *speaks* or that God *hears*? On the *pashut* conception, God is an entity who causes certain people to hear certain words, and whose mind comprehends words spoken by people. But if we do not conceive of God as an entity, what can it mean to believe that God speaks or hears? On the present view, to say that *God speaks* is to say that there are occasions when humans have certain auditory and/or visual experiences which play a crucial role in bringing about the great end toward which the universe is heading. These auditory or visual experiences may include verbal content or "information" that in some way advances the cosmic process. To believe that *God hears* is to believe that what human beings say (even in private) can have a profound effect on what happens in the world. This is not explicable in terms of the laws of nature or scientific laws; it is explicable only in terms of the divine principles, or *sefirot,* that supervene the natural order of things.

For Judaism, one very crucial aspect of divine prophecy involves the giving of *mitzvot,* or commandments. To believe that God commands or forbids certain actions is (in part) to believe that on certain occasions, humans have had certain auditory or visual experiences in which they have learned that doing or refraining from certain actions is crucial for advancing the cosmic goal. Putting the point colloquially, God does not merely "suggest" or "recommend" what we need to do to advance toward the end. Rather, God *commands* us to do those actions that are *necessary* for reaching the divine end.[7] The fulfillment of those commandments is a crucial part of the cosmic process. Moreover, Judaism teaches that Moshe was the prophet *par excellence* who received the revelation of the commandments for Israel, and he communicated these commandments to them.[8] What is more, he did not merely receive a collection of com-

---

6. More on the divine revelation at Sinai follows, in the next chapter.

7. We must leave room for the possibility of *tshuvah* (repentance) as well. Human failure to keep the commandments does not ruin the chances of getting to the great end. The possibility of *tshuvah* itself says a lot about the nature of God's benevolence and compassion. Not surprisingly, in Kabbalah, *tshuvah* is connected with the upper *heh.* But the teaching that *tshuvah* is possible does not mean that the *mitzvot* are *un-necessary.* On the contrary, the idea of *tshuvah* is that past failures can be overcome, and that one is given a new opportunity to get it right – i.e., to do *mitzvot.* In the next chapter, we shall see that, in a higher sense, *tshuvah* is associated with the *yod.*

8. The expression *Torah mi-Sinai* is used often by the Sages. It emphasizes that there was a specific time and place where the Torah was given to the people of

9

mandments; he received and transmitted to Israel the Torah, which is an entire system of commandments that make up a way of life. We shall have more to say about the unique nature of Torah in the next chapter. In any case, Judaism teaches and Kabbalah stresses that by keeping the *mitzvot*, human beings (especially the people of Israel) play a central role in advancing the process toward the cosmic goal.

Concerning the cosmic goal and cosmic process, we must ask two questions. First, *what* is the goal, and the process by which we are supposed to get there? A second and more difficult question is, *why* is the divine goal what it is? In other words, is there an explanation for *why* that is the divine goal, or even why God has any goal at all? In this chapter, we shall begin to describe the Jewish teaching regarding *what* is the cosmic goal, and the cosmic process that leads toward that goal. We will address the second question as best we can in the next chapter on the *yod*, which represents God's will and wisdom.

Israel. The revelation was not an ahistorical event. As the Torah says (Exodus 19:1) "It was in the third month after the exodus. . . ." This is a crucial doctrine for traditional Judaism. Divine revelation is not a metaphysical event that is outside of time, but rather an "irruption" into time and space.

SOVEREIGNTY (*MALCHUT*)

WE HAVE SAID THAT *BINAH* signifies divine intelligence or the providential governance of the world. Just as a good king providentially governs his country, so too, the world is providentially governed by God. It follows that *binah* has a close connection with the notion of God as Sovereign, or *Melech*.[9] The notion that God is Sovereign is closely related to the notion of divine *achdut* (oneness). In speaking of God as *melech*, we are speaking of God as the *single*, Master of the Universe (*ribbono shel olam*). The notion of *melech* is also connected to divine *kedushah*, that is, his transcendence or separateness from everything else.[10] For, it is in virtue of his separateness from all else that God is the

---

9. In the first chapter, we said that the term *malchut* is associated with the *lower heh*. In the second chapter, we said that the term *Ha-melech* is associated with the *vav*. Yet now we are saying that *malchut* is associated with the *upper heh*. This happens frequently in Kabbalistic literature. The same term may apply to different *sefirot*, depending on what aspect of that term one has in mind. See Ramak, *Pardes Rimonim, Erchei Hakinuyim*. (We saw something similar in the case of the Name itself. It stands for the entire array of *sefirot*; it also stands specifically for the *vav*. Something similar is true for colors.) The explanation is that there are three different aspects of *malchut*. An analogy may help to explain this point. Imagine a King in his private chamber, as he plans the overarching goal toward which he wishes to lead and guide his kingdom. This aspect of the King corresponds to the upper *heh*. Once he has that goal in mind, the King then chooses the proper tools by which to reach that goal. The "tools" are the governing principles that he uses to run the affairs of his realm, so that his goal will be realized. This aspect of the King corresponds to the *vav*. Finally, the King interfaces with the citizens and carries out his plan on a daily basis and throughout the entire realm. This aspect of the King involves his omnipresence; it corresponds to the lower *heh*.

10. Earlier we said the *vav* is associated with the name, *Hakadosh Baruch Hu*. Yet

unique King. In this way, *malchut, kedushah,* and *achdut* constitute a triad of integrally related aspects of God.

Now we come to the all-important question: *According to Judaism, what is the cosmic goal toward which all things are heading?* A complete articulation of this goal is beyond the scope of this book. Indeed, certain aspects of this goal are mysterious and beyond human comprehension. Still, some articulation of the goal is necessary for our purpose. In order to make progress on the spiritual journey we must have some grasp of this great end. Kabbalah teaches that the more we understand the goal, the better we will be able to participate in bringing it about.[11] And, the more accurate our understanding is of the end, the more accurate a sense we shall have about what are the *limits* of our understanding.

One way in which Jewish texts describe this goal is in terms of *malchut shaddai,* that is, *the Kingdom of the Almighty.*[12] Sometimes the phrase is used, "*letaken olam bemalchut shaddai*" – "to mend the world so that it constitutes the kingdom of the almighty." The goal is the establishment of God's kingdom. The endeavor to bring about or promote this end is sometimes called *Tikkun Olam*[13] or *mending the world.* Now, in some sense, God is already King. Indeed, we spoke about this in earlier chapters. The lower *heh* signifies that God is King in the sense that God is omnipresent; the *vav* signifies that God is King in the sense that the world is governed in accord with the six active attributes associated

---

here we are saying that *kedushah* is signified more properly by the upper *heh.* The explanation is simple. The upper *heh* connotes God's separateness or transcendence, that is, *kedushah.* The *vav* connotes the fact that *despite* his holiness or separateness, He is *baruch,* that is to say, the source of blessing. Kabbalists put this point by saying that the *vav* connects the upper realms with the lower realms. We noted the connective aspect of the *vav* in the previous chapter.

11. Kabbalists strongly emphasize the importance of understanding and intent (*kavannah*) in performing the *mitzvot.* See Ramak, *Or Ne'erav* 4:2. Hence the need for the prefatory "*leshem yichud*" before *mitzvot.* In the Kabbalah of the Ari, *kavvanot* are extremely important.

12. See the *Alenu* prayer, and the *Amidah* for Rosh Hashanah. Divine *malchut* is a central theme of Rosh Hashanah.

13. Maimonides alludes to the notion of *tikkun olam* in his discussion of the Messiah (*Hilchot Melachaim* 11:4). The phrase, *tikkun olam* is used in several different contexts and by different groups of people. For example, in the Talmud, *tikkun ha-olam* is the basis for instituting certain policies that are intended for the general welfare of society, or to protect vulnerable groups (*Tractate Ketubot* 52b). In some contemporary circles, *tikkun olam* refers to policies that promote social justice and/or world peace.

with the *vav*. If God is already King, what can it mean to speak of the *establishment* of God's kingdom?

To understand this, consider the case of a human king. For his kingdom to be *established*, two related things must happen. First, he must exercise fully his power and dominion, in the sense that his policies for the operation of the kingdom need to be fully implemented. All of the policies must be working in concert. Now, the king's policies are a reflection of the king's personality. (A corrupt king has corrupt policies; a good king has good policies.) It follows that, if and when the kingdom is "established," the kingdom will be a *reflection* or *expression* of the king himself. Second, it is one thing for there to be a king, and quite another for all the citizens of the realm to recognize, acknowledge, and serve him as king. This service would include not mere lip service but actually doing those things that implement the King's plan for the kingdom. When all of this happens, the kingdom is "established."

Similarly, the establishment of God's kingdom involves two things. First, God's "policies" for the operation of his kingdom need to be fully implemented. The divine policies are the six *sefirot* of the *vav*. In the previous chapter, we noted that while those *sefirot* are operational, they are not as of yet *fully* operational. As it is, the world does not fully exhibit God's benevolence, compassion, and justice. Moreover, as of now, the six *sefirot* are not operating in concert. In other words, the six *sefirot* seem to operate independently of one another. For example, there are awesome natural events that wreak havoc and destruction, such as earthquakes. This seems like a conflict of *hod* and *rachamim*. There are also beautiful people that are unjust and cruel. This seems like a conflict of *netzach* and *gevurah*. When *tikkun olam* is complete, this will no longer be the case. The divine kingdom will be "established" only with the full operation of the six *sefirot* of the *vav* at their greatest capacity and in full concert.

Second, the establishment of God's kingdom includes the service of God as King, by not only the congregation of Israel, but also by all humanity.[14] To serve God as King, one must recognize and appreciate some fundamental things about God. One does not need to know everything about God that a human might be able to know. But, one has to recognize, and appreciate at some level, God's ultimacy or transcendence (*kedushah*), and God's oneness (*achdut*). Hence, service to God includes recognizing God's *kedushah* and *achdut*. Moreover, that service will include not merely paying respects every now and then, but actively participating in the cosmic process that brings about the divine goal. It

---

14. Again, see the *Alenu* prayer, and the prayers for Rosh Hashanah.

is important to note that *tikkun olam* is a *collective* or *social* project. It is something that humanity needs to work on as a whole, not merely as individuals. As we shall see later, this has important consequences for the *middot* of the upper *heh*.

An important aspect of this teaching is that it is by divine design that the world is incomplete or "broken." This raises the age-old theological problem, which surfaced in previous chapters. If indeed God is perfect and the world is an expression of God, why isn't the world *already* perfect? In other words, why didn't God create the world in such a way that *chessed*, *rachamim*, and *gevurah* are already fully operational and in full concert? One classic explanation is that the world is created in such a way as to give human beings the opportunity to play a role in fixing the world.[15] In this way, the end that is achieved is all the much better for being earned rather than given to us on a silver platter. The reason for why *chessed*, *rachamim*, and *gevurah* are not yet fully operational is because in the long run, a greater good will thereby be achieved. Ironically perhaps, the only way that God can express or manifest Himself fully is by *not* doing it all at once, but rather by doing it in such a way that humans play a role in completing the process. We shall return to this point later in our discussion of the *middot* associated with the upper *heh*.

When the divine kingdom is established, the world will be a more complete reflection or expression of God himself. In effect, the establishment of the divine kingdom will involve a manifestation or expression of divine *kedushah* and *achdut* in the world. In previous chapters, we alluded to *kedushah* and *achdut*, but we must now address them more directly. Once we have a better grasp of divine *kedushah* and *achdut*, we will then be able to understand what it means for them to be expressed or manifest in the world. This is turn will help us understand the process that is leading toward the cosmic goal of *malchut shaddai*.

---

15. See Ramchal, *Derech Hashem*, chapter 2. This is also a major theme in his *Da'at Tevunot*. This harks back to the theme of existential shame discussed in the previous chapter.

ONENESS (*ACHDUT*) AND HOLINESS (*KEDUSHAH*)

FIRST, LET US REFLECT on divine oneness, or *achdut*. Traditionally, the notion of divine *achdut*, or oneness, is understood to mean that God is *unitary* and *unique*. If one thinks of God's essence as an entity, then one might understand the doctrine of God's *unity* as saying that God is a being who does not have parts, and one might understand the doctrine of God's uniqueness as saying that there is only one such being as God. In order to believe in divine unity on the common view, one must believe that there exists such a being, and that this being is radically unique and radically one.

However, if we think of God's essence as *Being itself*, we may, and indeed we must, understand divine *achdut* in a different way. We may say the following. Being itself is unitary in the sense that although the universe is made up of parts, Being itself doesn't have parts; we must not confuse Being itself (which does *not* have parts) with the universe itself, or the sum total of all beings (which *is* made up of parts).[16] Furthermore, Being itself is "unique" in the sense that despite the diversity of things in the world, they are *all expressions of the very self-same Being*. To understand this idea better, consider the following. In the world, we find trees, fish, humans, rivers, flowers, etc. All of these things are very different. Trees express or manifest being in one way, and fish express being in another way, which is very different from humans, etc. *Yet all of these express or manifest Being*. While fish and humans are not the same, and trees and flowers are not the same, we must still surely say that all of these different things manifest the *very same* Being. To put the point

---

16. It may be helpful for the reader to review the discussion in the Introduction on p. 20ff.

bluntly and perhaps inelegantly, it would not make sense to think that
there are two or more *Being Itselves*. Rather, it is that very self-same
Being itself, which is manifest or expressed in the many and composite
things of this world.

It turns out that, if one thinks of God as Being itself, one arrives
rationally at the conclusion that God is one, or unitary. Philosophers
distinguish between *necessary* and *contingent* truths.[17] God's essential
oneness is a *necessary* truth. A necessary truth is one that cannot possibly be false. Divine *achdut* is a necessary feature of Being itself. God's
essential oneness may be known by anyone using reason and common
experience, without reliance on the *mesorah* (tradition) or divine revelation.[18]

Next, let us reflect on *kedushah*. Again, the term *kadosh* means *separate, set apart*, or *transcendent*. On the common, or *pashut*, view, to say
that God is *kadosh* is to say that the entity, God, is a being that is separate
and radically different from any other being. In order to believe this, one
must believe that there is such a being and that this being is radically
separate and different from all else. On the present view, *kedushah* has
to do with the special status of *Being itself* insofar as it may be contrasted
with *beings*. On this view, it is a necessary truth that God, i.e., Being,
is *kadosh*. By reflecting on the nature of Being one arrives rationally at
the conclusion that *Being* is radically different from *beings*. It does not

---

17. For example, consider the rule, "If A is identical with B, and B is identical
with C, then A is identical with C." This must be true and cannot possibly be false.
It is a *necessary* truth. On the other hand, a *contingent* truth is one that could have
been false. For example, "George Washington was President" could have been false.
Sometimes this is known as an "empirical truth." Most Jewish philosophers (and
Kabbalists) would say that "God created the world" is a contingent truth, for God
could have chosen not to create it. Similarly, it is a contingent fact that the cosmos
has a certain goal, for God could have chosen not to construct the world with a
specific purpose, or he could have designed the world with a different goal. The fact
that some end is divinely ordained does not make it *necessary* – this is a mistake
and in fact to think so would contradict the notion that God is "free." (See *Likutei
Moharan* 52.) One should also not make the mistake of thinking that a contingent
truth is one that is shaky or dubious. It is a contingent truth that George Washington
was President, but there is little doubt about it. Also, a contingent truth is not an unimportant or an "accidental" truth. It was not an accident nor was it "unimportant"
that George Washington was president. Nor was it accidental or unimportant that
God created the world.

18. This is the view of Jewish thinkers such as Bahya Ibn Pakudah (*Chovot Halev-
avot: Shaar Hayichud*), Maimonides (*Guide to the Perplexed* Part II) and Ramchal
(*Derech Hashem*, chapter 1). They hold that there are certain necessary features of
God; these matters do *not* require some special act of faith or revelation to be known.

require some special act of faith or reliance on revelation to believe that Being itself is separate from beings. It is rather a self-evident truth.

There is a tension between *kedushah* and *achdut*. In a way, they are opposites. Actually, they are two sides of the same coin. *Kedushah* has to do with the radical *difference* between God and all else. *Achdut* on the other hand has to do with the fact that anything and everything expresses the very same divine essence, that is, Being. When we think about *kedushah* we are thinking about God's otherness, transcendence, and difference, from all else. When we think about God's oneness, or *achdut*, we are thinking of how close God is to all else. As the Maharal writes, because God is the true *nivdal*, that is why he is associated with anything and everything, both noble and simple, grand and plain.[19] In other words, precisely because God or Being is *kadosh*, it is also true that *melo chol ha-aretz kvodo*, the earth is filled with his glory. Being is separate from all beings, but it is also expressed everywhere in the universe.

---

19. *Gevurot Hashem*, Second Introduction.

THE COSMIC PROCESS (*TIKKUN OLAM*)

SO FAR, WE HAVE SEEN that *achdut* and *kedushah* are necessary features of God. Judaism teaches that there is a cosmic process going on, such that divine *achdut* and *kedushah* are progressively expressed in the world. This requires explanation.

First, let us focus on the expression of *achdut*, or unity. In certain ways, it is already the case that the universe exhibits unity. There is, as far as we can tell, only one universe. There may be many levels and dimensions of reality, but in the final analysis, all of reality makes up one universe. The fact that there is one universe is an expression of the oneness of God or Being. Moreover, as discussed above, the universe is a *cosmos*; it has an order or structure. There are regularities or uniformities in nature that are sometimes called scientific laws or universal laws of nature. Any order or harmony that we find in the natural world is an expression of unity. To take a simple example, the fact that the sun comes up and goes down every day is an expression or exhibition of unity, in the sense that the solar system obeys *one* set of physical laws over time. More generally, the fact that all physical objects obey the same basic set of natural laws is an expression of unity, in the sense that all physical objects obey that same *one* set of laws.

There is another more fragile kind of unity that may be found in human society. Unity or oneness is found wherever there is peace, justice and brotherly love, or *chessed*. Indeed, love itself is a profound kind of unity, or oneness, between people. From the Jewish point of view, the very phenomenon of love is an expression of divine unity. Of course, there is disorder and lack of unity in human society, wherever there is chaos, strife, and war. Hatred – especially, *sinat chinam,* or baseless hatred – is a lack of unity, and therefore it belies the expression of divine unity in the

138

world.[20] The human is often at odds with himself and his environment. We live in a "broken" world. Clearly, the unity, or *achdut,* of the divine essence is not as fully expressed as it might be. Judaism teaches that we are undergoing a process in which human history is heading, slowly but surely, to that great day when the world will be whole and at peace.

Judaism teaches and Kabbalah stresses that everything that happens in world history is part of the cosmic process. But, there are certain key events in human history that play a pivotal role in the process. The Hebrew Scriptures may be regarded as an account of those key events. Abraham was the first person to be truly committed to recognizing the oneness of God and to making it known in the world. It is not a coincidence that Abraham is also regarded as a man of *chessed.*[21] Later, the exodus of the Israelites from Egypt and the subsequent giving of the Torah to Israel were major steps along the way. Through these events, the *achdut,* or oneness, of God was made manifest even more. It is no coincidence that many of the commandments involve the performance of acts of *chessed,* since this, too, manifests unity in human society. The great prophets such as Isaiah and Jeremiah taught that there will come a time when there will be social harmony in the world, during the Messianic age. From a Jewish point of view, the growth and spread of Monotheism among the nations may also be viewed as progress toward the cosmic goal.[22] When divine benevolence, compassion, and justice fill the earth, the *achdut* of God will be more fully expressed and recognized.

Jewish tradition relates this teaching to the verse (*Zechariah* 14:9) "*And it shall be that* י-ה-ו-ה *will be King over all the earth; on that day,* י-ה-ו-ה *will be one and his name will be one.*" On the surface, this is a very strange verse. After all, isn't God one already? The answer is that, while God himself is essentially and eternally one, that oneness is not fully *recognized* or *manifest.*[23] God's essential and necessary oneness never changes; what changes is the *manifestation* of that oneness in the contingent world. In other words, although God is king, his kingdom is not *established.* As long as there is evil in the world, God's oneness

---

20. Thus, Judaism teaches that one of the worst sins is baseless hatred. *Tractate Yoma* 9b: "Baseless hatred is equivalent to the three severe transgressions: Idol worship, forbidden sexual relations, and murder (!)."

21. Maharal, *Netivot Olam: Netiv Gemilut Chassadim* 1.

22. Maimonides. *Mishneh Torah: Hilchot Melachim* 11:7. In that passage, he uses the phrase, "*u-letaken et haolam*" (to fix the world) in the sense intended here.

23. This is a major theme in Ramchal's works. In *Da'at Tevunot,* the full expression of divine *achdut* is the essential goal. See also *Derech Hashem* (chapter 2 and his discussion of *Shema* in Part 4).

is not fully manifest. Scripture also represents this teaching by saying that until that time, God's *Name* is not "complete." Since י-ה-ו-ה represents the modes or ways in which Being is manifest/expressed in our world, another way of talking about this goal is to speak of *yichud shmo*, or the *unification of his name*. When the goal is reached, all humanity will recognize that it is no cosmic accident that the world is governed with benevolence, compassion, and justice. In Kabbalistic terms, all humanity will recognize that the six *sefirot* of the *vav* are rooted in divine *binah*.

Next, let us consider how *kedushah*, or holiness, is expressed or manifest in the world. As explained above, God is *kadosh*, or holy – indeed necessarily and eternally so. That which is holy is set apart, transcendent, and radically different from anything else. At first glance, the notion that something which is *kadosh* may be expressed in the world may seem like a contradiction. How can that which is *separate* from all else be expressed *in* the world? However, Judaism teaches that, at least to some extent, divine holiness is (already) expressed in the world in a number of ways. Certain things are *set apart* from others, in such a way that those things reflect or in some way express God's holiness or "apartness." But, there are also certain things that humans can do to express or manifest this holiness even more. Let us discuss some examples.

In the Torah, the first example of the expression of divine holiness in the world is the holiness of *Shabbat*. The Torah teaches that the world was created in six days, and on the seventh day God rested and made it holy. During the six days, the process of creation took place, new things were generated, and then, that process came to a halt. The stopping or cessation of the creation process is symbolized by *Shabbat*, which means cessation. The period of cessation is radically different from the rest of the days of creation, when the divine work was going on. This period of cessation is *kadosh*, set apart from the other days. Hence, there is a parallelism between God himself, who is separate from all beings, and the seventh day, which is separate from the six days. Furthermore, when the congregation of Israel *observe* the *Shabbat* and *"remember it to keep it holy,"*[24] this increases the manifestation or expression of God's holiness in the world.[25] To the degree that non-Jews are aware of and respect

---

24. Exodus 20:8.

25. Judaism teaches that *Shabbat* hints at something even grander and holier, namely, *olam haba*, or the World to Come. This is the *"Shabbat* of the universe." Just as the six days of creation culminate in the *Shabbat*, world history will culminate in the World to Come. The precise nature of the World to Come is

the holiness of the *Shabbat* – this too adds to the expression or at least recognition of *kedushah* in the world.[26]

Another way in which divine holiness is expressed in the world is in the special designation of the People of Israel as the *am kadosh*, or holy people. Just as the *Shabbat* is set apart from the rest of the week, the people of Israel are set apart from the nations. Furthermore, there are various divine commandments about how the people should act, in order to live a life that is *kadosh*. When the people of Israel keep the *mitzvot*, and act in a holy manner, the holiness of God is further expressed in the world.

In general, divine *kedushah* is expressed within the world when it is recognized and respected by humans. When divine holiness is disparaged or disrespected or degraded – that is a violation of God's holiness. Like God's essential oneness, God's essential holiness is never affected one way or the other by what humans do. What is affected is the *manifestation* or *expression* of that holiness or oneness in the world. At the present stage of human history, God's holiness – like God's oneness – is not expressed or recognized in the world as fully as it might be. The completion of this process will take place only during the Messianic age.

Our account of the cosmic goal of *tikkun olam* is vague in some of its details. One might wonder, when the Messiah will come, whether it will involve extraordinary miracles, whether it will be preceded by some kind of world upheaval, whether all non-Jews will end up converting, and so on. The nature of the World to Come is an even greater mystery. However, we do not need to know exact details in order to participate in the cosmic process, which consists in doing our part to bring about *tikkun olam* by living a moral life, and by fulfilling the *mitzvot*. Some *mitzvot* focus on promoting *achdut*, and others promote *kedushah*. For

---

unknown, as is its relation with other traditional notions about the end of days, including the Messianic age and the Resurrection of the Dead. However, it is worth adding that Kabbalah teaches that on every *Shabbat*, something occurs which is called *"hitkallelut ve-hitkashrut"* (integration) of the *sefirot* of the *vav*. This has as much to do with *achdut* as it does with *kedushah*. It relates to the point made earlier that *tikkun olam* involves all the six *sefirot* working in concert under the guidance of *binah*. This is the major theme of the passage (*Kegavna de-inun*, etc.) from the *Zohar* (2:135a) recited (by some) immediately before the evening service for *Shabbat*. A more advanced work on Kabbalah would delve into this subject.

26. According to Torah law, non-Jews are *not* supposed to refrain from work on the *Shabbat*. (*Mishneh Torah: Hilchot Melachim* 10:9). However, this does not stop them from respecting or acknowledging the holiness of the *Shabbat* in other ways. Many Noahides mark the *Shabbat* as holy, even if they do not refrain from work.

example, we promote the expression of *achdut* through acts of *chessed*, *tzedakah* (charity), social justice, not worshipping idols, and the affirmation of the oneness of God in *Shema*. On the other hand, we manifest or express *kedushah* by keeping *Shabbat*, sanctifying God's name, and maintaining the "apartness" of the people of Israel. Some *mitzvot* involve the recognition of God's kingdom, or *malchut*, very directly – e.g., celebrating Rosh Hashanah with the blowing of the *shofar*, and, when the time comes, properly identifying and showing allegiance to the genuine Messiah. Moreover, insofar as there are certain aspects of the cosmic goal and the cosmic process that are unknown or mysterious to us, there are some commandments (known as *chukim*, or statutes) which may not make sense to us at least on the surface. However all the *mitzvot* taken together promote the expression of *kedushah* and *achdut*, and thereby promote the establishment of divine *malchut*.

Earlier we noted that God's essential oneness and holiness are necessary truths. However, the Jewish teaching that there is a cosmic process and that it is leading to a certain cosmic goal is *not* a necessary truth. Rather, it is a *contingent* truth. The fact that there is such a cosmic goal at all is a result of divine free choice. God could have chosen otherwise than he did. Judaic belief in the cosmic process is based largely on the collective religious and historical experience of the people of Israel. The record of that experience which is transmitted from one generation to the next is the *mesorah*, or tradition, which includes the Written and Oral Torah. To some degree, belief in these matters may also be based on personal experience (i.e., religious experience of the individual devout Jew). We shall return to this issue later.[27]

A few more general points about the upper *heh* are necessary. In virtue of *binah*, Kabbalists sometimes refer to God as *Imma*, or Mother. Just as the lower *heh* has a feminine character, so too, the upper *heh* has a feminine character. Kabbalah teaches that all of the active and receptive *sefirot* that are associated with the *vav* and lower *heh* are guided by divine intelligence. Hence, like a mother who gives birth and guidance to her children, divine intelligence, or *binah*, is metaphorically referred to as the "mother" of those *middot*.[28] The six *sefirot* associated with the

---

27. See below, the discussion of whether it is rational to engage in *kabbalat ol malchut shamayim* and *kabbalat ol mitzvot*.

28. See *Igerret Hatshuva*, chapter 9. There is another reason why *binah* is considered feminine; the upper *heh* is receptive *relative to the yod*, which is the masculine principle above it. Through *binah*, the plans of the *yod* are implemented. But this cannot be explained until later.

vav, together with the *Shekhinah* that is associated with the lower *heh*, are represented metaphorically as the "children" of the mother. In other words, the "lower seven" *middot* of God are "offspring" of divine intelligence. Hence, the Kabbalists sometimes refer to the *vav* as *ben* (son) and the lower *heh* as *bat* (daughter). The *middot* are not blind or haphazard; nor are they disconnected. All of the *middot* are ultimately working together so that the ultimate end or goal will be met.

In the previous chapter, we saw that sometimes the name י-ה-ו-ה connotes divine compassion, or *rachamim*, while the name *elohim* (which means ruler or judge) connotes justice. We also noted that some of the *sefirot* of the *vav* are right-sided while others are left-sided and others are central. In Kabbalistic literature, the divine name often associated with *binah* is י-ה-ו-ה itself, but pronounced or vocalized as if it were written *elohim*.[29] This represents the notion that *binah* is the root of both *rachamim* and *gevurah*, and indeed all the six *sefirot* of the *vav*. However, *binah* itself is generally considered a left-sided *sefirah*. The reason is that *binah* is "restrictive" in that the order or structure of the world limits or defines what may happen in the world. There are certain natural laws that govern the world, and so certain things are ruled out from happening given those natural laws. The fact that there is a certain cosmic goal is also "restrictive," for in virtue of that goal, certain things must happen and certain other things will not happen. In the next chapter, we shall see that, in contrast, *chochmah*, or wisdom, is a right-sided *sefirah*.

Finally, in previous chapters we noted the Kabbalistic teaching that different colors represent different aspects of God's manifestations, and so, different colors correspond to different letters of the Name. Recall that the color red symbolizes the lower *heh*, while the color green symbolizes the *vav*. Again, red is the color of the earth, while green is the color of grass and vegetation. The upper *heh* is symbolized by the color blue. As we look upward from the red earth, to the green grass and leafy trees, the next color we see is the blue of the heavens or the sky. It is from the sky that the earth receives its rain, which makes the grass and the vegetation grow. Interestingly, the color blue is rarely found in the vegetable and animal realm. Perhaps the fact that it does *not* occur commonly in nature – with the exception of the sea and the heavens – is re-

---

29. Jewish tradition teaches that certain words in the Hebrew Scriptures are written (*ketiv*) one way and pronounced (*keri*) another way. See for example, *Obadiah* 1:1. There, the word י-ה-ו-ה is supposed to be pronounced as *elohim* rather than the usual *Adonai*.

lated to the fact that blue is considered an elegant color that symbolizes royalty or kingship. In Scripture, the sky or the heavens represent God's throne or kingdom.[30] God "looks down" from the heavens and governs the earth.[31] The color blue represents God's sovereignty, or *malchut*.[32] Hence, the color blue symbolizes the upper *heh*.

30. See Isaiah 66:1; Psalms 11:9, 103:20.

31. Psalms 33:16.

32. Ezekiel 23:6; Esther 1:6, 8:15. More on *techelet* follows below.

EXISTENTIAL DESPAIR (*ATZVUT*)

WE ARE ALMOST READY to discuss the *middot,* or spiritual virtues, that correspond to the upper *heh.* One preliminary is necessary. As explained earlier, the incentive to advance to a higher stage comes in part from a realization of the inadequacies of one's present stage. Before we can move to the *middot* associated with the upper *heh,* we must first recognize and confront the inadequacies of the *middot* associated with the *vav.*

Recall that in the *vav* level, one seeks to alleviate existential shame by cultivating the active virtues. By cultivating the moral *middot,* a person becomes a *giver* rather than merely a receiver, and shares his gifts with others who are in need. To a lesser degree, one also alleviates existential shame by cultivating esthetic and creative accomplishments, and by making one's mark on the world. However, it does not take much reflection to realize that no matter how moral, esthetic, or creative one may be, the truth is that it is impossible thereby to *eradicate* existential shame. To use a medical analogy, the *middot* of the *vav* treat the symptom, but not the cause, of existential shame. We have already discussed some of the limitations of the virtue of diligence, as well as the limitations of the esthetic and creative virtues in alleviating existential shame. Suppose the poor man refuses a "handout" and instead works for his bread, and thereby earns it. The problem is that although he may have earned *his bread,* he has surely not thereby earned his *natural gifts,* without which he would not have the ability to earn anything at all. The same problem plagues one's esthetic, creative, and even moral accomplishments. Whether one paints a beautiful painting or writes a great book or builds a great empire, one still has not thereby earned one's capacity to do these things. The same thing is true if a person is benevolent, compassionate,

145

or just. No matter how benevolent I am, I cannot escape the fact that I am a receiver. Even if I share most or all of what I have, I still do not thereby deserve or merit what I have. I cannot, it seems, do anything to deserve my natural gifts.

Our esthetic, creative, and moral achievements are limited in other ways. For one thing, they are largely a result of luck or *contingency*. The greatest artist in the world may be responsible for his achievements to some degree, but he is not responsible for so many contingent factors, such as the natural talent with which he was blessed, his upbringing, his teachers, and the general amount of good fortune which must fall in to place to allow any person to become "great." For example, J.S. Bach could not have been the great composer if not for the centuries of musicians that preceded him. Bach's achievements are therefore not entirely *his own*. The same holds true for any great (or not so great) athlete, politi-cian, architect, etc. Even a moral hero, so to speak, is a product of his upbringing, his parents, his social milieu, and so forth. Surely, it makes sense to praise and thank a moral hero. But a person who takes full credit for his moral actions is actually deluding himself. Much of what we achieve in life is due to circumstances that are beyond our own control. Just the mere fact that a person is born in reasonably good health and is able to survive through infancy and childhood and then continue on to live a normal human existence – without the ravages of disease, famine, war, etc., is a result of circumstances for which the person himself is not responsible. The role that luck plays in our esthetic, creative, and moral achievements is often underestimated. Once we face up to how little we are actually responsible for our achievements, this undermines any prospect that we can rid ourselves of existential shame through such accomplishments.

Another limitation is that, ultimately, one comes to realize that one's esthetic, creative and even moral "accomplishments" are in some sense superficial and vain. To use a well-known cliché, our accomplishments are "here today, and gone tomorrow." To use philosophical terminol-ogy, our esthetic, creative, and moral accomplishments are *infected by temporality*. Most of our esthetic actions wither with age. If we paint beautiful paintings or cook fine meals, if we build nice houses or even formidable empires, if we accomplish athletic feats or we invent new inventions – most of the time, these things are gone after some time. Even if we perform moral actions such as helping people or curing people – eventually, those people die. This may seem like a morbid and depressing thought, but we must face up to this fact. What do we re-ally accomplish by doing any of these actions? Ultimately, our moral, esthetic, and creative accomplishments have little or no permanence, or *kiyyum*. They are not grounded or anchored in anything that is eternal.

In sum, by behaving morally, esthetically, and creatively, a person can *alleviate* existential shame, but cannot *eradicate* it. This disturbing realization leads to a bitter experience, which we may call *existential despair*.[33] This is *worse* than existential shame. The term *shame* connotes a negative experience or bad feeling about oneself, but which is something that may be overcome, if only one takes the right steps. The term *despair* connotes a realization that a certain negative situation cannot be overcome. This occurs when one faces up to the fact that all of one's accomplishments, whether moral, esthetic, or creative are ineffective to eradicate existential shame. It is (in part) this bitter experience of existential despair, which makes a person dissatisfied with the *middot* of the *vav*, and inspires one to look for something higher.

It is worth dwelling on some of the differences between existential shame and existential despair. Existential shame is something that even children or young persons can feel. It is also something that children can alleviate by engaging in esthetic, creative, and moral behavior. A child can and should be proud of his esthetic, creative, and moral achievements. We pat them on the back and tell them they are wonderful. We should never downgrade or mock their achievements. In other words, one should never encourage a child to feel existential despair. This is expecting too much. Existential despair is something that generally one experiences only after some maturity. As we get older, we realize, or rather, we should realize, how vain our "accomplishments" really are. That doesn't mean we shouldn't do them. Yet, as we grow and understand better the bigger picture, we should realize how insignificant these "accomplishments" really are in the scheme of things. We should also realize that our responsibility for our "accomplishments" is really much less than it may seem at first glance.

This is one way of understanding what is probably one of the most difficult books of the Hebrew Scriptures; namely, Ecclesiastes, or *Kohelet*. Jewish tradition teaches the book was authored by Solomon. Why does he choose to call himself *Kohelet* rather than use his real name? Another puzzling thing is that the book makes no mention of many traditional Jewish teachings, such as God's interaction with the patriarchs, the Chosenness of Israel, the exodus from Egypt, and so forth. Although the

---

33. The term *existential despair* is often associated with existentialist writers such as Kierkegaard and Heidegger. However, my use of this term does not necessarily agree in all respects with their use.

book makes ample reference to God as "*elohim*," it makes not a single mention of the Holy Name of God (י-ה-ו-ה).[34] Indeed, this book seems to convey a very depressing message. "All is vain, proclaims *Kohelet*." Even the wise, wealthy, and accomplished "King *Kohelet*" falls into despair, when he recognizes that any achievement requires luck or fortune, and any achievement can conceivably be undone after one's life is over. If one succeeds in making a fortune, it is possible that after one's death the fortune could be lost or turned over to one's enemies. If one succeeds in having good children, it is possible that after one's death, those children could die tragically; even if this does not actually happen, it is not due to anything a person has done but rather to luck. Nothing we do, it seems, adds up to all that much. In the grand scheme of things, what do any of our accomplishments really matter? *Kohelet* does not seem to provide an answer to this disturbing question.

Yet, there is the silver lining in the cloud of existential despair. Things seem bleak, but one can only recognize things as *contingent* and *temporal* if one already has in the back of one's mind the notion of the *necessary* and *eternal*. One senses a deficiency only because one also senses that perhaps there is something better than one's current level. As noted earlier, within the very recognition of the problem lies the seed of its solution. The way out of existential despair is to find a kind of meaning or purpose that escapes the contingency of the *vav* level. We shall soon see how we can escape existential despair by embracing a new set of *middot* – the *middot* of the upper *heh*.

We have said that the *middot* of the upper *heh* are motivated by the bitter experience of existential despair. However, there is also a more positive realization that inspires the movement to the upper *heh*. Again, the general rule is that all spiritual growth involves "graduating" from a relatively superficial and indirect relationship with God or Being to a deeper and more direct relationship or encounter with God. As we saw earlier, the advantage of the *middot* of the *vav* over the *middot* of the lower *heh* is that whereas the former are active, the latter are passive. This active engagement with God constitutes a more mature and direct relationship than does the merely passive *middot* of the lower *heh*. Similarly, we shall soon see that the *middot* of the upper *heh* allow us to engage in an even more direct relationship with God than is possible through the *middot* of the *vav*.

---

34. In the Hebrew Scriptures, the only other books that make no mention of the Holy Name are *Esther* and *Song of Songs*.

RECEIVING THE KINGDOM OF HEAVEN AND THE COMMANDMENTS (*KABBALAT OL MALCHUT SHAMAYIM U-MITZVOT*)

AT THE BEGINNING OF THIS CHAPTER, we saw that the upper *heh* represents a cluster of related concepts. Essentially, the upper *heh* represents *binah*, or divine intelligence. The upper *heh* also signifies that God is *Melech*, or sovereign King. This entails that God is "personal" in the sense that God has intentions, and his divine providence governs the world. God reveals himself, communicates with humans, and gives us commandments. Based on revelation, and based on the collective historical experience of the Jewish people, the congregation of Israel believe that world history is heading toward a great goal. That goal is *malchut shaddai*, which involves the full realization of the six *middot* of the *vav*, and the expression of divine *kedushah* and *achdut* in the world. By fulfilling the *mitzvot*, humans play a crucial role in *tikkun olam*, that is, the cosmic process that is heading toward this great goal.

In light of this, Judaism teaches that indeed there is a way to escape existential despair. The way to do so is by *accepting or receiving God as King*, and *taking upon ourselves a commitment to observe his commandments*. Since these are the commandments of the King, this is tantamount to taking upon ourselves a commitment to "serve" God as our King. To see how these commitments banish existential despair, we must first delve deeper into the root of existential shame, which stems from the fact that we have so much that we do not deserve. What does it mean to say that I have something *I do not deserve*? It means that I have it *for no sufficient cause that is due to my own activity*. Either I have it because of luck or chance, or because of some other cause that lies outside of me. So the question arises, what can I do to bring it about that there should be some *necessity* for what I have?

Putting the question differently, what can I do to escape the *contin-*

gency of my accomplishments? This may seem like an impossible task, and in a way, it is. Certainly, nothing I can possibly do is going to make my *existence* necessary. Only God, or Being itself is necessary. How then can I resolve this existential problem? Judaism teaches the resolution lies in accepting the Kingdom of God, and taking upon oneself the divine commandments. For, while it is true that only God or Being is necessary, it is also the case that Being is expressed or manifest in the contingent world. And, while it is true that God's *kedushah* and *achdut* are necessary, there is a cosmic process at work, which involves the expression of divine *kedushah* and *achdut* in the contingent world. The existence of humans is not an accident; humans exist because they are part of the divine plan, and, by serving God through keeping the commandments, humans can and do play a crucial role in fulfilling the divine plan. Thus, by doing *mitzvot* we can be genuinely worthy of what comes to us from God. In other words, by doing *mitzvot*, we can gain *schar* (reward) from God.

By accepting God as King and by taking upon oneself the *mitzvot*, one's life takes on supreme or cosmic significance. In a way, there can be nothing more important or meaningful than fulfilling a divine commandment. All other pursuits pale in comparison. Not only does a person thereby resolve the problem of existential despair, but this also brings about a feeling of pride (*gaiut*)[35] and joy, or *simcha*. Once we realize the noble role we can play in the grand cosmic process of *tikkun olam*, we are inspired with *simcha shel mitzvah*, that is, joy in doing or keeping *mitzvot*. By doing so, our time on this earth is transformed from a kind of meaningfulness that is contingent, to a kind of meaningfulness that is grounded in that which is necessary and perfect. We thus escape the "vanity of vanities" described by *Kohelet*. We become worthy not only of our natural gifts, but worthy of having been created.

The advantage of *kabbalat ol malchut shamayim* and *kabbalat ol mitzvot* over the *middot* of the *vav* can be seen in another way. Earlier we noted that the *middot* of the *vav* are infected by temporality. Our moral, esthetic, and creative accomplishments wither with age. Yet, this problem does not plague our performance of *mitzvot*, since they have a cosmic and everlasting significance. God is eternal, and the divine project is an expression of God. The *mitzvot* are a crucial part of the di-

---

35. One might ask, isn't pride sinful? Perhaps some forms of pride are not sinful. Alternatively, there is something problematic about this pride, and it is counteracted or rectified only through the *hitbatlut* (self-abnegation) of the next stage. See note 41 in the next chapter.

vine project. Hence, by fulfilling the *mitzvot* we participate in the divine project, which is an expression of that which is eternal.[36]

Let us return briefly to *Kohelet*. If we allow ourselves to read between the lines, perhaps this too is the message of Solomon in this amazing work. *Kohelet* is chosen as a "pen name" for Solomon because he has assumed a *persona* in order to write this book. He adopts a *persona* because he wishes to dramatize how depressing life would be, if things were different than they actually are. Solomon knows that there is a personal God; but his character "*Kohelet*" does not know of such a God, and therefore he is not familiar with the Holy Name or י-ה-ו-ה. Purposefully, there is no mention of traditional Jewish teachings regarding God's interaction with the patriarchs or the prophets. There is a God (*elohim*) of some sort, but God is not "invested" in human history; he is not directing the world toward the goal of *tikkun olam*. In such a world, there would be little or no place for *kabbalat ol malchut shamayim* and *kabbalat ol mitzvot*.[37] We would be left with the existential despair of the *vav* level. This bleak picture is presented in such a way as to make us realize how dismal life would be – if *Kohelet's* assumptions were correct. Thankfully, they are not correct, and there is a way out of existential despair!

We need to be careful in understanding this teaching. Some people may interpret *Kohelet* to be saying that if God had not given the Torah, life is utterly meaningless or worthless, and that morality (as well as esthetic and creative behavior) is a sham. However, that is not our interpretation here. *Kohelet* affirms that even without Torah, there are some things in life that are good to pursue, and some bad things to avoid. Our achievements do matter; they just don't matter *enough* to banish existential despair and render a person genuinely worthy of his gifts. The message of *Kohelet* is that even though we can and should cultivate the moral, esthetic and creative virtues, we are still left with existential despair – if that's where we stay.[38]

---

36. This is related to the Scriptural teaching that God's relationship with Noah, with Abraham and with the people of Israel involve a *brit*, or covenant, that is eternal. See Genesis 9:16, 17:7; Exodus 31:16.

37. The notion that there are some divine *mitzvot* is (barely) found in *Kohelet* (8:5, 12:13). However, missing is the notion that one can establish an interpersonal relationship with God through keeping *mitzvot*. Also missing is the notion that God is involved in guiding the world toward *tikkun olam*, and that we can play a role in bringing about *tikkun olam* by doing *mitzvot*.

38. This is also the message of the passage, *Leolam yehe adam*, which occurs in the first stage of *Shacharit*. This is the preamble to the "little *Shema*." This passage quotes *Kohelet* and expresses the notion of existential despair. It goes on to affirm

We have said that accepting the divine kingdom and the commandments takes us beyond the *middot* of the *vav*. However, this does not mean that one *leaves behind,* or *gives up,* the moral, esthetic, or creative virtues of the *vav*. As the Sages teach, *derech eretz kadmah la'torah,* which means, "proper human conduct is a prerequisite for observance of Torah." The moral, esthetic, and creative virtues are not merely a stepping-stone to keeping the *mitzvot*. Rather, they are an ongoing prerequisite for the proper performance of *mitzvot*. In taking upon oneself the *mitzvot,* one builds on the *middot* of the *vav,* and transforms them into something higher. Indeed, many *mitzvot* involve acts of benevolence, compassion, and justice – at an extremely demanding level. The committed Jew does these things then, not only because they are morally right or praiseworthy (which they would be, even if God didn't command them) but also because they are commanded by God. In doing so, he not only does what is moral but also participates in the divine project of *tikkun olam*. One should bear in mind that *tikkun olam* is not *merely* moral and socially productive behavior. *Tikkun olam* involves promoting the divine project of the expression of God's unity and holiness, which *includes* as part of that project, the social unity and harmony of humankind.

A crucial question arises regarding *kabbalat ol malchut shamayim* and *kabbalat ol mitzvot*. Is it *rational* to make these commitments? Does it *make sense* for a person to make these commitments, or is it a matter of blind acceptance? This is a major issue in Jewish Philosophy. A full treatment of this issue is impossible here. However, some discussion is necessary. The *middot* of *kabbalat ol malchut shamayim* and *kabbalat ol mitzvot* are associated with the upper *heh,* which signifies not only divine intelligence but also human intelligence. It is with the *mind* that one recognizes God as King, and it is with the *mind* that one comprehends the commandments. Hence, these commitments can and must be, to some extent, *rational* commitments. Indeed, part of the spiritual journey involves growing in one's cognitive awareness of God. Judaism and especially Kabbalah place a high premium on understanding God – *to the degree that such understanding is possible*.

So, in what way are these commitments rational? Some Judaic teachings are rational to accept without reliance on revelation. First, as explained earlier, if God's essence is understood as Being itself, the crucial Judaic teachings regarding the essence of God are *necessary* truths.

---

that we are fortunate (*ashreinu*) in that we have an interpersonal relationship with God, and that by receiving the kingdom of heaven we are able to overcome existential despair.

Divine *achdut* and *kedushah* are necessary features of Being. The belief in these truths is as rational as the belief in mathematical truths. Second, as explained earlier, ordinary experience tells us that the contingent world has structure and order. Now, to believe in divine *binah* is in part to believe that the world has a structure. Hence, to some extent, the belief in divine *binah* is rational based on ordinary experience. Third, as discussed in the previous chapter, the belief that the world is governed in accord with the six *sefirot* is rational *to some extent*, insofar as divine benevolence, compassion, and justice (and the others) are to some degree exhibited in the natural course of our experience.

On the other hand, as explained earlier, some Judaic teachings do *not* fall into the category of necessary truths; nor are they clearly evident to ordinary experience. These include the teaching that there is a cosmic process heading toward *malchut shaddai*, that is, the expression of divine *kedushah* and *achdut* in the world. These also include the teachings that God reveals himself, that God communicates in prophecy, that he issues *mitzvot*, or commandments, and that there will come a day when the six *sefirot* are fully operational. Still, Judaism does not expect that we blindly accept these optimistic teachings. *Kabbalat ol malchut shamayim* is based on the collective religious and historical experience of the people of Israel. It is based on a claim of revelation and the *mesorah*, or tradition, which is a record of that revelation. We shall return to this issue in the next chapter.

Kabbalat ol malchut shamayim and *kabbalat ol mitzvot* are associated with the feminine letter, *heh*. Like the *middot* of the lower *heh*, the *middot* of the upper *heh* have the feminine character of *openness* or *receptivity*. Yet, there is a difference. The receptivity of the lower *heh* is a more basic kind of receptivity. The lower *heh* involves receptivity to one's natural gifts, which are obvious to all humans. The receptivity of the upper *heh* is a cognitive or intellectual receptivity to the *mesorah*, to the kingdom of God, and to the commandments. (One cannot possibly engage in this *kabbalah* unless one is exposed to the *mesorah*.) Still, both forms of receptivity involve a kind of pliability or openness. A person who is not "open" will not fully receive and appreciate his natural gifts; a person who is not open might be too skeptical or stubborn to accept the *mesorah*. It requires a certain kind of intellectual humility to accept the *mesorah*, for one can always play the skeptic if one wishes to do so.

Earlier we noted that Kabbalah teaches that the lower *heh* corresponds to the *nefesh*, or lowest part of the human soul, while the *vav* corresponds to the *ruach*. The upper *heh* is associated with the part of the soul known as *neshamah*. The term *neshamah* is associated with *sechel*, that is, the mind, or the intellectual capacity of understanding. The mind governs speech and bodily motions. Hence, *neshamah* is viewed as superior to *ruach* and *nefesh*. It is with the mind that one accepts or intellectually receives the Kingdom of God and the commandments. Also, it is with the mind or the intellect that we can understand that God is One and Holy, and it is with the mind that we can learn the *mitzvot*, and direct our emotions and our bodily actions and even our speech toward the service of God. Just as the universe has a structure and a plan, so too the human being can use the mind to structure and organize his or her life in such a way that it is devoted to participating in the cosmic process, which is heading toward the great end of *tikkun olam*.

In accepting upon oneself the commandments, one also accepts upon oneself the duty *to learn* and to *teach* the commandments. Obviously, one cannot fulfill the commandments if one does not know them. The mind's engagement with Torah is a crucial part of this third stage. One needs to *learn* in order to *do*. Indeed, learning itself is a commandment; learning (even without doing) advances the cosmic process. The commandment to study and teach Torah has a very special place in Judaism. Especially when we study Kabbalah we are studying the cosmic process itself and what role is played in that process by our performance of *mitzvot*. The commandments themselves are rooted in divine *binah*; when we use our own intelligence or *binah* to study Torah we are in touch with the very root of the commandments themselves. Moreover, for various practical reasons, there are some commandments that we are not able to fulfill. By studying them, we are involved in those aspects of the divine project. Nevertheless, whenever we learn, we should learn not merely out of intellectual curiosity but rather *al menat la'asot*, that is, in order to do the *mitzvot*. In the next chapter, we shall see that study plays a crucial role in enabling a person to reach the *yod* level.

REVERENCE (*YIRAH*) AND LOVE (*AHAVAH*) FOR GOD

SO FAR, WE HAVE seen that the third stage of the Jewish spiritual path involves *kabbalah,* or acceptance, of God's *malchut* and *mitzvot.*[39] The acceptance of God's *malchut* and *mitzvot* is linked with two other very important *middot,* namely, *yirah* (reverence) and *ahavah* (love) of God. This is true in two ways. First, it is not enough that we accept the kingdom of heaven blithely. We must accept them with the right attitude, and that is, with *yirah* and *ahavah.* In this sense, some level of *ahavah* and *yirah* precedes or perhaps coincides with the acceptance of God's *malchut* and *mitzvot.* Second, it is through acceptance of God's kingdom and especially God's *mitzvot* that we can reach higher levels of *ahavah* and *yirah.* In this way, the acceptance of God and his *mtizvot* precedes *ahavah* and *yirah.*

In cultivating *yirah* and *ahavah,* one cultivates an *interpersonal* relationship with God. Much has been written about these notions. Our main effort here will be to explain that while *yirah* stems from recognition of divine *kedushah* (transcendence) and *malchut* (sovereignty), *ahavah* stems more from recognition of divine *achdut* (oneness). It is crucial that we understand these points, if we hope to cultivate properly these *middot.*

In a way, *yirah* and *ahavah* are opposites. *Yirah* involves a movement *away* from something or someone; it involves restraint, withdrawal, even fear. *Yirah* stems from a recognition that someone or something is *other* than oneself, and is therefore in some way *alien* or *forbidding.* On the other hand, *ahavah* stems from recognition that there is some fun-

---

39. On the association of *ahavah* and *yirah* with the upper *heh,* see e.g., *Iggeret Hatshuvah,* chapters 4 and 9.

damental *kinship* or *unity* between oneself and someone or something else. It also involves a passionate drive to become close to the beloved. Speaking colloquially, whereas *yirah* involves giving another person his or her "space," *ahavah* involves entering into another person's "space."[40]

Developing this point further, *yirah* of God stems from recognition of divine *kedushah* (transcendence, otherness) and *malchut* (sovereignty or power). On the other hand, *ahavah* for God stems from recognition of divine *achdut* (oneness). *Yirah* stems from recognition that God's essence or Being is radically different from and radically more powerful than everything else.[41] On the other hand, *ahavah* stems from recognition that there is some fundamental *kinship* or *similarity* between oneself and God; it also involves a passionate drive to come "close" to God. Earlier, we noted a tension between divine *kedushah* and divine *achdut*. Correspondingly, there is a tension between *yirah* and *ahavah*. Using Kabbalistic imagery, *yirah* is a left-sided *middah*; *ahavah* is a right-sided *middah*. Despite the tension between *yirah* and *ahavah*, Jewish tradition teaches that it is a divine commandment to have both *yirah* and *ahavah* for God. Like *kedushah* and *achdut*, they are two sides of the same coin.

To understand love of God, we must answer two questions. First, what is the fundamental kinship between the human and God? After all, if God is radically different from anything, how can we have a kinship with him? Second, if love involves "coming close" to one's beloved, how can one do that in the case of God? After all, if God is radically different from us, how can we become "close" to God?

What kinship do we have with God? First of all, anything that exists has some kinship with God, for any being manifests or expresses Being. But, our kinship goes further. As explained in previous chapters, humans have the image of God, or *tzelem elokim*, insofar as the structure of the human being mimics the way in which God's essence or Being manifests himself in the universe. We do have a great kinship with God – despite the fact that his essence is radically different from us or anything else.

Second, in what way can we become "close" to God? Obviously, we cannot get *physically* close to God. Rather, closeness to God has to do

---

40. For those familiar with some of the Ari's teachings, the *tzimtzum* was an act of withdrawal that allowed a *chalal* (void or empty space) in which the world could exist. The *tzimtzum,* or withdrawal mimics *yirah*. On the other hand, the *kav* (ray of energy) that comes into the *chalal* and begins to create the world mimics *ahavah*.

41. This is what Ramchal (*Mesilat Yesharim*, chapter 24) calls *yirat ha-romemut* as opposed to *yirat ha-onesh* (fear of punishment). The connection between reverence and God's radical otherness was discussed by Rudolf Otto in his classic work, *The Idea of the Holy*.

with things such as thinking about God, knowing God to the degree that we can, and caring about God. This involves fulfilling God's commandments; that is, participating in the divine project of divine expression, and helping to bring about *malchut shaddai*, in short – walking in the *derech Hashem*, or way of God. In this respect, "closeness to God" is similar to what is involved in love of another human, for love includes caring about the beloved and helping the beloved to reach his or her goals.

Ahavah and *yirah* are rooted in *binah*, or intelligence.[42] When we recognize certain features of Almighty God, we are lead rationally to cultivate reverence and love. *Yirah* of God stems mainly from recognition of divine *kedushah*, or transcendence, or *radical otherness*. When we contemplate God, we *should* be awed. If we can be awed by a powerful thunderstorm or a marvel of nature such as the Alps or the Grand Canyon; if we can be awed by the starry skies; even more so, we should be in ultimate awe when contemplating God Himself who is the source of these things. Similarly, when we contemplate divine *achdut*, we are lead rationally to cultivate love for God. Any relationship of love involves a kinship between the lover and his beloved; *achdut* is harmony and oneness itself. Thus, *achdut* is a condition for the very possibility of any love whatsoever.[43] Moreover, the people of Israel especially are called upon to love God, for the special generosity and benevolence of God, as displayed in God's choosing of the people of Israel and God's communicating to them the *mitzvot*, which allow Israel to form an interpersonal relationship – again, a kind of unity – with God. The love Israel has (or should have) for God is not a wild-eyed, irrational love. It is a love that is rooted in comprehension, or *binah*.[44]

It is worth noting that, like all of the *middot*, there are "degrees"of *yirah* and *ahavah*. A person can have some *yirah*, a lot of *yirah*, or a great deal of *yirah*. A person can have some *ahavah* at one point, and

---

42. This is a rationalistic way of understanding *yirah* and *ahavah*. For the idea that love should be governed by understanding, see Maimonides, *Mishneh Torah: Hilchot Tshuvah* 10:6; *Tanya*, chapter 3; *Shaar Hayichud Ve-ha'emunah*, chapter 8. This is not to deny that there may be a kind of love or an aspect of love that "goes beyond" reason. More on this topic follows in the next chapter.

43. Later, in our discussion of the first portion of *Shema* we will discuss further aspects of the connection between love and *achdut*.

44. This should not be taken to mean that Israel's love for God is rational *independently of the tradition of prophecy and revelation*. As stated earlier, it is through prophecy and revelation that we learn that God is King; that divine providence governs the world, and that God has a special relationship with Israel. On the notion of rational love and its connection with *olam habriah* (which corresponds to the upper *heh*) see *Tanya*, chapter 39.

then develop greater *ahavah* later. Also, some persons can have these *middot* at a higher degree than others. Needless to say, the more *yirah* and *ahavah* one has, the better.

Earlier we noted the parallel between the basic kind of receptivity associated with the lower *heh* and the more advanced, cognitive receptivity associated with the upper *heh*. Here we may add that, respectively, the love and reverence of the upper *heh* parallel the other *middot* associated with the lower *heh*, namely, gratitude and humility. Moreover, each of the *middot* of the upper *heh* is an advanced version of some *middah* of the *vav*.

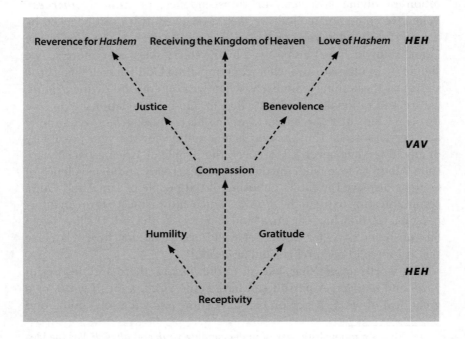

As the chart indicates, receptivity, compassion, and the receiving of God's kingdom and his commandments are central *middot*. The central *middot* are the root from which the other *middot* stem. Just as receptivity forms the basis of gratitude and humility, so too, the receiving of God's kingdom and his commandments form the basis of love and reverence. On the left side are humility, justice and reverence. Humility involves recognizing and acknowledging one's dependency and frail nature. Humility is achievable by anybody, and does not require or depend on accepting the *mesorah*. The same is true of the virtue of justice. Justice involves self-restraint and self-control; reverence for God demands even greater self-restraint. However, reverence before God is a more advanced, cognitive matter. It requires and presupposes an exposure to the *mesorah*. Still, as noted earlier, it takes a certain kind of humility to accept the *mesorah*. These are all left-sided *middot*.

On the other hand, gratitude, benevolence and love of God are positive, or active modes, of behavior. Yet, the activity involved in committing oneself to pursuing an interpersonal relationship with God is far more demanding than the activity involved in giving thanks or even doing benevolent actions. Love of God involves a passionate commitment to fulfill the *mitzvot*. It also requires or presupposes an exposure to the *mesorah*.

Despite the fact that *ahavah* and *yirah* are rationally grounded, it is also true that they both have an *emotional* and *practical* component. The emotional aspect of *ahavah* and *yirah* are feelings or passions – these are hard to describe in words, but as the saying goes, *you know it when you feel it*. Love involves a positive feeling of some sort; in its extreme case, it involves bliss or ecstasy. On the other hand, reverence involves a sobering or disconcerting feeling; in its extreme case it involves trembling and fright. The practical component of *ahavah* involves a drive to *do* what God has commanded and to "serve him" with all our heart, soul, and might; this is *avodah mi-ahavah* (service from love). The practical side of *yirah* is a drive to *avoid* anything wrong in God's eyes. This is *avodah mi-yirah* (service from reverence). It has been said that *yirah* is the root of our observance of the *negative* commandments, while *ahavah* is the root of our observance of the *positive* commandments.[45] Again, *ahavah* is a right-sided virtue and *yirah* is a left-sided virtue. Yet surely, a person can do a positive action out of reverence for God; one can also avoid doing something that God has forbidden, out of love for God. Ideally, the committed Jew strives to fulfill all of the commandments with both reverence and love.[46]

---

45. *Zohar* 3:121b; *Tikunei Zohar* 5a. Ramban, *Commentary on the Torah*, Exodus 20: 8. Maimonides, *Commentary on the Mishnah, Mishnah Avot* 3:1. *Tanya*, chapter 4.

46. Judaism teaches that love and reverence for God are *themselves* commandments. This raises a much-discussed question, namely, how can one be *commanded* to have love or reverence for God? It seems that love and reverence are *emotions*, and if so, they are not under our control. Either you feel love or you don't; but how can one be commanded to love? There are several possible answers to this question. One answer is that, as noted above, love and reverence for God are rationally grounded. They are not emotions but rather *cognitive attitudes*. Therefore, they are under one's control after all. Another answer is that one can *indirectly* manage one's emotions,

While *yirah* and *ahavah* should pervade our performance of all the commandments, there is an especially strong link between *ahavah* and the study of Torah. A person who has genuine love for God fervently wishes to study Torah. One reason is obvious. If one loves God, one wishes to serve Him and keep the commandments as fully and carefully as possible. And, in order to keep the commandments rigorously, one must know what they are, in the most precise way. Apart from that, study of God's word is *in and of itself* an act of love. If I really love someone, I want to know what he has to say, not only so that I can do his bidding, but also because I simply want to know what's on the mind of my beloved. Studying Torah is like finding out what's on God's mind. More on this point follows in the next chapter, on the *yod*.

Aside from *ahavah* and *yirah*, the recognition of God as our King, and in particular as our Savior (*Moshia*) and Redeemer (*Goel*) involves *simcha*, or joy. Throughout Jewish texts, we find that *simcha* is linked with acknowledgment of God's *malchut* and his *yeshuah*, i.e., salvation of Israel. Earlier we spoke about the joy of doing a commandment (*simcha shel mitzvah*). Here we are speaking of a different aspect of *simcha*. Like *ahavah* and *yirah*, this kind of *simcha* is rationally grounded. It makes sense for a person to feel joy at the fact that God is our King, and that God has saved us and redeemed us from our national troubles. Like *ahava* and *yirah*, *simcha* has an emotional and practical component as well. Again, the emotional aspect is hard to describe, except by using synonyms such as exhilaration, elation, delight. Again, *you know when you feel it*. The practical aspect of joy is that it brings exultation. There are physical symptoms of joy, such as, singing, clapping, and dancing. Joy also brings an enthusiasm and zest to a person's activities. If a person experiences joy in some activity, he is likely to continue it with fervor, and to do it again on a regular basis. Our worship of God should be with joy.

---

by doing certain actions that cultivate those emotions. On this view, the commandment to love is really the commandment to engage in reflection on those things that will bring about love. (See the Introduction to *Shaar Hayichud Ve-ha'emunah*, and *Netivot Shalom* on *Veahavta* in *Parshat Ve-etchananan*.) Another possibility is that, as noted above, love and reverence have a practical dimension. Therefore, the commandment to love/revere God is really a commandment to *act* lovingly/reverentially toward God. Still another possibility is to deny the premise of the question, and to insist that even if it is difficult to so, we *can* control our emotions, at least to some degree. For example, sometimes it is wrong to be angry; one needs to learn how to repress certain emotions, at least some of the time. After all, it is not always easy to control our actions either; yet we regard actions as subject to commandment. There are elements of truth to all of these answers.

Finally, another *middah* associated with *kabbalat ol malchut sha-mayim* and *ol mitzvot* is *faithfulness* or *loyalty*, or *ne'emanut*. If we recognize and accept God as our King and Savior, and take upon ourselves the commitment to keep the commandments, then we should remain loyal to this commitment. This is a *rational* kind of faithfulness.[47] It is like the faithfulness of a citizen to a noble and just king who has protected his citizens in the past, and made a commitment to protect them in the future. Judaism teaches that God has committed himself to a special providence over the people of Israel; hence, the Israelite should remain faithful to his commitment to serve God as King and keep the commandments.

In sum, the *middot* of the *heh* include *kabbalat ol malchut shamayim*, *kabbalat ol mitzvot, ahavah, yirah, simcha*, and *ne'emanut*. By cultivating these *middot*, a person not only escapes existential despair, but also relates more directly to God than is possible through the *middot* of the *vav*. The relationship one has with God through the *middot* of the *vav* is *impersonal*. By cultivating a relationship of *yirah* and *ahavah* for God, one establishes an *interpersonal* relationship with God. Such a relationship is possible only in virtue of the fact that God is intelligent, revelatory, and providential. If God were *not* personal, we would be living in the cold world depicted by *Kohelet*. We would be trapped in existential despair, and we would not be able to engage in an interpersonal relationship with God involving reverence and love.[48]

Earlier in this book, we discussed whether and to what extent agnostics or naturalists could pursue or possibly even attain certain levels of the Jewish spiritual path. We had said that they could surely attain the lower virtues of receptivity and humility, and to some degree grati-

---

47. A Biblical source for the notion of a rational kind of faithfulness is in Psalms 78, where some form of the term *emunah* comes up several (three) times. The Psalmist faults Israel for their lack of faithfulness, precisely because after experiencing God's miraculous providence they stupidly and stubbornly fail to keep faith with God. The notion there is clearly that of a *rational commitment based on experience of God's providence*. There is no inkling here of a faith that is anti-rational or trans-rational. In the next chapter on the *Yod*, we shall see there is another kind of faithfulness, that is, a commitment that goes *beyond* rationality or comprehension. To keep the two concepts separate we shall call the rational kind of faith *ne'emanut* and the trans-rational faith *emunah*.

48. A passage in the liturgy which expresses this idea is found toward the end of the morning prayer in *U-va letzion*. This passage expresses the prayer that "God should open our hearts in his Torah, and place in our hearts love and reverence for Him, so that we may do his will with a full heart, so that we will not strive for emptiness, and we shall not bear children in vain."

tude. They could also cultivate the moral, esthetic, and creative virtues. However, it should be clear that one who does not accept (for whatever reason) the teaching that God is King, or that God has given the *mitzvot* cannot reach the level of the upper *heh*. For, the acceptance of these teachings is itself part of the third stage. The agnostic and the naturalist remain trapped in existential despair and at best an impersonal relationship with God.

However, another question remains. Must one become a Jew, that is, a member of the Congregation of Israel, in order to cultivate the *middot* of the upper *heh*? In fact, one does *not* need to be Jewish to reach the level of the upper *heh*, *at least to some degree*. What a person needs to do is accept the yoke of heaven and the commandments. According to Jewish tradition, all humans have commandments, which are known as the Noahide commandments.[49] Non-Jews can participate in *tikkun olam* by fulfilling the Noahide commandments. They do not need to accept the entire Torah. However, the matter is different for those who are already members of the congregation of Israel. The congregation of Israel has already accepted the Torah; for Israelites, the minimum of *mitzvot* is the entire Torah (by tradition, *Taryag,* or 613, *mitzvot*). Moreover, as we shall see in the next chapter, the role played by Israel in keeping Torah goes beyond facilitating the process of *tikkun olam*. Hence, for Israelites, the commitment to keep the commandments entails the commitment to keep the entire Torah.

This concludes our discussion of the *middot* of the upper *heh*. We shall soon see how the third stage of *Shacharit* helps us cultivate these *middot*. First, we must discuss the crucial transitional passages between the second and third stage of *Shacharit*. These passages convey important lessons regarding how to make the transition from the *vav* to the upper *heh*.

---

49. See *Mishneh Torah: Hilchot Melachim* 9.

THE TRANSITION TO THE THIRD STAGE OF *SHACHARIT*: *YISHTABACH, KADDISH,* AND *BORCHU*

EARLIER WE SAW THAT the second stage of *Shacharit* involves *shevach,* or praise, of God insofar as God or Being is manifest within the everyday natural wonders of the world. Our enthusiastic and songful expression of our appreciation of God as manifest in the natural wonders of the world inspires us to cultivate the moral, esthetic, and creative virtues. However, as wonderful and beautiful as the natural world is, it does not and cannot fully express the divine essence. As we come to the end of the second stage, we begin to recognize and articulate the fact that God's essence or Being is *kadosh* (transcendent) and *echad* (unique). No particular thing or set of things within the world can fully express the essence of God or Being. Thus, before we move on to the third stage of the prayer, we must recognize and articulate the limitations of praise or *shevach.* Essentially, the transitional phase between the second and third stages of *Shacharit* involves a shift away from a focus on *shevach* for God as manifest in nature, and toward a focus on God himself, and in particular, on divine *kedushah* and *achdut.*

References to *kedushah* and *achdut* already find their way into the end of *PZ.* In the Song of the Sea, some form of the term *kadosh* is mentioned three times in close succession. This is striking in light of the fact that throughout most of *PZ* the term *kadosh* occurs rarely. At the very end of *PZ,* we find the verse (discussed earlier)[50] which speaks of the future manifestation of God's *achdut.* This is the only place in *PZ* where the notion of God's *achdut* is explicitly mentioned, and it is the first time since its initial mention in the little *Shema* all the way back in the first stage. These references to *kedushah* and *achdut* toward the end

---

50. See above, p. 139.

163

of *PZ* forecast what will be two of the main themes in the third stage of *Shacharit.*

The transition from the second to the third stage consists in *Yishtabach, Kaddish,* and *Borchu.* While *Baruch Sheamar* is the blessing that introduces *PZ, Yishtabach* is the blessing that concludes *PZ.* Although properly speaking *Yishtabach* is the culmination of *PZ,* we are now in a better position to understand and appreciate the contrasts between *Baruch Sheamar* and *Yishtabach,* and the lessons that are conveyed therein for the Jewish spiritual path. Both blessings involve praise and song for God. On the surface, these two blessings may seem similar, but a close reading shows that they are quite different. These differences reflect the shift from a way of thinking about God as associated with the *vav,* to a way of thinking about God associated with the upper *heh.*

As noted in the previous chapter, great emphasis is placed in *Baruch Sheamar* on speech, both divine and human.[51] Indeed, *Baruch Sheamar* is wordy (87 words) when compared with the much more concise *Yishtabach* (53 words). In *Baruch Sheamar,* the word *baruch* (blessed) is repeated thirteen times, two forms of the word *amar* (spoke) occur, as well as the words *peh* (mouth) and *lashon* (tongue, language). None of this occurs in *Yishtabach.* The lesson is clear. As we reach the end of the *vav,* we begin to focus on the *limits* of effusive speech about God. We are preparing to go to the next level, where speech is still important but what is more important is *thought,* and where we need to restrain ourselves to speak more concisely and with greater care, and indeed with some trepidation. This relates to the fact that whereas *PZ* corresponds to the part of the soul known as *ruach* (spirit), the third stage corresponds to *neshamah* (intelligence).

Another striking difference is that *Baruch Sheamar* refers several times to God as compassionate (*rachaman*). Indeed, in *Baruch Sheamar* we refer to God as "*ha-av ha-rachaman,*" or "the compassionate father." We also refer to the notion that God is just, in that he rewards the righteous (*meshalem schar*). On the other hand, *Yishtabach* makes no reference whatsoever to God's benevolence, justice, or compassion. At first glance, this may seem odd. However, the explanation is that the main purpose of *PZ* is to praise God insofar as He is manifest *within* the natural world. Indeed, *PZ* is filled with references to God's benevolence, compassion, and justice. Hence, as we begin *PZ,* we are thinking about God as He is manifest within the natural world as we know and experi-

---

51. See the discussion of *Baruch Sheamar* in Chapter 2. See also the discussion of the repetitive nature of *PZ.*

ence it. We focus on God's moral attributes, the *middot* associated with the vav. But, as we near the end of *PZ*, our focus shifts. The purpose of *Yishtabach* is to recognize that although God is worthy of praise and song, he *transcends* the natural world. Therefore, references to his moral attributes fall away.

A related difference is the following. In the rather lengthy blessing of *Baruch She'amar* there is no reference whatsoever to the notion that God is *kadosh*. On the other hand, in *Yishtabach*, we find two explicit references to the *kedushah* of God. Again, the explanation is that the focus of *PZ* is on God as manifest *within* the natural world. Therefore, as we begin *PZ*, the concept of *kedushah* is not on our minds or lips. However, as we conclude *PZ*, we recognize and articulate the fact that ultimately God is *beyond* the natural world. Therefore, *kedushah* is mentioned only in *Yishtabach*.[52]

Another difference is as follows. In *Baruch Sheamar* we say, ". . . . we shall make you great, we shall praise you, and we shall extol you . . ." We then conclude *Baruch Sheamar* with the blessing that God is "the King who is extolled through praises." Notice how much power or credence we give ourselves here, as if to say that *we* make God's Name great by praising and extolling Him. Similarly, the implication of the end of the blessing is that God or at least God's Name is elevated through our praises.[53] However, in *Yishtabach*, we say, "for unto you, song, praise, and exaltation is fitting."[54] Notice the change from the language in *Baruch Sheamar*. Instead of saying that *we* make God great through praise, here we say rather that praise is *fitting* to God. The emphasis here is not on what we achieve, but on what is "fitting." Furthermore, we conclude

---

52. As a general rule, we find in Hebrew liturgy and texts that reference to *kedushah* comes toward the end of a segment. Examples are, the three portions of *Shema*; the Song of the Sea; Psalm 145; Psalm 93; the first three blessings of the *Amidah*; the five Halleluyahs; the account of Creation in Genesis. Also in the blessing of *ga'al yisrael*, the term *kadosh* appears only twice toward the end. This is logical; *kedushah* is a relatively high level of attainment. This is indicated by *Mesilat Yesharim* as well as the teaching of R. Pinchas b. Yair upon which Ramchal based his book. *Kedushah* comes toward the culmination of the spiritual journey.

53. In fact, this raises a philosophical conundrum. How can Almighty God be "elevated" by our praises – or indeed, anything that we do? One possible answer is that although in truth we really have no effect on God's essence, nevertheless our praise of God elevates His *manifestation* or *expression* within the world.

54. The Hebrew: In *Baruch Sheamar* we say, "*negadelcha, ve-neshabechacha, ve-nehallelcha*, etc." and we conclude with "*Melech mehulal batishbachot.*" In *Yishtabach* we say "*ki lecha naeh shir ushevacha, hallel*, etc." and we conclude with "*habocher beshirei zimra . . . melech el chei haolamim.*"

Yishtabach by blessing "the King who chooses songs of musical praise, the King who is God of Living Eternity." In contrast to *Baruch Sheamar* where no such phrase is used, the implication of *Yishtabach* is that God *has chosen* to be praised. Had he not chosen to be praised, it might not be appropriate to praise him at all.

Another difference is that in *Baruch Sheamar* we say that God is "*merachem al ha-aretz*," that is, compassionate *on the earth*. Throughout the entire *Baruch Sheamar*, no reference is made to *shamayim* - the heavens. However, in *Yishtabach* we acknowledge straightaway that God is "great and holy *in the heavens and the earth*." The absence of the term *shamayim* (heavens) in *Baruch Sheamar* underscores the point that whereas in that opening blessing our focus is on how God is manifest *on earth*, when we reach *Yishtabach* we are thinking of how God is great in the upper realms, as well as the lower realms. The term *shamayim* is not only a reference to the physical heavens but also to the angelic realm, which is a major theme in the third stage of *Shacharit*.

Finally, although in *Baruch Sheamar* we refer to God's eternality (*chei ha-olamim*), the conclusion of that blessing is *melech mehulal batishbachot* (the King who is elevated through praises). Contrastingly, in *Yishtabach* the conclusion of the blessing is a reference to the King who is "living eternity." The conclusion of any blessing is considered its most important part. Thus, while *Baruch Sheamar* focuses more on praising God insofar as he is manifest *within* the world, *Yishtabach* focuses more on the fact that God is eternal and transcends the world.

After *Yishtabach*, the *Kaddish* is recited by the leader, or *chazzan*, (in the presence of a *minyan*, or quorum). Without actually using the Name, the *Kaddish* expresses the prayer that "his great name" should be magnified and sanctified, blessed and praised. The "great name" is an allusion to the י-ה-ו-ה.[55] The first half of the *Kaddish* expresses the prayer that God's *kedushah* should be recognized in the world. The second half of the *Kaddish* declares that God should be "*praised and exalted beyond all blessings and songs that can be said in the world*." In between the first and second half, the communal response is recited, "May the great Name be blessed for ever and ever."

The *Kaddish* formally and publically recognizes the *kedushah*, or transcendence of God. It coincides with recognition of the *limitations* of our blessings and praises for God. There is something of an irony here. After having just gone through *PZ* – a litany of praises of God – we now

---

55. See *Mishnah Berurah* s.k. 2 on *SA:OC: 56*.

assert that all the praises in the world are *inadequate*.[56] As one reaches the *climax* of praise, one realizes its *limits*. Although God is expressed in the natural world, He is not *fully* expressed therein. Since He transcends the world, ultimately praise is inadequate to describe him.[57] We shall return to this issue later.

Although the name י-ה-ו-ה is not mentioned explicitly in the *Kaddish*, the structure of the *Kaddish* mimics both the structure of the Name and the entire structure of the *Shacharit*. (See the table below.) However, there is a wrinkle in this parallelism.

Yitgadal veyitkadash, etc.	י-ה	*Kriyat Shema* and the *Amidah*
Yehey shmeh, etc.		*Borchu*
Yishtabach veyitpaer, etc.	ו-ה	*Birchot Hahsachar* and *PZ*

The wrinkle is that in *Shacharit*, we start at the *lowest* level and culminate in the *highest* level. In the *Kaddish*, we start at the *highest* level and conclude with the *lowest* level. This recalls a point made earlier regarding the spiritual journey. As we make the effort to go up the spiritual ladder, God comes down the ladder as well. Our prayer of *Shacharit* is an effort to go up the ladder; the *Kaddish* describes the process of divine "downflow." Thus, the first part of the *Kaddish* corresponds to the *yod* and the upper *heh*; the latter part of the *Kaddish* corresponds to the *vav* and the lower *heh*. The first half of *Kaddish* parallels the fourth and third stages of *Shacharit*, for it is in these stages where we find the sanctification of God's Name. The second half of the *Kaddish* parallels the first and second parts of *Shacharit*, for it is in the lower parts where we praise and bless God's Name. Moreover, just as the *Borchu* is placed directly between the two lower and two upper parts of the *Shacharit*, so too the phrase "*yehe shmeh Rabbah mevorach* etc." is situated between the lower and upper parts of the *Kaddish*. In this way, the phrase *yehe shme mevorach, etc.* corresponds to *Borchu*. This is not surprising, since

56. On the inadequacy of praise, see *Tractate Brachot* 33b and Maimonides' discussion of this passage in *Guide to the Perplexed* I: 59.

57. This point is made even more explicitly in *Nishmat*, which is said immediately before *Yishtabach*, but only on *Shabbat* and other Holy Days. Since on those days we aspire to a higher level of holiness, we need to be even more emphatic about the inadequacy of praise. Our recognition of divine holiness is proportionate to our recognition of the inadequacy of praise.

both *yehe shmeh* and *Borchu* are essentially blessings of God's name in a very general way.

Kaddish and *Borchu* can be said only in the presence of a *minyan*, that is, a quorum made up of at least ten Jewish adults. (An individual praying alone would simply skip *Kaddish* and *Borchu*.) The general rule is that a *davar she-bikdushah* (something which involves the declaration of God's holiness) can only be performed by the congregation of Israel, rather than individual Jews acting on their own. A *minyan* constitutes the minimum representative body of the congregation. The lesson is that God's *kedushah* can only be adequately recognized or articulated by the *community* of Israel, rather than by individuals. God's transcendent nature is in some way beyond what any individual can properly recognize.

Earlier we touched upon the importance of one's pose during various parts of *Shacharit*. It is proper to stand during the recitation of the *Kaddish*. As noted earlier, standing connotes action. When we seek to accomplish something or effect a change outside of ourselves, we stand. The *Kaddish* (like the *Amidah* later) is active, because it is an attempt to accomplish something, namely, to bring about that God's name is sanctified, glorified, blessed, etc. On the other hand, as we shall see shortly, the recitation of the *Shema* is a receptive matter. Thus we generally sit during the recitation of the *Shema*.

We noted that the *Kaddish Yatom* (Mourner's *Kaddish*) functions as a transition marker between the first and second stage of *Shacharit*. As explained, the *Kaddish* focuses our attention on the divine Name, and reinforces the link between the various stages of the *Shacharit* and the letters of God's *Shem*, or Name. Similarly, the *Kaddish* after *Yishtabach* functions as a transition marker from the second stage and the third stage. Yet, at this stage the *Kaddish* is more important than before. Halachically, there is no need for a mourner's *Kaddish* between the first and second stage; if a mourner is present, then there is a mourner's *Kaddish*. But, between the second and third stages, the *Kaddish* is an obligatory part of the service (if there is a *minyan*).

After *Kaddish*, we say *Borchu*. Halachically, *Borchu* is considered the beginning of *Birchot Kriyat Shema* (and not the end of *PZ*).[58] The *Borchu* is a rather unique blessing. It does not have the usual structure of any other blessing. All other blessings in Jewish liturgy describe something specific for which God is blessed. Thus, the typical form of a blessing is, "Blessed are you O God, King of the universe, who has done thus and such . . ." Here, instead of blessing God for something specific, we

---

58. See *Mishnah Berurah* s.k. 13 on *SA:OC*: 54.

bless God in general – for the very fact that He is blessed! What is the meaning of this unusual blessing?

We may explain it as follows. In going through the morning blessings and *PZ*, we recognize God as the source of many things. We sing God's praises for all the numerous and varied things that are in the world. Now, in saying *Borchu*, we recognize and express the fact that God is the source of all blessing, *beyond specific description*. In contrast to the contents of the world, God is one and transcendent. Based on what was said earlier, we can also understand why *Borchu* is considered a *davar she-bikdushah*, even though it does not mention any form of the word, *kadosh*. *Borchu* is not a blessing for anything specific; it represents an acknowledgement of God as the transcendent source of all. Like *Kaddish*, it requires a *minyan*. Thus, *Borchu* is a fitting introduction to the coming section, where our attention will be focused on the *achdut* and *kedushah* of God.

THE THIRD STAGE OF *SHACHARIT*: THE READING OF *SHEMA* AND ITS BLESSINGS

THE THIRD STAGE OF *SHACHARIT* corresponds to the upper *heh* of the divine Name. The central purpose of this stage is to receive the divine kingdom and the commandments (*kabbalat ol malchut shamayim* and *kabbaat ol mitzvot*). One does this by reading aloud the three portions of *Shema*. The Talmud teaches that the reading of the *Shema* is itself a divine commandment. Additionally, the purpose of this stage is to arouse within oneself the *middot* associated with the upper *heh*, namely, *yirah* and *ahavah*. To do this properly, a person must focus intently on divine *kedushah* and *achdut*. Although references to *kedushah* and *achdut* occasionally emerged in *PZ* (especially toward its end), in the third section these are the main themes. Finally, the latter portion of this stage helps a person cultivate the *middot* of *simcha* and *ne'emanut* and brings him or her to the brink of the fourth stage of the spiritual path, the *Amidah*.

At the outset, it is worth noting some parallels between the first stage of *Shacharit* and this third stage. Perhaps the most obvious one is that both sections contain some form of the *Shema*.[59] Another parallel is that both stages involve a variety of texts, including selections from Scripture, rabbinic blessings, poems, etc. Neither the second nor the fourth stages of *Shacharit* have this variety. Finally, another parallel concerns the crucial role played in both the first and third stages by the *tzitizit* and *tefillin*. This will be a major theme in our discussion below.

The elevated status of this third stage relative to the previous two stages is reflected in the fact that the *halachot*, or rules, regarding permitted interruptions (*hafsakot*) during this section are even more strin-

---

59. However, see footnote 21 in Chapter 1.

gent than during *PZ*. For example, while in the earlier section one could interrupt to say *amen* to any blessing, in this section one may interrupt only between the various sections or chapters of the *Shema* and its blessings.[60] This increased stringency reflects the fact that the *middot* of the upper *heh* are on a higher level than the *middot* of the *vav*.

The third stage is composed of two rabbinic blessings, the reading of the *Shema*, and then another rabbinic blessing. We shall discuss these in turn. Our purpose in what follows is to illuminate how this section of *Shacharit* helps a person cultivate the *middot* associated with the upper *heh*.

Yotzer Or

After *Borchu*, the first blessing is *yotzer or* (he who forms light). This blessing begins by recognizing God as the one "who forms light and darkness, who makes peace, and who creates all."[61] Here we express wonder at the work of creation, and the wisdom (*chochmah*) evidenced by the cosmos.[62] We cite the verse *"mah rabbu ma'asecha hashem, kulam be'chochmah asita."* (*How many are your works, Hashem; you have made them all with wisdom.*) This verse may be interpreted as saying that through reflection on the contents of the cosmos, a person may be lead naturally to a belief in a wise creator. It is only in this section that we find the divine name *Shaddai*; this brings to mind the notion of *malchut shaddai* discussed earlier.[63] Certainly, the dependence of the entire cosmos on a wise and powerful God is a major theme of this blessing. The cosmos includes not just the planets and the luminaries, but also the realm of angels and other celestial beings. The latter are not things we are familiar with on a daily basis, but they are part of the cosmos. Of

---

60. *SA:OC:* 66. For a convenient summary, see *Artscroll Siddur* p. 85.

61. Indeed, the original verse upon which this blessing is based reads, "He makes peace, and creates evil (!)" (Isaiah 45:7). In other words, even that which is evil comes ultimately from God, and it serves a divine purpose.

62. It is noteworthy that the word *chochmah* occurs here – a term that is entirely absent from *PZ* and occurs only once before in the entire Service – in the blessing of *Asher Yatzar* (said after using the bathroom) where we bless God for forming the human with wisdom. Note also that both blessings use the term "formed" – *yatzar* and *yotzer*. Both blessings recognize God for his wisdom in forming or creating something – in one case the human, in the other case, the cosmos.

63. The term *shaddai* occurs once again in *Alenu*, but nowhere else in *Shacharit*. (However in *nusach sefard* it is mentioned in a short series of verses recited by some after *Modeh ani*.) On *Shabbat*, the term *Shaddai* is not found in this blessing; but the term *binah* is mentioned.

course, belief in such entities is based on prophetic experience as recorded in Scripture. They are included here, as the point of this blessing is to recognize God as the intentional and providential source of *all* the contents of creation.[64]

The blessing continues with a recounting of the *Kedushah*,[65] or sanctification, of God, by the angels described in the books of Isaiah 6 and Ezekiel 3. As explained earlier, the notion that God is the source of all is integrally linked with the notion that God is *kadosh,* or transcendent. It is only because God is transcendent that He can be the source of all, including all opposites such as light and darkness (and even good and evil). The contrast between the *PZ* and this first blessing of *Shema* is striking. Whereas *PZ* focuses on the expression of God or Being *within* the wondrous workings of nature, the first blessing of *Shema* focuses on how God *transcends* nature, and in some way, transcends all opposites. Naturally, then, there are almost no references to angels and other celestial beings in *PZ*. In sharp contrast, this first blessing here recounts angelic activity in some detail. For most of us, it is difficult to imagine or fully comprehend the angel's sanctification. Indeed, one might wonder why the Rabbis chose to include the recitation of the *Kedushah* of the angels in our daily service. However, there are several important lessons we can learn from this section, that are relevant to the Jewish spiritual path.

A close look at the liturgy in this section reveals that the notion of *yirah* plays a strong role in the angels' sanctification of God. The angels are depicted as "sounding the voice of God with *yirah,*" and "doing the will of their creator with trembling and *yirah*" and finally as "saying with *yirah, kadosh, kadosh, kadosh,* is *Hashem* the Lord of Hosts, the world is filled with His glory." Thus in the space of just a few lines the term *yirah*

---

64. On *Shabbat*, the text of the first blessing before the *Shema* is expanded and altered in certain ways, to include a focus on *Shabbat*. Yet, the rest of the blessings before and after *Shema* are the same as on the weekday. The reason is simple. Since the first blessing focuses on creation and on *kedushah,* a special mention of *Shabbat* is relevant. *Shabbat* was the culmination of creation, and it is also the day of holiness or *kedushah.*

65. Until now, we have been using the word *kedushah* as an abstract noun to mean holiness or sanctity. However, the same term is also used to describe the "sanctification" or proclamation of God's holiness, made by the angels in Isaiah 6. It is also used to describe the sanctification made by the Jewish people later in the *Amidah.* In this latter sense, the term *Kedushah* refers to a *liturgical formula* that proclaims the holiness of God. In what follows, we shall use the lower case *kedushah* to refer to holiness, and the upper case *Kedushah* to refer to the liturgical proclamation of God's holiness.

occurs several times. This underscores the point explained earlier that the recognition of God's *kedushah* must be done with *yirah*.[66] On the other hand, nowhere do we find that the angels are depicted as having a *love* for God. In fact, the term *ahavah* is almost entirely absent from this first blessing.[67] This stands in sharp contrast to the second blessing, where the notion of *ahavah* plays a major role. A related point is that neither the term *simcha*[68] nor the term *ne'emanut* occurs in connection with the angels; these terms occur only later in the second and third blessings in connection with the people of Israel. We shall return to these points shortly.[69]

Just as humans can fully sanctify God's name only in the context of a *minyan*, so too the angels are depicted as "collectively as one" saying their *Kedushah*.[70] Even angels say the *Kedushah* only *as a group*, and only when each one "gives permission to the other." The same applies to the *Kedushah*, which we will say later in the *Amidah*. Ideally, everyone

---

66. *Nusach sefard* makes this point even stronger for here it adds the word *aymah* (trembling).

67. The only place where any form of the term *ahavah* emerges is where the angels themselves are referred to as *"ahuvim"* or beloved. In *nusach sefard* the angels themselves are referred to as having love for each other (*venotnim beahavah reshut zeh lazeh . . .*).

68. On *Shabbat*, in the expanded first blessing, we do find the term *smaychim* (joyous) – but there it is a metaphorical reference to the joy of luminaries (*meorot*) in fulfilling the word of God. The angels are not described as having *simcha*.

69. It is worth noting that when we describe how the angels recite the *Kedushah*, the text reads, ". . . they all as one open and say (*onim ve-omrim*) with reverence (*yirah*), "Kadosh, Kadosh, Kadosh is Hashem, etc." Immediately afterward, when we describe how the lower celestial beings respond after the angels, we say that they "elevate themselves and *praise and say (meshabchim ve-omrim) Blessed is the Glory of Hashem from His Place.*" There are two crucial differences here. In the first case, (1) the angels are described as "saying" and not as "praising," and, (2) the angels say the *Kedushah* with *yirah*. In the second case, (1) the response of the celestial beings is described as giving praise (*meshabchim*) and, (2) no mention is made of *yirah*. The explanation is that *Kedushah* is not a form of *shevach*, or praise (even when it is recited by the angels); rather, it is a recognition of God's transcendence or separateness. It is done with *yirah*, even by the angels. However, the blessing of God's *Kavod*, or "glory," made by the lower celestial beings refers to the expression of God that emanates from Him. This is a matter of praise, and, in that case, *yirah* is not particularly relevant.

70. There is a halachic discussion of whether our own recounting of the *Kedushah* recited by the angels requires a *minyan*. *SA:OC:* 59:3. The prevailing opinion is that it does not. Still, the fact that some say it does require a *minyan* is instructive. It underscores the notion that individuals acting on their own cannot adequately recognize divine transcendence.

must say the *Kedushah* together in unison. Shortly, we shall discuss the important lessons this conveys regarding *kedushah* and *achdut*, as well as *yirah* and *ahavah*.

In sum, the main function of the first blessing is to recognize and express verbally with *yirah* that God is the source of the entire cosmos, and that even the celestial beings recognize with *yirah* that God is the transcendent, or *kadosh*, source of all. Even though it may be difficult for us to appreciate the angel's sanctification of God, the point is to underscore that God is not just one being among many celestial beings. Even the angels recognize and express that God radically transcends anything and everything else in the cosmos. Another reason is that our own *Kedushah*, or sanctification (which we will say later in the *Amidah*), is modeled on the *Kedushah* of the angels. Therefore, it is crucial to acquaint and reacquaint ourselves with the *Kedushah* of the angels on a daily basis.

Ahavah Rabbah and the Three Portions of Shema

A brief overview of this segment of the third stage will be helpful. The second blessing is *Ahavah Rabbah* (Great Love). This blessing is the prelude to the first portion of *Shema*. The blessing recognizes God as one who loves Israel and chose Israel for a special mission by giving us the *mitzvot*. Belief or acceptance of divine revelation is implicit here, for we know about the *mitzvot* only through revelation. In the first portion of *Shema*, we affirm the oneness, or *achdut* of God, and we accept upon ourselves the kingdom of Heaven (*kabbalat ol malchut shamayim*) as we recite the first verse, *"Hear, O Israel, Hashem our God, Hashem is One."* Just this affirmation alone plays a great role in *tikkun olam*. In the second portion, we accept upon ourselves the commandments (*kabbalat ol mitzvot*) and we affirm that the material welfare of the people of Israel depends on their keeping the commandments. This relates to the principle of *schar va-onesh* (reward and punishment for keeping or violating the commandments). In the third portion, the section dealing with *tzitzit* (fringes), we recall that God took Israel out of Egypt in order to make us holy with his commandments. Just as God is holy, or *kadosh*, so too, we have a mission to be *kadosh*, through the observance of the commandments. The *tzitzit* are a visual reminder of the divine exodus as well as our duty to obey the commandments.

It may seem curious that in this blessing, we do *not* mention the event of *Matan Torah* at Sinai. It is implicit, but not explicitly mentioned. In this same vein, it is worth noting that in the Talmud (*Tractate Brachot*

2:2), Rabbi Yehoshua ben Korcha refers to the second portion of the *Shema* as *kabbalat ol mitzvot* and not as *kabbalat ol torah*. Another seeming oddity is that we refer to the patriarchs at the beginning of the blessing when it would seem we should have referred to Moshe, the man who gave us God's Torah. The fact is that this blessing focuses on the notion that God has given *mitzvot* to Israel. As intimated above, the giving of the Torah represents an even higher level of connection with God, as we shall explain in the next chapter, on the *yod*.

Clearly, the major theme of *Ahavah Rabbah* is love. The blessing begins with the word *ahavah* and ends with the word *ahavah*. It speaks of God's love for Israel but also calls upon God to inspire us to love God. Here we contemplate the special generosity and benevolence of God in choosing the people of Israel and giving the *mitzvot* to Israel, and the opportunity this provides us to attain an interpersonal relationship with God. This serves as a lead-in to the *Shema*, in which we affirm God's *achdut* and accept upon ourselves the divine kingdom with love.

While the blessing does mention *yirah*, the emphasis is clearly on *ahavah*. The term *yirah* occurs only once; some form of the term *ahavah* occurs six times. So too, a form of the term *kedushah* occurs only once. Note the sharp contrast with the previous blessing of *yotzer or*. Much of *yotzer or* focuses on divine *kedushah*; hence, the emphasis is on *yirah*. In contrast, *ahavah rabbah* leads up to the recognition of God's *achdut*. As explained earlier, recognition of divine *kedushah* inspires *yirah*; recognition of *achdut* inspires *ahavah*. Indeed, the first portion of *Shema* itself expresses this connection in a striking way. In the first verse, we affirm God's *achdut*. Immediately, in the next verse, we describe the commandment to love God, "with all of your heart, all your soul, and all your might."

The contrast between recognition of *kedushah* and recognition of *achdut* emerges in two other ways. Earlier we noted that the *Kaddish* and the *Kedushah,* or sanctification (said later in the *Amidah,*) may be recited only in the presence of a *minyan*. The same is not true of the *Shema*. While it has become customary to say (especially the first verse of) the *Shema* aloud and in unison when praying with a *minyan*, it is not necessary to do so. Halachically, *Shema* is not regarded as a *davar shebikdusha*, that is, a matter that involves divine holiness. A person may fulfill (and is obligated to fulfill) the commandment of reading the *Shema* without a *minyan* just as much as with a *minyan*. We shall return to this point shortly.

While the declaration of God's *kedushah* is made by the angels, the declaration of God's *achdut* is made by humans, that is, the people of

Israel. Even when we say our own *Kedushah* later in the *Amidah*, we do it by way of imitating the angels. Yet, when we affirm God's *achdut* in the *Shema*, there is no mention of angels whatsoever, and the text we use is one that was taught to us by a human, namely, Moshe (Deuteronomy 6:4). There is also a rabbinic teaching that this verse was first uttered by the sons of Jacob.[71] We explicitly mention the name "Israel" in the first verse of *Shema*; in *Kedushah* we do not do so. Rather, we speak of God as the Lord of Hosts – another reference to angelic beings. It is also worth noting that in *Ahavah Rabbah* we refer to God as *our father* numerous times. Yet, we do not find even one place in Jewish literature where angels refer to God as their "father."

Maharal expands on this theme.[72] As angels are separate from material existence, they are better able to grasp and appreciate God's separateness, or *kedushah*. As humans are physical beings, our grasp of God's *kedushah* is not so sharp. We can barely appreciate the transcendence of angels, not to mention, the transcendence of God. On the other hand, our ability to recognize *achdut* is linked to the fact that we have free choice and bodily inclinations that we must overcome. According to Maharal, angels do not have free will, but humans do have free will. Therefore, unlike angels, we have both the challenge and the opportunity to connect even our bodies to God by doing physical *mitzvot*; the angels do not have this opportunity. The depths to which we can take the process of the expression of God's oneness in the world is far deeper than anything the angels can do. Thus, Maharal explains that the task more suited to the human is *yichud* and love; the task suited to the angel is sanctification alone. Nevertheless, humans need to have both, and can have both. Angels only have reverence for God, but not love!

In sharp contrast to the *Kedushah*, the first portion of *Shema* is in certain ways a private and personal matter. Each Israelite is supposed to love God with all one's heart, soul, and might. Now surely, every Israelite's "heart, soul, and might" are different. Each Israelite is supposed to speak and think of these words, ". . . . when you sit in your house and walk along the way; when you lie down and when you wake up." Lying down for sleep and waking up from sleep is generally a personal matter that is done in private. In contrast to the public and communal recognition of divine *kedushah*, the recognition of divine *achdut* involves the awareness that our closeness or intimacy with God is so intense, that God can be with us, even in our bedroom. Extending this point even further, insofar

---

71. *Tractate Pesachim* 56a.
72. Maharal, *Tifferet Yisrael*, chapter 24. See also *Kedushat Levi*, on *Shmini*.

as every individual person is unique, the precise nature of God's loving relationship with each person is unique.[73] The oneness or intimacy that God might have with an individual person is so intense that it differs from person to person. Therefore, the declaration of God's oneness, and the related commandment to love God, is more of a private matter than a public one. In this light, we may well understand why the recitation of the *Shema* does not require a minyan.

It is worth dwelling on the term, *Shema*. It is often translated, *"Hear."* However, in Hebrew the term *Shema* does not only mean *hear*; it also means *comprehend, listen,* and *accept*.[74] The affirmation in the *Shema* is an intellectual or cognitive act, as well as a bodily act involving the producing and hearing of sounds. The practice of covering one's eyes during the recitation of the first verse is designed to help concentrate one's mind on the meaning of the verse.[75] The use of one's hand to cover one's eyes is itself a physical or bodily act. Indeed one might wonder, why is it necessary to cover one's eyes with one's hand – why isn't closing one's eyes enough?[76] The truth is that although the *Shema* is a cognitive act, it is also a *bodily* act as well. After all, many if not most of the *mitzvot* involve bodily actions (or bodily restraint), and so, when we accept upon ourselves the *mitzvot*, we are accepting the *mitzvot upon the body*. Again, the *mitzvot* are given to human beings, not angels. The bodily nature of the *Shema* emerges in several other ways. We shall return to this point shortly when we discuss *tefillin, mezuzah,* and *tzitzit*.

In the same vein, the manner in which one is supposed to recite all three portions of *Shema* is unique when compared to the other stages of the Service. The halacha is that we should be careful to pronounce aloud and enunciate clearly all the words of the *Shema*. The halachic works go into detail on this; for example, one is supposed to make sure to distin-

---

73. Something similar is true in human-to-human relationships. When I respect someone, I respect him insofar as he or she is a human. Respect focuses on the *humanity* of a person – that humanity is shared by others. Respect is in a sense *impersonal*. On the other hand, when I love someone, the relationship is tailored to the individual. For example, if I have many children, the loving relationship with each one is unique. Love focuses on what is unique about an individual; each individual is a world unto himself.

74. Targum Onkelos translates *vehayah im shamoa tishmau*, as, *V'yehe im kabbala tekablun* (And it shall be that if you receive). Yet, interestingly, in the first portion, he translates *Shema* as *Shema*.

75. *SA:OC:* 61:5

76. There is a contrast here with the *Amidah* on this point. Some say it is best to pray the *Amidah* by heart, and the advice given is simply *close one's eyes*, but *not* to cover one's eyes with the hand. We shall return to this issue in the next chapter.

guish the *z* sound from the *s* sound when saying *lema'an tizkiru*. In part, this is related to the fact that the portions of *Shema* are selections from the Scripture, and to the fact that it is a divine commandment to read the *Shema*. But there is something else going on here. In contrast to *PZ*, the *Shema* is not supposed to be *sung*; it is supposed to be *chanted*, ideally with cantillation notes, or *trop*. The chant, or the *trop*, is not singing, or *zemer*; it is rather a matter of grammar and proper phrasing. The chanting of *Shema* reflects the fact that it is more cerebral and intellectual than *PZ*. Also, there is much less repetition in this section, when compared to *PZ*; since it is not *shevach*, repetition is out of place. Music and dancing is out of place when reading the *Shema*, but not so for *PZ*.

On the other hand, in contrast with the *Amidah*, the *Shema* is said aloud rather than in a whispering voice. Indeed, the practice is to say the first verse "*be-kol ram*," or in a raised voice, to arouse *kavanah* (intent).[77] All of these features reflect *the intellectual nature* of the *Shema* when contrasted with *PZ*, but also the *bodily nature* of the *Shema* when compared with the more elevated *Amidah*.

Let us move on to the second portion, *Vehayah im shamoa* (And it shall be that if you listen, etc.). Here we engage in *kabbalat ol mitzvot*, that is, we accept upon ourselves the commandments. We also affirm the principle that the material well-being of the people of Israel depends on our service of *Hashem*. This is a fundamental principle of *schar ve-onesh*, that is, divine reward and punishment for obedience or violation of the commandments.[78] In accepting upon ourselves this principle, we affirm that we have the ability to merit or earn what we have by keeping the commandments. As explained earlier, this is one of the motivations for accepting upon ourselves the divine commandments. In order to escape existential shame, we need to be in a position where we can earn or merit our material (and spiritual) blessings. In fact, the notion that

---

77. The phrase *baruch shem kvod malchuto leolam vaed* is said silently. A number of reasons are given for this, one of which is that it is rabbinic rather than scriptural. Possibly another reason is that since God's *achdut* is not yet fully recognized and expressed in the world, we say it silently, as way of indicating that this goal is not yet fulfilled. On Yom Kippur when we are like angels, we say it aloud, as angels are not under the same veil of ignorance that humans are, and can see that God's kingdom will be established in the future.

78. According to many sages, such as Maimonides, material success is not really the reward for obedience. See *Mishneh Torah: Hilchot Tshuvah* 9. Rather, material blessing is promised by God because it enables the people to continue serving God well. The true reward and punishment takes place in the next world. Furthermore, there is a level of service where "reward" becomes irrelevant altogether. We shall see this in the next chapter.

we can escape shame by fulfilling *mitzvot* is hinted at in the previous blessing, *ahavah rabbah*.[79] For there we say, "And give us our share in your Torah, and make our hearts cleave to your *mitzovt*, and designate our hearts to love and to revere your name *so that we will not be embarrassed forever*." What is the "embarrassment" referred to here, if not the embarrassment of existential shame? Furthermore, by accepting upon ourselves the commandments, we commit ourselves to participate in the divine project of *tikkun olam*. In making this commitment, we escape the existential despair associated with the *middot* of the *vav*.

Both the first and second portions of *Shema* include the commandment to teach "these words" to one's children. As mentioned earlier, this is an extension of *kabbalat ol mitzvot*. Despite the fact that halachically it is not a *davar she-bikdushah*, the commitment to *mitzvot* is essentially a collective or social commitment that Israel makes *as a people*. Thus, in committing oneself to *mitzvot*, one naturally commits oneself to teach them to one's children. The great importance of this commandment is self-evident, as it insures the transmission of the *mesorah* to the next generation. Furthermore, as mentioned earlier, learning and teaching the commandments are acts of love. If we love *Hashem*, we want to learn the commandments not only to do them, but also as a way of gaining a close relationship with *Hashem*. Also, if we love *Hashem*, we want not only ourselves, but others too, especially our children, to know and recognize the *achdut* of *Hashem*. For again, the *achdut* of *Hashem* is the root of our love for him, and indeed, the root of any love. Hence, learning and teaching (especially about divine *achdut*) is a labor of love.

Earlier we noted that the *kabbalah*, or reception, involved in the *Shema* is not just a cognitive process but also a bodily process. The *Shema* has a tactile quality. One way this emerges is in that both the first and second portions describe the commandments of *tefillin* and *mezuzah*. The *tefillin* are supposed to be a "sign upon one's arm and a jewel between one's eyes" (Deuteronomy 11:18). The *tefillah* that goes on the arm signifies the commandments that involve action; the *tefillah* that goes on the forehead signifies the cognitive dimension of the *mitzvot*. Although the *mezuzah* is not a garment worn on the body, it is affixed to the *mezuzah*, or doorpost, of a physical dwelling. It serves as a symbol of divine providence over Israel, as it recalls the daubing of the blood of the Paschal lamb on the doorpost, which was a prelude to the smiting

---

79. It may seem counterintuitive to say that serving God with *ahavah* is connected with the pursuit of *schar*, or reward. This issue will be addressed more in the next chapter.

of the Egyptian first born and the subsequent exodus. Both *tefillin* and *mezuzah* are physical objects that are symbolic of the relationship between God and the *bodies* of the Israelite people. It is no accident that the custom is to touch and feel the *tefillin* while reciting the *Shema*. We shall return to this point later, as we shall find that the fourth stage, the *Amidah*, is rather different in this regard.

The third portion of the *Shema* is a brief Scriptural passage that mentions God's taking us out of Egypt, as well as the commandment to wear *tzitzit*, or fringes, on the *tallit katan* or *tallit gadol*. This portion is in a somewhat different category than the first two. The Talmud teaches that the reading of the first two portions is a divine commandment. The third was chosen by the Sages for recitation because it fulfills the divine commandment to recall the exodus daily. The Sages could have chosen many passages for this purpose. They chose this one because the *tzitzit* reminds us not only about the exodus, but also about all the *mitzvot*.[80] As the verse reads, "*And you shall see it [the tzitzit], and you shall remember all of the commandments that I have commanded you, and you shall not stray after your hearts and eyes which you are tempted to follow thereafter.*" The passage goes on to say that by keeping the commandments, we become holy, or *kadosh*, unto God, and it concludes with the reminder that that God took us out of Egypt in order to be "our God." In other words, God took Israel out of Egypt in order to establish a devotional or interpersonal relationship between Himself and Israel. For those wearing *tzitzit*, it is customary to hold them while reciting the passage, and to kiss them upon mention of the word *tzitzit* during the recitation, and again at the conclusion of the portion. It is also customary to gaze at the *tzitzit* while reciting the verse just quoted. The *tzitzit* serve as a visual aid to remember our God and our commitment to keep the *mitzvot*. While the first and second portion of the *Shema* focus on "hearing," this last portion focuses on "seeing." Once again, note that all three portions have a tactile quality.

Clearly, this portion expresses key themes associated with the upper *heh* and the divine *sefirah* of *binah*. Recall that *binah*, or divine intelligence, signifies that there is a divine plan, and world history is heading toward *malchut shaddai*. God's taking Israel out of Egypt is the primary divine intervention in the natural course of events. It is one of those critical or "watershed" historical events that is part of the cosmic process described earlier. This is one reason for why the remembrance of the

---

80. *Tractate Brachot* 12b.

exodus is a central theme throughout many *mitzvot*.[81] In taking Israel out of Egypt in miraculous fashion, God made his Name known to the world. He also established Israel as his chosen nation, and prepared Israel for its great mission, which is to play the pivotal role in bringing about *tikkun olam* through keeping the *mitzvot*. As we read the portion of *tzitzit*, we call to mind that foundational event that established our devotional relationship with God, and its corollary, namely, our obligation to fulfill the commandments.

Like the *tefillin*, the *tzitzit* are worn on the body. However, the *tzitzit* play a somewhat different role than the *tefillin*. The *tefillin* symbolize the special relationship between God and Israel, through the exodus and the giving of the commandments. The *tefillin* themselves are holy, as they contain portions of scripture. The *tzitzit* are rather a reminder that one should not be drawn astray by temptation to violate the commandments.[82] The *tefillin* may be compared to a locket that a lover wears around his neck. Inside the locket is a love-letter from his beloved. The locket sits upon his heart and reminds him of his beloved. On the other hand, the *tzitzit* may be compared to a simple string that a lover might tie around his finger that reminds him to be true to his beloved. Like the locket, the *tefillin* are more precious; but it is not practical or proper to wear the locket all the time. Thus, for example, *tefillin* may not be worn in an unclean place; *tzitzit* may be worn anywhere. The *tzitzit* are less precious, but precisely for that reason the *tzitzit* can be worn at all times. The *tzitzit* serve as a constant reminder "not to stray" from the commitment to the beloved. One needs the reminder precisely when one is far removed from one's beloved.

In this passage regarding *tzitzit*, the Torah prescribes that a "*petil techelet*" should be placed on the corner of the garment with the *tzitzit*. The *petil techelet* is a string (or set of strings) that has a blue dye, made from a rare snail known as the *chilazon*. Indeed, the snail is so obscure that for many centuries, the exact knowledge of this *chilazon* was lost. The practice of adding the blue string fell by the wayside. Only in recent years, after some great rabbinic scholars claimed to identify the *chila-*

---

81. See Ramban on Exodus 13:16.

82. Numbers 15:37ff. Indeed, the *mitzvah* of *tzitzit* was instigated by a violation of *Shabbat* (the *mekoshesh*). Based on a *midrash*, *Orach Chaim* (15:37) comments that since we do not wear *tefillin* on *Shabbat*, Moshe asked God for some commandment that might keep us from violating *Shabbat*. *Tefillin* are associated with specific positive commandments (sanctification of the first born, the Paschal offering, learning and teaching Torah). The *tzitzit* are primarily intended to keep us from violating *any* of the negative commandments.

zon, a growing number of Jews are once again wearing the blue *techelet* on their *tallit katan* and/or *tallit gadol*.

There is something of a mystery here. It is clear that the fringes of the *tzitzit* serve as a reminder of the exodus and as a reminder of all the *mitzvot*. Yet, the Torah does not explain the significance of the blue color of the fringes that are made from the rare snail. The key to the explanation lies in the following Talmudic teaching. "The *techelet* is similar [in color] to the sea; the sea is similar to the heavens, and the heavens are similar to the throne of glory."[83] When we gaze at the blue color of the *techelet* we are inspired to think of the majestic sea, which leads us to think of the still more majestic sky, which leads us to think of the still more majestic divine royalty itself. The awesome quality that we find in the sea and the sky is only a reflection of the awesome transcendent God and adds to the impact of the visual aid, which is the very purpose of the *tzitzit*. We should be inspired to keep the commandments not only out of a sense of obligation, but also out of a sense of pride in our allegiance to the divine and royal king. One might go so far as to suggest that it is *only* by contemplating the divine royalty of the king that a person will be able to master the temptations of the "eyes and heart" that lead us astray from keeping the commandments.

As suggested earlier, the color blue symbolizes the upper *heh*. The rarity and preciousness of *techelet* is linked with what it symbolizes – royalty. Its rarity is essential to its nature – it symbolizes that which is *unusual, set apart, kadosh*. It is no accident that while in the first stage of *Shacharit,* we find numerous references to the reds of blood and earth; in the second stage we find reference to the greenery of the grass and the forest; it is only in the third stage where we find reference to the royal blue *techelet*. Similarly, in the case of the spiritual journey, it is only after having worked through the first two lower stages of the lower *heh* and the *vav* that one may reach the august level of the upper *heh*.

Earlier we noted a parallel between the *middot* of the lower *heh* and upper *heh*. The basic receptivity of the lower *heh* corresponds to the cognitive receptivity involved in the upper *heh*. Kabbalistically speak-

---

83. *Tractate Menachot* 43b. It is also possible to see a connection between the *tzitzit* and the *tzitz* (head plate) of the High Priest. The *tzitz* was tied around the head with a string of *techelet* (Exodus 28: 37) and it bore the phrase, "Holy unto י-ה-ו-ה" (*kodesh la-Hashem*). The *tzitz* is worn like a "holy crown" (*nezer ha-kodesh*), and thus signifies royalty. The root of both words *tzitz* and *tzitzit* may come from the word for gazing or looking (*le-hatzitz*). (See *Da'at Mikra* commentary on Numbers 15:38.) By looking at the *tzitz* and the *tzitzit* we are inspired with awe. This helps us avoid violating the commandments, and thereby reach *kedushah*.

ing, these are feminine *middot*. We find a similar parallel between the first stage and third stages of *Shacharit*. In our discussion of the lower *heh*, we noted that the first stage of *Shacharit* involves donning *tzitzit* and *tefillin*. By putting on *tzitzit* and *tefillin*, one literally accepts upon one's body a relationship with God, that is, one physically receives the divine presence, or *Shekhinah*. Later, upon reaching the third stage of *Shacharit*, we focus intellectually on the meaning and significance of these *mitzvot*. We read with great care the passages which refer to *tzitzit* and *tefillin*. As we mention the Scriptural terms for *tefillin* and *tzitzit*, we touch them and we kiss them. Whereas in the lower *heh*, the donning of *tzitzit* and *tefillin* help us receive God's presence, or *Shekhinah,* in a general way, in the upper *heh* we are more cognitively engaged in focusing on the meaning or significance of the *tzitzit* and *tefillin*.

Note that the *tzitzit* and *tefillin* do not play much of a role in the *vav* section. Although men are supposed to wear *tzitzit* and *tefillin* throughout the whole *Shacharit*, there is only *one* occasion during *PZ* when we hold the *tzitzit*, and one occasion where we touch the *tefillin*. In the *yod* section there is not a single occasion when we do this. As we shall see, in the *yod* section one is not supposed to be touching or feeling the *tzitzit* or *tefillin*. All of this reinforces the point that there is a commonality in the two *heh* sections that is not shared by the *yod* and *vav* sections. The bodily aspect of the human is given more attention in both the lower and upper *heh*. Since the *yod* and the *vav* do not involve receptive *middot*, garments and visual aids do not play a significant role. We shall return to this point in the next chapter.

Despite the fact that the *Shema* involves a cognitive reception of the kingdom of heaven, the bodily nature of the *Shema* is expressed in a teaching of the *Zohar* that has generated a universally accepted practice among all Jewry. According to the Talmud, a human has 248 separate bodily parts. The Zohar notes that there are 245 words in the three portions of *Shema*.[84] In reading the *Shema*, we are supposed to accept the divine kingdom upon each and every one of our limbs. To symbolize this, it is customary for the *chazzan,* or leader, to repeat the last three words of the final portion. In this way, we reach 248 words. By making

---

84. See *Tikunei Zohar* 25b. The number 245 includes the six words, *baruch shem kvod malchuto leolam va'ed*. When praying in private with no *minyan*, the three words *"el, Melech, ne'eman"* are said just before the beginning of the *Shema*. When praying with a *minyan*, the *chazzan* repeats the last two words of the final portion together with the word *emet*, which is the first word of the following blessing. See *SA:OC*: 61:3.

this addition, we demonstrate that we are accepting *ol malchut sha-mayim* and *mitzvot* upon *all* of our limbs.[85] There is a profound lesson here. According to Judaism, the spiritual journey is not just a journey that involves the spirit or the mind. It involves the body as well. Even when it comes to such a lofty thing as the love of God, it is not just with the soul that one loves God, but also with the body – indeed "with each and every limb."

Ga'al Yisrael

The final section of the upper *heh* begins with the phrase "*Emet ve-yatziv*" (true and permanent) and ends with the blessing, *Ga'al Yisrael* (redeemer of Israel). In this blessing, we recognize that God is the king who not only redeemed Israel in the past by taking us out of Egypt but also the king who continually redeems Israel throughout the generations. In this context, "redemption" means a material or bodily saving (*yeshuah*) of the people of Israel from oppressors. It also hints at the fact that by taking us out of the land of *Mitzrayim*, and then giving us the commandments, God spiritually redeemed Israel, by uplifting them from a lower form of mere material existence.[86] The foundation of our relationship with God was the exodus from Egypt, and that relationship has remained in place throughout the ages.

The notion that God is our king is also a major theme in this blessing. Although the conclusion of the blessing ends with "redeemer of Israel," the notion that God is King is mentioned repeatedly.[87] God is committed to providential care for us, and we are eternally bound by our commitment to serve the king by fulfilling the commandments.

Another theme of this blessing is that the redemption of Israel was *miraculous*. The exodus from Egypt was miraculous, and the divine revelation of the commandments was miraculous. Throughout the earlier stages of the service, we had thanked and blessed God for our natural gifts, and we praised and blessed God for the wondrous workings of

---

85. *Tikunei Zohar* (132a) teaches that the Israelite must accept God's kingdom "on each and every limb" (*al kol ever ve-ever*).

86. This is a major theme in Maharal's *Gevurot Hashem* and in Chassidic Literature. For example, see *Tanya* 31.

87. Some form of the word *melech* occurs nine times in *emet ve-yatziv*. Interestingly, in this blessing the term *kadosh* is almost absent; it occurs only twice toward the end of the blessing. This represents a sharp contrast with the first blessing, in which *kedushah* plays a major role.

the natural world. The main focus was not on extraordinary miracles.[88] Here, in the upper *heh*, especially in the final blessing, God's miraculous intervention in the ordinary course of things is a major theme. The upper *heh* signifies that God is not just the God *of nature*; God is *supernatural*. This ties in with the point made earlier regarding *kedushah*. Since God transcends nature, God is able not only to manage natural events but to intervene in the course of nature. The exodus of a slave nation from the most powerful kingdom on earth is the paradigmatic example of such an intervention. Indeed, toward the end of the blessing we explicitly link the notion of *kedushah* with miracles, as we say, "*Mi kamoch ba-elim Adonai, mi kamocha, needar bakodesh, nora tehillot, oseh feleh.*" ("Who is like unto you among the powerful ones, O Lord; who is like unto you, noble in *holiness*, awesome in praises, doer of *the miraculous!*")

Another theme in this last blessing is joy, or *simcha*. This emerges in two ways. First, we say "*ashrei ish sheyishma le'mitzvotecha, v'torat-cha u'dvorcha yasim al leebo.*" ("Happy is the man who listens to your commandments and who places your teaching and your words upon his heart.") There is a kind of joy here which is related specifically to keeping the commandments. In rabbinic terms, this is known as *simcha shel mitzvah*. Shortly thereafter, we recall the Song of the Sea, which was said *be-simcha rabba* (with great joy). Here, the *simcha* is a response to salvation (*yeshuah*) and redemption (*geulah*). We exult in God's salvation of Israel from Egypt at the sea and his continual salvation of Israel throughout the generations. Clearly, the intent of this passage is to recognize God as King and Redeemer, *with joy*.

Finally, another theme of this blessing is *ne'emanut*, or faithfulness.[89] We recognize God as a faithful God who keeps his commitment to Israel, throughout the generations, by continually redeeming us from potential destruction. We reciprocate by expressing our intent to remain faithful to our commitment to God and the commandments. Again, this kind of faithfulness is a rational faithfulness, borne out of the collective experience of the people of Israel. Essentially, this is a reaffirmation of what we just affirmed in the *Shema*. In simple terms, we made a commitment – and we plan to stick to it. This is the virtue of *ne'emanut*.

---

88. As noted earlier, the Song of the Sea was originally *not* part of PZ. In light of the present discussion, we can understand a little better the (apparently defunct) custom of delaying the Song until after *Yishtabach*.

89. Some form of the word *emet* or *ne'emanut* occurs ten times in this blessing. The word *emet* is usually translated as "true." In this blessing, it often means "true" in the sense that a dedicated friend or spouse might be "true" or "loyal."

In summary, the major themes of the third stage of *Shacharit* are divine *malchut*, *kedushah*, and *achdut*, the revelation of *mitzvot* to Israel, and God's special providence over the people of Israel. We recognize God's *kedushah* with *yirah*; we recognize and accept God's *achdut* and the *mitzvot* with *ahavah*; we declare that God is our king and savior with *simcha*; we affirm our commitment with loyalty, or *ne'emanut*. As the major theme of this section is receptive, it is generally said while sitting (even though it is permissible to say it while standing). Of course, in order for the *Shacharit* to serve as a vehicle for spiritual growth, it is not enough merely to say the words. Rather, our *Shacharit* should set the tone for the rest of the day. A person must carry through with service and devotion to God with *ahava*, *yirah*, *simcha*, and *ne'emanut*, throughout the rest of the day, by fulfilling the *mitzvot* and living a life that is *kadosh*.

At this point, the reader may wonder, can there possibly be a level higher than serving God with reverence, love, joy and faithfulness? Could there be some flaw in the *middot* of the upper *heh* that needs to be repaired or fixed – as we found in the case of the lower stages? We shall find that this is true in one sense, but not true in another. The *middot* of the upper *heh* lead naturally and seamlessly to the *middot* of the *yod*. At the same time, the *middot* of the *yod* constitute a significant advance over the *middot* of the upper *heh*. Let us proceed without delay to the next and final chapter.

י

YOD

knowledge and understanding, *chochmah* has more of a creative or inventive connotation. *Binah* involves computation, comprehension, logic, analytical ability; *chochmah* involves creative thought, invention, and originality.[2] Thus, a *mavin* (from the word *binah*) is someone who understands things or figures things out; a *chacham* (from the word *chochmah*) is more of an original thinker. Kabbalistically speaking, *binah* is a receptive or feminine quality, whereas *chochmah* is more of an active or masculine quality. This should not be taken to imply that women are more intelligent than men, or that men are more creative than women. Again, as stated in previous chapters, both men and women have feminine and masculine qualities.

In the same vein, *chochmah* is regarded as an expansive or right-sided *sefirah*; *binah* is regarded as a restrictive or left-sided *middah*. *Chochmah* represents God's ability to have creative ideas; *binah* represents God's ability to implement those creative ideas. Thus, *binah* involves limiting and defining the original creative idea in certain ways; this is a restrictive process.

Chochmah plays a role in God's creation of the world in the following way. When God created the world, he did so in just such a way as to meet the goal he had in creating the world. God does not choose blindly, and when he does choose, he tailors his actions so that this goal will be reached. If God had so wished, he could have created a universe without any order or structure; but he chose to create an orderly world. Furthermore, he did not just create *any* order, but rather a world that has a specific order. In other words, God wisely designed his creation so that it meets the end for the sake of which he created it. In this way, the world is not only an expression of divine will, but also *chochmah,* or wisdom.

Now let us face the question that we had pushed off earlier. Namely, *why* did God create the world at all, and why did God create the specific world that he did? The question may be restated as follows. Based on the previous chapter, much of what God does can be explained in terms of the fact that God has the goal of establishing *malchut shaddai.* God's actions make sense in light of that goal. However, this only pushes our question back. Is there an explanation for *why* God has the goal of establishing *malchut shaddai*?

Some might be tempted to say that, ultimately, there is *absolutely no reason* for why God has the goal of establishing *malchut shaddai,* or any other goal for that matter. God simply chooses his ultimate goals by

---

2. On the difference between *chochmah* and *binah* see Maharal, *Tifferet Yisrael,* chapter 31.

"divine *fiat*." However, if that were so, the universe would be a complete accident, for God could have just as easily chosen not to create at all, or to create a world that has no order whatsoever, or a world in which people suffer endlessly for no reason. That doesn't seem correct; it doesn't seem to fit the idea of God as reasonable and benevolent. (Alternatively, the problem would be that God is benevolent only by accident; accidental benevolence doesn't seem like genuine benevolence at all.)

Another response might be that indeed there is some divine reason for why God created the world, and why the world is the way it is, but we cannot ever hope to know or understand it. Perhaps that is so. But, if there is an available explanation that we can understand, or even a partial explanation, we should keep looking for it. For, if we can know even something of why God created the world, such knowledge might be helpful or perhaps even integral to our fulfilling our mission in the divine plan. So, let us keep looking.

One classic explanation sometimes given for why God created the world is the following. It is in the nature of a good being to do good for others. The classic Hebrew phrase for this notion is *teva ha-tov, lehetiv*.[3] By nature, God is benevolent, and a benevolent being does benevolent things, such as, share his goodness with others. In order to share his goodness, God had to create a world. Therefore, God created the world out of benevolence, or *chessed*. This sounds plausible, but it raises yet another question. Does God *need* to be benevolent? If so, then God is not truly free, for he is "forced" by his nature to create the world. On the other hand, if God does not *need* to be benevolent, then the question returns – why did he bother? Another point is that *chessed* is only one of God's traits. So, this answer seems to imply that the other traits of God has are not relevant to his creation of the world.

It seems wrong to say that something *outside* of God caused him to create the world. It must be that something *inside* God led him to create the world. On the other hand, we do not want to say that anything inside God *compelled* him to create the world. This leads to the following suggestion. The world exists and is the way it is because God is engaged in a grand cosmic act of *free self-expression*. God's reason for creating the world is internal, but it is also not something he was compelled to do.

The Rabbis allude to the notion that God created the world as a form of divine self-expression in *Mishnah Avot*, chapter 6: "*Kol mah shebara,*

---

3. See R. Yosef Irgas, *Shomer Emunim* page 18. Although Ramchal does not use this exact phrase, the idea is found in *Derech Hashem* 1:2. Some base this notion on the verse in Psalms 89:3, "*olam chessed yibaneh*." See *Kli Yakar* on Deuteronomy 32:6.

lichvodo bara." "Everything that God created, He created for his glory."
What does it mean to say that God created everything "for his glory"?
If this means he did it to be glorified by others, that would seem problematic. Why would God need glorification from others? Rather, what
it means is that ultimately everything God does is an *expression of His
glory*, that is, it is a matter of self-expression. The world and all of its
contents are an expression of God himself. This could also be understood as the meaning of the phrase said in *Kedushah*, "*melo kol ha-aretz
kvodo*" – all of the world is full of his glory.

We find an allusion to the notion of divine self-expression in the following rabbinic teaching. Rabbi Shmuel son of Nachman said, "When
God created the world, he desired to have a *dirah batachtonim*," that
is, a dwelling place in the lower realms.[4] How can we understand this
teaching? It is surely not in a physical sense that God might "dwell" in
the lower realms. Rather we may understand it to mean that in creating
the world, God seeks to manifest not only some or even all of his powers.
Rather God seeks to "dwell" in the world; that is, God seeks to express
his divine nature as fully as possible within the world. We have already
made use of the notion of divine self-expression in the previous chapter,
but in what follows, we shall make use of this concept even further.

The notion of divine self-expression may best be understood by the
following analogy. God is like a great artist. Why does a great artist
produce a work of art? A great artist has within himself the potential
to produce a great work. Does this mean that he is forced or compelled
to produce the work? No. He *can* produce the artwork, but he is not
thereby *compelled*. Furthermore, the work will have a certain character,
namely, it will represent or express what is within the artist. The work
is not arbitrary or merely whimsical. The fact that the artist created the
work *makes sense* and the content of the artwork *makes sense* in light of
the nature of the artist. The explanation for the existence and nature of
the artwork is *not* that is was created primarily in order to give something to others to enjoy. However, that may happen incidentally as well.
If the artist is a benevolent person, his artwork will express benevolence,
along with all the other features of the artist. Indeed, that might be one
of his intentions in creating the work. Still, even if others enjoy the artwork once it is there, that is not the primary reason for the creation of
the artwork. It was an act of self-expression. God, too, creates the world
as an act of self-expression.

---

4. *Midrash Tanchumah,* Numbers 16. Later, we shall discuss how this goal of
dirah batachtonim includes but also surpasses the goal of *tikkun olam.*

It turns out that this answer to the question of why God created the world *includes* within it the idea mentioned earlier that God created the world because he is benevolent (*teva ha-tov lehetiv*). Since God is benevolent by nature, his creation of the world is an expression of his benevolence. However, this answer is broader than that, for God has attributes aside from benevolence. In some way, the world is an expression of *all* of God's features – including his very being, his oneness, and even his necessity. On this approach, the contingent universe is an expression of God. It didn't *have to* exist, but it *makes sense* that it exists, and ultimately, what happens in the universe *makes sense*, even if it is not necessary.

One final comment is necessary here. Normally, when an artist produces a work of art, the work is produced as a finished project. The expression of God in the world is not like that. It is not yet finished; it is a work in progress. Human beings, and especially the people of Israel, play a crucial role in this process. We shall return to this point later.

Maximal Divine Self-Expression

So far, we have described the notions of *keter* and *chochmah* on the *pashut* conception of God as an entity. We have also grappled with the question of why God created the world. In this book, we aim to think of God's essence not as an entity; rather, God's essence is Being itself. On this view, what can it mean to speak of divine wisdom and divine will? And, on this approach, how might we answer the question, *why* does our world exist, and why does it exist in the way that it does? Although it must be couched in different terms, the answer is similar to what was said above. The explanation for why the world exists has to do with *maximal divine self-expression.*

Like all *sefirot*, *keter* and *chochmah* have to do with *the way or ways in which Being is manifest or expressed.* The essence, or *atzmut*, of God is *Being itself.* It is a plain and self-evident fact that Being has certain necessary and fixed features. At the same time, there is also a realm of possibility or contingency. On the one hand, there are certain necessary and eternal truths. On the other hand, there are an infinite number of possible things that could exist and an infinite number of possible events that could happen. The world that we live in is a contingent world. Many things exist and many events happen that could have easily not happened.

Now, to speak of *keter*, or divine will, is to say that *the contingent world is headed toward the fullest possible expression of the necessary nature of God.* At first glance, this may sound problematic – how can the *necessary* nature of God be expressed at all in the *contingent* world? But we have already touched on this notion in previous chapters. For example, we said that *kedushah* and *achdut*, which are necessary features of Being, are expressed to some degree in the world. Yet, now we are saying something even stronger. *Keter* signifies that the contingent world is not merely a *partial* divine expression; rather, it is ultimately going to be *the most complete possible* expression of *ein sof*, or infinite Being. Of course, *ein sof* cannot ever be *completely* manifest or expressed in the contingent world. For, that would mean that the contingent universe itself would become God! Rather, *keter* signifies that there is a process that is heading toward the *most complete possible* expression of *ein sof*.[5] That is the explanation for why the world exists, and why it is the way it is.

Again, as before, one might still be inclined to press the question, *why* is this happening? That is, *why* is there a process afoot such that the universe is headed toward the fullest possible expression of Being? This is another way of asking, "Why did God create the world, and why is the world this way rather than some other way?" or "Why is there a contingent world, and why does it have the features that it has, rather than other ones?" The answer is that although it is *not* a necessary thing to have happened, it is *reasonable* that it has happened, given the nature of Being. The universe "freely flows from God's necessary nature."

We have said that *keter* represents that the contingent world is headed toward the most complete possible expression of Being. On this view, how might we understand *chochmah*? *Chochmah* signifies the fact that *Being is "channeled" in just such a way so that its fullest possible expression will occur in a contingent universe.* Of course, the term "channeling" is a metaphor here. The explanation is as follows. Since God or Being is essentially necessary and infinite, a "constriction," or *tzimtzum*, is required in order for there to be a contingent universe. This is one reason why *chochmah* is represented by the *yod*, the letter that comes closest to constituting a single tiny point. The single tiny point represents the constriction or concentration of God's infinite and unlimited nature.[6] At the same time, this "channeling" represents something positive, for some amount of energy or being is transmitted through the channel. This is

---

5. Arguably, this process may take forever. If so, this would explain the need for a world that never ends. This is the traditional notion of *olam haba* (the world to come).

6. See *Shaar Hayichud Ve-ha'emunah*, chapter 9. Relative to the infinite essence, or *ein sof*, *chochmah* is finite.

also represented by the *yod* in that, despite the fact that it is merely a point, it is after all, a point, not an empty space.

The notion of divine self-expression has already played an important role throughout this book. In the first chapter, we said that *malchut* signifies that there is *some* expression of Being itself in any particular thing, even in such things as pebbles or sand. In the second chapter, we said the six *sefirot* of the *vav* signify the various ways in which Being is manifest or expressed in the natural world. In the third chapter, we said that *binah* represents the fact that there is an orderly structure to the world. We also said that *kedushah* and *achdut* are necessary features of God or Being, and there is a cosmic process at work, such that there is an expression of those necessary features in the world. That process will reach its culmination when the world reaches *tikkun olam bemalchut shaddai*. Now we are saying that in virtue of *keter*, there is something of an *explanation* for why the world is headed toward *malchut shaddai*. It is headed toward that end *because* it is headed toward the *fullest possible* expression of Being. In other words, *keter* underlies, or explains, *binah*. And, in turn, *keter* explains all the other *sefirot* as well. All the *sefirot* are what they are because they play a role in the grand cosmic process of maximal divine self-expression.

Moreover, in virtue of *keter*, two further dimensions are added to the cosmic process. First, the goal of the cosmic process involves something that encompasses, but also goes beyond, the goal of *tikkun olam bemalchut shaddai*. It involves the "divine desire" to establish a *dirah batachtonim*, that is, a "dwelling place in the lower realms." Second, in the virtue of *keter*, there is, so to speak, a *divine guarantee* that this process is going to be completed. Earlier we had noted that human free will plays a crucial role in the cosmic process. Now we are saying that even though that remains true, it is still the case that one way or another, the goal of maximal divine self-expression will be reached. These points will be explained in the following sections.

The Difference between *Tikkun Olam* and *Dirah Batachtonim*

Recall that *tikkun olam* involves the expression of divine unity and holiness in the world. It also involves the attainment of world justice and peace, and the universal recognition of God as the holy and sovereign king. However, as we shall now explain, the goal of *dirah batachtonim* includes, but surpasses *tikkun olam*.

The Rabbis teach that there are certain historical events that exhibit the divine aim to attain a *dirah batachtonim*. One is the revelation of

God at Sinai. During that event, God "came down upon the mountain" and revealed himself within the world, in a way that he had never done before. The imagery of God's "coming down" upon the mountain matches the imagery of God's seeking a dwelling "in the lower realms." The purpose of that event was to reveal Himself in the world, and to give the Torah to Israel. He revealed himself in the divine utterance, *Anochi Hashem Elokecha* ("I am the Lord your God"). The giving of the Torah is also regarded as a revelation of God. Judaism teaches, and Kabbalah emphasizes, that the Torah is the quintessential expression of God, in way that goes beyond His expression in the various commandments that he had issued until that point.[7] In any commandment, God's will is expressed to some degree. But, the totality of God's commandments in the Torah (by tradition, *Taryag,* or 613, commandments) represent God's will – or rather, God himself – in a more complete fashion.[8] The Torah is not merely a collection of many commandments; it is a whole that is greater than the sum its parts. Furthermore, the culmination of the process of *dirah batachtonim* is the resting of God's presence in the *mishkan* (tabernacle) and later in the *Beit Hamikdash,* or Temple. The Rabbis teach that the *mishkan* and later the Temple are ways of making permanent that original act of divine "resting" or "descent" that took place upon Mount Sinai.[9] The indwelling of God's presence in the Temple represents the climactic goal of God's self-expression in the world.

In order to achieve *tikkun olam bemalchut shaddai,* none of these things was necessary. Imagine a world in which all humans live in peace and harmony, and worship only one God. For that to happen, God had to give *some* commandments, and he had to make himself known in the world *to some extent.* As discussed in the previous chapter, God made himself known not just to Israel but to the world, through the exodus and its miracles. Perhaps it was necessary for God to designate a "chosen people" who would play the central role in leading the world toward the goal of *malchut shaddai.* But, it was not necessary for God to reveal

---

7. The patriarchs were given a number of *mitzvot* (e.g., circumcision). During the exodus, the Israelites were given a few more *mitzvot* (e.g., Passover, *tefillin*). Shortly after the exodus but before the revelation at Sinai, a few more *mitzvot* were given (e.g., *Shabbat*).

8. Thus it is taught that the Torah is one long name of God (*Zohar* 3: 99a). *Tikunei Zohar* (21b) teaches that God and the Torah are one (קוּדְשָׁא בְּרִיךָ הוּא אִיהוּ אוֹרַיְיתָא). On that notion, see *Tanya,* chapters 4 and 23. The difference between a *mitzvah* or even a collection of *mitzvot* and the Torah is a major theme in rabbinic and Kabbalistic literature. See, e.g., *Tractate Sotah* 21a; Maharal, *Ner Mitzvah* (toward the end).

9. Ramban, *Commentary on the Torah,* Exodus 25:1.

himself at Sinai, give the Torah, nor to rest in a temple. These actions represent that God seeks to establish a much more intimate connection with the world than merely *tikkun olam*.[10]

In the previous chapter, we found that the upper *heh* stands for divine *malchut,* or sovereignty. The upper *heh* also reflects the divine goal of *tikkun olam bemalchut shaddai*. In contrast, the *yod* stands for divine will and wisdom. The *yod* reflects the goal of *maximum* divine self-expression, or *dirah batachtonim*. The revelation at Sinai, the giving of the Torah, the building of the *mishkan* and later the *beit mikdash* are all aspects of this higher goal. Later we shall see how this shapes the *middot,* or spiritual virtues associated with the *yod*.

The Divine Guarantee

In the previous chapter, we noted that human free will plays a crucial role in the achievement of the divine goal of *tikkun olam*. It also plays a role in the attainment of *dirah batachtonim*.[11] For God to dwell within the lower realms, humans must do certain things that will allow that indwelling to take place. As the Kotzker Rebbe said, in answer to the question, "Where is God?" – "God dwells wherever a person lets him in!"

Yet, if matters were left *completely* up to human free will, it is possible that humans might actually fail and then the divine goals would not be reached. Judaism insists that this will not happen. Indeed, *keter* represents the fact that there is a cosmic process occurring, such that maximal divine self-expression *will be reached*. In other words, in virtue of *keter* there is a "divine guarantee" that these goals will be attained. To

---

10. Indeed, the very term *shaddai* hints at the fact that *malchut shaddai* is *not* the highest level of divine revelation. The name *shaddai* suggests there is still some dimension of God that is hidden. See Exodus 6:3 and Ramban's *Commentary on the Torah,* ad loc. A close study of *Alenu* also supports the thesis that it is reasonable to distinguish *tikkun olam* from *dirah batachtonim*. *Alenu* is a prayer for *tikkun olam be-malchut shaddai*. In the first half of *Alenu,* the distinction of Israel from the nations is celebrated, not for having received the Torah, but rather for having been drawn away from idol worship, which is something that all peoples are supposed to avoid. The second half of *Alenu* is essentially a prayer for *tikkun olam*. We pray that "the wicked of the earth" shall one day turn toward God and recognize him. No mention is made of the giving of the Torah at Sinai, nor do we pray here for the building of the *beit mikdash*. The reason is that *Alenu* focuses on *tikkun olam* and not *dirah batachtonim*.

11. This is clear from the remainder of the *midrash* quoted above (see note 4). It is through human failure (sin) that God is banished from the world; it is through human achievement that God is able to dwell in the world.

put the point bluntly, human history is "rigged" so that the divine goals of *tikkun olam* and *dirah batachtonim* will be reached.[12]

This seems to raise a philosophical problem. If things are rigged so that the end will be reached, doesn't this imply that, in the final analysis, human free will is irrelevant to the attainment of the goal? For, no matter what humans do, the end will be reached! However, that doesn't follow. What does follow is that human free will can be weakened or diminished by God, if we stray too far from the divinely ordained goals of creation. God has designed the world in such a way that humans will freely do what they need to do in order to reach the goal. The question is how much of it will be due to our freedom, and how much of it will be due to divine coercion. The more God intervenes, the less is the ultimate result due to our own free will, and the less grand is the achievement. In other words, the world is structured in just such a way that human freedom is maximized, but only up to the point where more freedom would wreck the whole project.

An important aspect of all this is that God forgives sins or mistakes, if a person does *tshuvah*, or repentance. Indeed, not only does God forgive; God wipes the slate clean. Thus, Kabbalists relate *keter* to the "thirteen attributes of mercy"[13] by which God not only forgives sin but also "atones" and "purifies" the sinner. These thirteen attributes of mercy transcend the ordinary lower level *rachamim* (which is associated with the *vav*). For, it is one thing to forgive sins. It is quite another to wipe the slate clean. This is associated with the possibility of not only *tshuvah* but rather *kapparah* (atonement) and *taharah* (purity) from mistakes or sins that would otherwise ruin the fulfillment of the divine project. This is associated with the power of Yom Kippur. It is also associated with the revelation at Sinai. As explained earlier, the event at Sinai was more than just a "law-giving" event; it was a divine revelation of the highest order. Thus, the *luchot* (tablets) contained the *Anochi* as one of the ten sayings. After the first tablets were broken due to the sin of the golden calf, the second tablets were brought down by Moshe on Yom Kippur.[14] This hap-

---

12. This concept of God's "rigging" things to ensure that his goals will be reached may be seen in the *midrash* that God compelled Israel to accept the Torah with a threat of death (*Tractate Shabbat* 88a). While the people of Israel are given credit for freely accepting the Torah, the *midrash* teaches that God *insisted* that the Torah be accepted. In this way, it is guaranteed that the divine project will succeed. Since God himself is engaged in the project of maximal divine self-expression, He will see to it that the divine goals will be reached, even if it means tinkering with human free will.

13. Exodus 34:6–7.

14. See Rashi, *Commentary on the Torah*, Exodus 33:11.

pened only after the revelation of the thirteen attributes of *rachamim* to
Moshe. In this revelation, Moshe reached the pinnacle of his prophetic
career, and the most intimate bond with God. That is to say, he reached
a level where he had prophetic contact with the highest aspect of God,
namely, *keter*.

Having said all this, we may now consider whether it is rational to
believe in *keter* and *chochmah*. Is it rational to believe that there is a
process of maximal divine self-expression at work in the universe? Here
we must say something similar to what we said in the previous chapter
regarding the belief in the cosmic process of *tikkun olam*. Based on ordinary or everyday experience, one would not necessarily conclude that
the universe is headed toward completion or perfection. Judaic belief in
keter and *chochmah* is based largely on the *mesorah* of revelation. The
Hebrew Scriptures are one long account of the divine attempt to achieve
dirah batachtonim. But we may add something else. Recall the notion
suggested earlier that the contingent universe is an expression of God.
The existence of the contingent universe is not *necessary*, but it does
exist, and if it is an expression of God, it *makes sense* that it exists. If
the contingent universe is an expression of God at all, it would make
sense that the universe should be the *fullest possible* expression of God.
Otherwise, God is like great artist, who fails to express himself fully
in his artwork. Hence, we may say that the belief in maximal divine
self-expression is a form of *rational optimism*. It is *rational*, because
if one reflects on the nature of Being, it *makes sense* to think that this
process of maximal divine self-expression should occur. But it is *optimistic*, because it is not *necessary* that such a process must occur. It
is also optimistic because, if this process is occurring, it means there
is a way out of existential despair and a way of engaging in the grand
project of *tikkun olam bemalchut shadday*. It also means that the world
is headed toward the fullest possible expression and manifestation of
Being, in other words, *dirah batachtonim*. We shall touch on this issue
again, when we discuss *da'at Hashem* or knowledge of God.

Final Points about *Keter* and *Chochmah*

Kabbalah regards *keter* as the most important and fundamental of all the
sefirot. It is in virtue of the fact that God seeks to express himself as fully
as possible that all the other *sefirot* are what they are. All the other *sefirot*
are explained by *keter*, that is, maximal divine self-expression. Yet there
is a still a difference between *keter* and *ein sof*, the infinite essence of
Being itself. Being itself is not the same thing as the *maximum possible*

expression of Being. Going back to our analogy above, no matter how great an artwork is, it is not identical with the artist himself.

All of these points are alluded to by the very shape of the *yod*. Just as the tip of the *yod* points upward indicating the infinite *ein sof*, or essence of God, *keter* symbolizes the fact that the contingent universe expresses the infinite *ein sof*. Just as the tip of the *yod* points upward toward infinite empty space, the contingent universe "points" toward the infinite *atzmut* of God. Nevertheless, *keter* requires *chochmah*; it is impossible for *keter* to function without *chochmah*. The expression of the artist in an artwork requires a certain wisdom; otherwise it is not an expression of anything coherent but merely a random outburst. Thus, there is no such thing as a tip of *yod*, without the body of the *yod*. *Keter* requires *chochmah*.

Earlier we had noted the kinship between the *yod* and the *vav*. Kabbalah teaches that, just as the *vav* has a masculine character, so too, the *yod* has a masculine character. The *yod* represents the potential for action, and the *vav* represents the actualization of that potential. At this point, we are in position to understand that on a deeper level. The *yod* represents will and wisdom; the consequence of will and wisdom put into practice are the six *middot* of the vav. Action flows from will and thought.

In Kabbalistic literature, *Keter* is sometimes symbolized by *atik yomim* (Ancient of Days) or *erech anpin* (Patient Countenance). The image is one of an elderly gentleman who is filled with grandfatherly patience. *Chochmah* is sometimes referred to as *Abba,* or Father, the mate of *Imma* (Mother or *binah*). The six *middot* associated with the *vav,* together with the *Shekhinah* that is associated with the lower *heh,* are represented as the "children" of the mother and father. Like parents, *chochmah* and *binah* are the origin of the six *middot* and the divine presence. In other words, the "lower seven" *middot* of God are the "offspring" of divine intelligence, wisdom and will. In some cases, where the Father and Mother might be more stern with the children, the Grandfather may be inclined to "spoil" his children. This links back to the point about the thirteen attributes of mercy mentioned above. Still, as one family, all of the *middot* work together so that the ultimate end or goal will be met. This imagery represents the fact that the "father" (the *yod*) and "mother" (the upper *heh*) have a more intimate bond with each other than do their children (the *vav* and the lower *heh*).[15] More on that point follows shortly.

---

15. *Zohar* 3:4a. But see Ramak's complex discussion of this matter in *Pardes*

The divine name associated with *keter* is *"ehyeh asher ehyeh"* which means, *I will be what I will be* (see Exodus 3:14). This name alludes to God's power to choose, and to choose whatever He wishes, even if it sometimes goes against the natural course of things and even if it goes against the way God normally operates. The name associated with *chochmah* is ה-י (*yod-heh* or *Yah*) which are the first two letters of the Tetragrammaton. Kabbalah teaches that the close connection between the *yod* and the upper *heh* (when contrasted with the *vav* and lower *heh*) is signified by the fact that one of the names for God is *Yod-heh* just by itself. This is not the case with the *vav-heh*; the latter does not constitute a divine name by itself. Nor do the letters *yod-heh-vav* constitute a name. This indicates a special bond between the *yod* and the upper *heh* that is not found among the other letters in God's name. Still, the name *Yod-heh* is not the complete Name of God, and we find it used as an appendage to other words. The complete name is the *Yod-heh-vav-heh*, because only this name represents all aspects of God or Being.

Earlier we discussed the Kabbalistic teaching that different colors represent different aspects of God or Being; thus, different colors correspond to different letters of the Name. The lower *heh* is represented by earthy red; the *vav* is represented by leafy green; the upper *heh* is sky blue. The *yod* is in a completely different category altogether, for the color that corresponds to the *yod* is white. In Kabbalistic imagery, the color white is associated with the divine beard of the *atik yomin,* or Ancient of Days, that is, God in his guise as the grandfatherly figure described above. White is also the color of Yom Kippur; the color of the holy *Shabbat,* that stands apart from the rest of the week. In a sense, white is the *absence* of color. Perhaps this is why white represents purity. Even a tiny spot of dirt is noticeable on a white background. It is said that all the other colors are included in white. Similarly, all the other *sefirot* are contained potentially in *keter*.[16] The *yod* is also associated with a bright shining light, which is a universal metaphor for wisdom, or *chochmah.* Light is what makes all the other colors visible. Just as without light, no other color is visible, so too *keter* generates all the other *sefirot.*

Earlier we noted that the letters of the divine name correspond not only to various aspects of God, but also to various aspects of the human

---

Rimonim 8:14.

16. The color white also hints at the blank parchment on which the Torah is written. This relates to the notion that the Torah represents or expresses God's infinite will in the highest possible way – even beyond the letters of the Torah, which represent his will in a more concrete fashion. See *Ohev Yisrael* on *Parshat Tetzaveh* 3.

soul. Recall that the lower *heh* corresponds to the *nefesh,* or the animal soul; the *vav* corresponds to the *ruach* which is linked with the capacity for speech and emotion; the upper *heh* corresponds to *neshamah* which is associated with intelligence. Here we may add that the *yod* corresponds to the loftiest aspects of the soul, *chaya* and *yechidah,* which represent, respectively, the human capacity for wisdom and free will. Not surprisingly, as we shall soon see, the *middot* of the *yod* involve these higher aspects of the human soul.

THE LIMITATIONS OF LOVE
AND REVERENCE

WE ARE ALMOST READY to turn our attention to the *middot*, or spiritual virtues associated with the *yod*. Before doing so, we need once again to reflect on the limitations of the *middot* of the previous stage, namely, the upper *heh*.

Recall that in the upper *heh*, a person transcends existential despair, by engaging in *kabbalat ol malchut shamayim* and *kabbalat ol mitzvot*. Guided by comprehension – intellectual recognition – or *binah* – of the divine Being and the divine commandments, a person makes a rational choice to live a life whose meaningfulness is grounded in the necessary and eternal God. In the upper *heh*, a person cultivates the *middot* of *ahavah*, *yirah*, *simcha*, and *ne'emanut*. He fulfills the commandments, and thereby takes part in the grand cosmic process of *tikkun olam*. He becomes worthy of his natural gifts. Indeed, the *middot* of the upper *heh* are very lofty. If a person should reach this level and never move on, he or she would thereby live a deeply purposeful life. However, some reflection shows that there is still something missing if one remains at that level. This is true for several related reasons.

Let us go back to our starting point. The goal of the spiritual path is to attain a deep, meaningful, relationship with God or Ultimate Being. The closer, more intimate the relationship, the better it is. Now, in the upper *heh*, the relationship with God is an *interpersonal* one. I relate to God well by doing *mitzvot* and by cultivating *ahavah* and *yirah*, and I thereby live a life that has deep meaning because it is anchored in divine necessity. Yet, if I have an interpersonal relationship with God, then, I am *me*, and God is *he*. Hence, *there remains a chasm between myself and*

God.[17] The same point may be stated in a different way. The upper *heh* level involves accepting God as our King. If I think of myself as a servant to the King, a certain distance inevitably remains between myself and the King. While I can find great meaning in a life of devotion to a great King, the fact remains that there is a chasm between myself and the King. This raises the question of whether there is some way of closing this gap. This may seem like an impossible task. Won't there always remain a gap between myself and God? Surely Judaism doesn't teach that one can become *identical* with God! Nevertheless, as we shall soon see, the *middot* of the *yod* take us even closer to God than do the *middot* of the upper *heh*.

Another way to see the limitations of the *middot* of the upper *heh* is as follows. As explained earlier, any growth in spiritual maturity is based on a growth in intellectual comprehension or what is colloquially called "seeing the bigger picture." Now, the *heh* is the level of rational recognition of God or Being as the holy, one, creative source of all else, as well as the king of Israel, the redeemer, and the giver of *mitzvot*. In the upper *heh*, my choice to accept the kingdom of God, to commit to *mitzvot*, and even to cultivate *ahavah* and *yirah* – these are all driven by rational comprehension. Here then is a subtle but very profound point. When my choice to do some action is based on reasons, the connection between that action and myself is *mediated* by something, namely, those reasons.[18] The question arises as to whether there might be some way of relating to God that is *not* mediated by reasons. This does not mean that the reasons would fall away completely, but rather that in addition to there being reasons, there would also be some aspect of the relationship that transcends reason.

We can make the same point using Kabbalistic terms. Just as I am able to recognize that in God, *keter* and *chochmah* transcend *binah*, so too I am able to recognize and take stock of the fact that in the human being, the mind (*neshamah*) is not the highest aspect of the self. Ultimately, the powers of wisdom and will (*chaya* and *yechidah*) are higher than intellect (*binah*). If my relationship with God is mediated through *binah*,

---

17. See *Tanya*, chapter 35. The one who loves or fears God is still a *davar bifnei atzmo* (a separate entity). See also *Ohev Yisrael, Beshalach* 7.

18. If an action or commitment is totally based on reasons, it is open to being undermined by a potential argument against those reasons. Even if those reasons are good, they can *still* be attacked, even if the attack is frivolous or silly. In Kabbalistic and Chasidic literature, this is sometimes referred to as the doubt, or *safek,* of *Amalek.* See Tzemach Tzedek, *Derech Mitzvotecha* on *Amalek.*

the question arises whether there can be some mode of relating to God that goes *beyond* reason and that involves those higher powers. These will be the *middot* of the *yod*. A person comes to recognize that the relation between oneself and God that is based on *binah*, or rational comprehension, of God or Being and its characteristics only goes so far. One seeks to meet God more directly, with the higher powers of ones' being, namely, the capacity for wisdom and the will; and perhaps even something even beyond those two as well.

Another, related limitation of the *middot* of the upper *heh* is the following. One of the key *middot* of the upper *heh* is *ahavah*, or love. The truth is that this love involves a kind of self-interest. It is a very refined self-interest, but self-interest nonetheless.[19] The *middot* of the upper *heh* are motivated by the desire to escape existential despair and to be involved in the joyous and meaningful work of *tikkun olam*. One takes great pride (*gaiut*) in fulfilling the *mitzvot* of God. This is related to the fact that *schar va-onesh* is a major theme in *Vehaya Im Shamoa*. At the level of the upper *heh*, there is a reason for *kabbalat ol mitzvot*, namely, reward and the avoidance of punishment. This includes not only material reward and blessing, but also the higher kind of benefit one gets from doing *mitzvot* – the escape from existential despair, the sense of pride and joy one derives by participating in *tikkun olam*, and the spiritual reward – the bliss and ecstasy involved in having a loving relationship with God. Anyone who has been in a loving relationship gets some kind of "kickback" from the relationship, some kind of satisfaction or pleasure or good feeling. Some kind of self-interest keeps the engine of love churning, so to speak. This is not a bad thing, but there is room for improvement – if that's the *only* motivation for serving God.

The bottom line is that while the *middot* of the upper *heh* are very noble, there remains a gap between the spiritual seeker and God himself. This leaves us looking for a more direct yet also selfless way of relating to God Himself than is possible through the *middot* of the upper *heh*.

---

19. In other words, it is an *ahavah* that is *tluyah badavar*, that is, dependent on something and therefore not the best or purest form of *ahavah*. See *Mishnah Avot* 5:16. Another way to put the point is that this *ahavah* involves worship that is *al menat lekabel pras* (for the sake of reward). See *Mishnah Avot*, chapter 1:3. One might say that if this is the problem with the *middot* of the upper *heh*, then the solution is not necessarily to move to a new *middah*, but rather to fix the *ahavah* to be a better kind of *ahavah*! Indeed, it is possible to view *devekut* as an advanced form of *ahavah*. See below, p. 212.

BONDING (*DEVEKUT*) AND ABNEGATION (*HITBATLUT*) OF THE WILL

How can one close the gap between the self and God? How can a finite and contingent creature close the gap between oneself and perfect, necessary Being? In some sense, the very first thing one must do at this level is acknowledge and accept the fact that one can never *totally* close the gap between oneself and God. Indeed, accepting this truth is *itself* part of the spiritual maturity associated with the *yod*. At lower levels, we found that there was some insufficiency that could, in some measure, be fixed. But at a higher stage, we realize that we have certain limitations that *cannot* be surpassed. Accepting these limitations may be difficult, but that too is part of the spiritual path. At the same time, it is also part of spiritual maturity to realize that even though one can never totally close the gap between oneself and God, there is always room for improvement; the fact that one can never reach total perfection should not prevent a person from striving to improve. The *middot* of the *yod* take us closer to God than do the *middot* of the upper *heh*. We shall see that although one cannot fully close the gap, there is a certain sense in which the gap can be bridged.

We noted earlier that the *yod* in the name of God corresponds to the *sefirot* of *keter* and *chochmah*. *Keter* corresponds to the highest part of the human soul, which is *yechidah*, or the will. *Chochmah* corresponds to *chaya*, which is the second highest part of the human soul, and it is associated with our capacity for wisdom. Hence, the spiritual virtues, or *middot*, of the *yod* have to do with the will and with our capacity for wisdom. The *middot* of the *yod* that concern the will are *devekut* (bonding) and *hitbatlut* (self-abnegation). The cognitive *middot* of the *yod* are *chochmah* (wisdom), *emunah* (faith), and *da'at* (knowledge).

Let us first discuss *devekut* and *hitbatlut*. *Devekut* may be translated as bonding or clinging. *Hitbatlut* may be translated as abnegation or sub-mission. These terms can be used in different senses and contexts.[20] We may distinguish two senses of *devekut* and *hitbatlut*. First, we can think of *devekut* (and *hitbatlut*) as a character trait or *middah*. A *middah* is a quality that a person can cultivate and have all the time. A second way of looking at *devekut* (or *hitbatlut*) is as an *event*, that is, as a spiritual oc-currence that can happen and then pass. A *devekut* (or *hitbatlut*) event might happen during prayer or meditation and then pass over. We may also distinguish different senses of *devekut* and *hitbatlut*, depending on what human function or power is involved. In what follows, we shall discuss a certain form of *devekut* and *hitbatlut* that involves the human will. Later, toward the end of this chapter, we shall discuss a higher kind of *devekut* and *hitbatlut* that involves the very core of one's being.

A starting point for our discussion is the following rabbinic teaching (*Mishnah Avot: 2*) that explicitly uses the words *ratzon* and *batel*:

> *Rabban Gamliel, bno shel Rabbi Yehudah Hanasi omer . . . Aseh retzono kirtzoncha, keday sheyaaseh retzoncha kirtzono. Batel retzoncha mipnei ritzono, keday sheyevatel retzon acherim mipnei retzoncha.*[21]

Literally, this translates as follows:

> Rabban Gamliel the son of Rabbi Judah Hanasi says, ". . . Make His will like your will, so that He will make your will like His. Nullify your will before His will, so that He will nullify the will of others before your will."

Here we find both a positive and a negative instruction. *Do* make your will like His – that is *devekut*. *Nullify* or negate your will before His will – that is *hitbatlut*. In other words, *devekut* and *hitbatlut* involve *con-forming one's will to God's will*. These two *middot* go hand in hand; they are really two ways of talking about the same thing. A person cannot have one without the other. Thus we will frequently speak of them as

---

20. For the idea that these two *middot* always go together, see *Netivot Shalom* Vol. 2, p. 25; Vol. 1, p. 64.

21. Perhaps we may homiletically interpret *retzon acherim* (the will of "others") to refer to the wiles of one's own evil inclination. (The term "*acherim*" often connotes the "other side," in the sense of the evil inclination.) The point of this statement is that if a person nullifies his will to God's will, then God will help the person by nullifying his or her evil inclinations.

a pair using the expression, *devekut/hitbatlut*. If I conform my will to God's will, that means both that I want only what God wants, and I do not want what God doesn't want.

Still, what exactly does it mean to make your will like His, and to nullify your will before His will? It seems to mean, doing what God wants us to do, and not doing what God does not want us to do. However, if this is what *devekut* and *hitbatlut* are, how is that any different from the *middot* of the upper *heh*, namely, the commitment to observe the positive commandments and not violate the negative commandments? As we shall explain, there are many differences. All of these differences revolve around the same point: *The bond with God established in devekut/hitbatlut is more total and complete than the bond that is established through ahavah and yirah.*

First, let us remind ourselves of one of the main differences between *binah* and *keter*. While *binah* is associated with the exodus and with the giving of a certain number of commandments to Israel, *keter* is associated with the revelation of God at Sinai and the giving of the Torah. Correspondingly, the *middot* of the upper *heh* are associated with *kabbalat ol malchut shamayim* and *kabbalat ol mitzvot*.[22] In contrast, the *middot* of the *yod* are associated with something more encompassing, namely, *kabbalat ha-Torah*. It is one thing to recognize God as the one King, and to accept a few *mitzvot*. It is quite another to accept Torah (*Taryag*, or 613 commandments) which governs one's entire life.

This, then, is the essential difference between the *ahavah* and *yirah* of the upper *heh*, and the *devekut/hitbatlut* of the *yod*. In theory, it is possible for a person to recognize God as King and to accept some *mitzvot*, without accepting upon himself the Torah. Indeed, this is precisely the level that the people of Israel were on, *before* they received the Torah. Moreover, according to Jewish tradition, this is the level of all other nations even to this day – they are supposed to recognize God as King and obey certain commandments, but they need not accept the Torah.[23] It is entirely conceivable that a human being might have a good relationship with God by keeping some *mitzvot*. One thereby escapes existential despair, and participates in the goal of *tikkun olam*. But, one cannot reach *devekut* without accepting and keeping Torah (*Taryag*, or 613 *mitzvot*), nor can one participate in the higher divine goal of bringing about *dirah*

22. See the discussion of Rabbi Yehoshua ben Korcha's terms, in the previous chapter, page 175.

23. See the discussion of the Noahide commandments in the previous chapter, on p. 162.

batachtonim. This is the special task and commitment of the people of Israel.

Another difference between the *ahavah* and *yirah* of the upper *heh* and the *devekut/ hitbatlut* of the *yod* is as follows: In the upper *heh*, devotion to God is motivated and mediated by *binah*. One's fulfillment of the commandments is based completely on understanding or rational comprehension. There is a kind of cold and calculating process, which leads one to commit to the *mitzvot* and serve God. In contrast, *devekut* involves bonding or connecting one's own will *with God's will itself*, in a way that goes beyond reason. At the *yod* level, the connection between the self and God is not completely mediated by reason (*binah*). There is a dimension of the relationship that involves a "leap" beyond what cool, calm and collected reason would dictate. *Devekut* of the will involves doing what God wants, *without hesitation or question*; *hitbatlut* involves not wanting what God does not want, *no matter how crazy it may seem*. In either case, this is different from wanting what God wants (or not wanting what God does not want) because of purely rational calculations.

A person who is still only in the upper *heh* level may actually have desires and wants that *conflict* with the commandments. To use rabbinic language, he may still have *hirhurim ra'im*, or negative thoughts. Yet, he overcomes those *hirhurim* and compels himself to obey the commandments because he has a love and reverence for God. He may even go so far as to give up his life for God and for keeping *mitzvot*. Yet if he does so, it takes a struggle and effort. On the other hand, a person who has reached *hitbatlut* and *devekut* does not even want anything that violates God's commands, and he wants only to fulfill what God commands. If the situation calls for giving up his life for God or for keeping the commandments, he does so without hesitation. Such a person does not have *hirhurim ra'im*; his thoughts are pure and clean. In this way, a person who has cultivated *devekut* and *hitbatlut* is closer to God than someone who has "only" the *ahavah* and *yirah* of the upper *heh*.[24]

Another point of difference is this. As explained above, the love involved in the upper *heh* is driven by a refined self-interest. It is linked with the aim to achieve some kind of *schar*, or reward. To be sure, the love is still wholehearted as long as the person carries through on the commitment by keeping the *mitzvot*, even if it is out of rational con-

---

24. This distinction here parallels the distinction between the *beinoni* (average person) and the *tzaddik* (saint) in *Tanya*, chapters 12–13. While not everyone can reach the level of a *tsaddik*, everyone can and should strive for that level.

siderations, and/or out of a desire to escape existential despair, and/or a desire for reward, whether material or spiritual. *Devekut/hitbatlut* is higher than that. In *devekut* of the will, a person simply *wants to do what God wants*, period. It remains true that there are great advantages in doing so, that it brings great joy, reward, meaningfulness, and so on. Still, in *devekut/hitbatlut*, any such motivation is secondary. The primary motivation is that *God's will should be done*, period.

This point relates back to the difference between *tikkun olam* and *dirah batachtonim*. As we said earlier, the upper *heh* is associated with *tikkun olam* whereas the *yod* is associated with *dirah batachtonim*. In the upper *heh*, I am looking at things from the point of view of the *receiver*. In other words, I am looking at things from the point of view of *what the world wants*. In the *yod*, I am looking at things more from the point of view of God. I am thinking about *what God wants*. In the *yod* I come to recognize that the divine project includes *tikkun olam* but also something even greater – God's maximal self-expression in the world. Insofar as that is my focus, I am no longer thinking about my benefit, nor even the benefit of the world. I care rather that "God's will be done." This is *devekut/hitbatlut* of the will. Another way of saying the same thing: I have to "forget myself" to reach *devekut/hitbatlut*.

Yet another point of difference is the following. A person who has *ahavah* and *yirah* fervently keeps those commandments that apply to him or her. But a person who has *devekut* and *hitbatlut* goes beyond the commandments and does what God would want him to do (or not do) *even without being told directly what to do*. A person who has the *ahavah* and *yirah* of the upper *heh* is like a loyal servant who does exactly what the king wants. He goes "by the book" without fail. He shows up on time for work, he does his job, and he leaves when the job is done. But a person who has *devekut/hitbatlut* is like a servant who knows the king so intimately that he anticipates and rushes to do what the king wants *even without being told*.[25] He doesn't even want to go home; he wants to hang around the palace all the time. (How is it possible for us to know what God wants us to do without being told? We will turn to that question in the discussion of *chochmah* below.)

In the previous chapter, we noted that there is a tension between *ahavah* and *yirah*. *Ahavah* involves going forward with positive emotion toward God; *yirah* involves reeling backward away from God. *Ahavah* is

---

25. This is related to the concept of "*kadesh atzmecha be-mutar lach*," or "sanctifying the permissible" (*Tractate Yevamot* 20b). See Ramchal, *Mesilat Yesharim*, on *prishut* and *chassidut*. See also, *Netivot Shalom, Parshat Vayetze*.

a warm and pleasant feeling; *yirah* is a scary and uncomfortable feeling. Kabbalistically, love is a right-sided *middah* and awe or fear is a left-sided *middah*. However, that same tension does not apply to *devekut* and *hitbatlut*. For, again, *devekut/hitbatlut* are really two names for the very same *middah*. If I have *devekut/hitbatlut*, all I want to do is exactly what God wants; this means that I want to do what God wants, and I don't want to do what God does not want. Kabbalistically, *devekut/hitbatlut* is neither right-sided nor left-sided; it is a central *middah*.

We have explained various ways in which *devekut/hitbatlut* of the will go beyond the *ahavah* and *yirah* of the upper *heh*. Despite all this, it would not be wholly incorrect to view *devekut* and *hitbatlut* as a highly advanced form of love and reverence. For, a love of God that involves a struggle against one's inclinations is surely not as pure a love as it might be. Similarly, a love that is dependent on reasons is not as pure as a love that goes beyond reasons. From this point of view the *middot* of *hitbatlut* and *devekut* do not really go beyond *ahavah* and *yirah*; *it is rather that ahavah and yirah when taken to their full extreme lead naturally to this more advanced state.* In different words, the cultivation of *devekut* and *hitbatlut* is the natural outcome of the life of Torah lived with *ahavah* and *yirah*. We shall return to this point later when we discuss the transition in the liturgy from the third to the fourth stage of the *Shacharit*. For the most part, in what follows we shall assume that *ahavah/yirah* is distinct from *devekut/hitbatlut*.

Earlier we noted that there are degrees of *yirah* and *ahavah*. A person can have some *yirah*, a lot of *yirah*, or a great deal of *yirah*, and so on. It also seems clear that with respect to something like *chessed* and *rachamim*, there are degrees of how giving or how compassionate a person might be. But here, in the case of *devekut/hitbatlut*, the matter is not so simple. Can there be *degrees* of *devekut/hitbatlut*? For example, can a person have some *devekut* at one time, then more *devekut* at another time? Can a person grow in *devekut*? Or, is it something that one has totally, or not at all?

On the one hand, *devekut* involves a total devotional commitment. Hence, if a person does not do, or at least try to do, all the *mitzvot* in the best way he can, there is a flaw in his *devekut*. However, perhaps it is possible to do even *just one mitzvah in a devekut-like manner* (rather than merely an *ahavah* type manner). One could be totally committed to doing a specific *mitzvah*, just because God commanded it, without thought of reward, and just because through that commandment one connects one's will with God's will. Even within one *mitzvah*, there are degrees of how *devekut*-like is the performance of that *mitzvah*. For example, the thought of reward may be very central, less central, somewhat weak, etc. We can safely say that although this is a flawed *devekut*, one can grow in terms of approaching *devekut* by doing more and more *mitzvot* in a *devekut*-type manner. Although *devekut* in its purest sense itself does not admit degrees, there are degrees of how close a person can get to *devekut*. Something analogous may be said regarding *hitbatlut*.

So far we have explained what is *devekut/hitbatlut* of the will. Next, let us consider the practical question, how does one attain or cultivate *devekut/hitbatlut* of the will?

Firstly, one does so by working hard at keeping Torah, that is, keeping all the positive and negative commandments, no matter how small or great. Again, there is a difference between *doing isolated mitzvot* (even a lot of them) and *keeping the Torah* – which goes beyond just doing *mitzvot*. One also needs to study Torah intensively – we shall return to this point in our discussion below of *chochmah*. By diligently working at keeping the *mitzvot*, a person may gradually train himself to attain *devekut/hitbatlut*. Yet, even if I *do* all the *mitzvot*, I might still not reach *devekut/hitbatlut*, for I might be doing them because "I should" and not because "I want to." Or I could fall into a pattern of doing them by habit. This is a serious threat that can befall the careful and devoted *mitzvah* observer. In order to reach *devekut/hitbatlut* one must do the *mitzvot with the specific intent (kavanah) to bond one's will with God's will.* Thus, Kabbalists recommend that before one performs a *mitzvah* one should verbalize one's desire to do it with proper *kavanah* (intent).

Second, while it is true that to cultivate *devekut/hitbatlut*, one needs to keep all the *mitzvot*, there are certain *mitzvot* in particular which help cultivate *devekut/hitbatlut* of the will. One such *mitzvah* which we do not have in our day is that of *korbanot*, or sacrificial offerings. In earlier times, a person or the community could cultivate *devekut/hitbatlut* by offering a *korban*, or sacrifice. This is something we cannot do in our day, until the Temple is rebuilt. But it is worth reflecting on what's involved in bringing a sacrifice. A sacrifice involves a *bittul* (nullification) of one's will to God. This is especially so for a commanded *olah* sacrifice, such as the *korban tamid* (the daily communal sacrifice). The idea is that we are willing to give up something precious for God. Furthermore, by doing what God has commanded, we create a *"re'ach nicho'ach"* for *Hashem*. Literally this means a pleasant smell. But the Sages explain that the *re'ach nicho'ach* is generated because "God said something and his will was done" (*amarti, ve-naasah retzoni*).[26] This expresses the fact that we

---

26. *Sifrei* on Numbers 118.

did something *just because God said so*. We don't necessarily get anything out of the sacrifice; the sacrifice does not involve doing good deeds in the humanitarian sense; nor does the sacrifice serve the purpose of reminding us of some historical event (such as eating *matzah* or sitting in a *sukkah*). Rather, the whole point of the sacrifice is to express submission and devotion to God.

Again, in our day we do not have sacrificial offerings. However, the Talmud teaches that the *Amidah* in some way takes the place of, or stands in for, the offerings (especially the *tamid*).[27] We shall see later that the primary way in which one cultivates *devekut/hitbatlut* is through *tefillah,* or prayer; that is, through the final stage of *Shacharit* – the *Amidah*.[28]

Can a person know if he or she is succeeding in achieving *devekut/ hitbatlut* of the will? This is not simple, for a person may keep many or even all of the commandments but not with the pure *kavannah,* or intention. Still, a sign that one is succeeding is that gradually one finds it easier and easier to keep the *mitzvot*. As R. Gamliel says, if you make His will like your will, *He will make your will like His will*. One might ask, if indeed one has made one's will like God's will, why is it necessary for God to do what we have already done? The answer is simple. The task of our making our will like God's will is not easy. But if we make the effort, God will help us complete the task, so that it is no longer a struggle but rather something we *want* to do.

So far, we have discussed *devekut/hitbatlut* of the *ratzon,* or will. There are also two cognitive virtues, or *middot,* associated with the *yod*. These are *emunah* and *chochmah*, which are the subject of the next two sections.

---

27. *Tractate Brachot* 26b. Another view is that the patriarchs established the prayers. Both views are accepted.

28. On the importance of prayer for achieving *devekut/hitbatlut*, see *Netivot Shalom* Vol. 1. *Netivei Hatefillah.*

FAITH (*EMUNAH*)

IN THE PREVIOUS CHAPTER, we noted that one of the *middot* of the upper *heh* is *ne'emanut*, that is, faithfulness or loyalty. This is a rational kind of faithfulness, because it is based on the collective national experience of the Jewish people over the ages. Here, at the *yod* level, a higher kind of faith that is *le-ma'aleh min ha-da'at*, or "trans-rational" comes into play. This is the *middah* of *emunah*.[29]

All the way up to and through the *heh* level, one's commitment to God is guided by reason. However, as explained above, *devekut* and *hitbatlut* go beyond *binah*, or intelligence. The devotion and dedication involved especially in *hitbatlut* of one's will to God's will requires a submission, or *bittul* (abnegation), of one's power to rationally understand God's will. At the *yod* level, one makes a total commitment to God that is "head over heels." One can reach *devekut* and *hitbatlut* only if one develops this type of *emunah*. Alternatively, this higher kind of *emunah* is itself part of *devekut* and *hitbatlut*.

In the previous chapter, to explain the notion of *ne'emanut* we used the analogy of the faithfulness or loyalty of a citizen to a benevolent and provident king. The citizen is faithful to such a king based on past experience. To explain *emunah*, consider a different analogy, namely, that of a couple who meet and get to know each other. After spending time together, they realize that they are suited to each other as companions. Each has good reason based on experience that the other person is worthy of courtship. They agree to continue to spend time together and in

---

29. See Maharal, *Gevurot Hashem* 9 and *Netivot Olam, Netiv Emunah*. See *Tanya*, chapter. 18 where the author writes that *emunah* goes beyond *da'at*. See *Netivot Shalom* Vol. 1, Chapter 1.

some way to be a couple. But, when it comes to getting married, do they really have enough objective evidence that the other person is worthy of spending one's life with? No. Yet they go out on a limb and make that commitment anyhow. And, precisely through that commitment they lay the foundation for developing a deep bond with each other – a bond that is much deeper than the bond between a couple that is merely courting.

Now, let us explain the analogies. The trust or faithfulness of the citizen to the king is comparable to the *ne'emanut* of the *heh* level. This is the kind of faith the Israelites had in God, when Moshe performed the signs in Egypt, and when they followed Moshe into the desert after the plagues. They also accepted upon themselves that *Hashem* was their God and they accepted some commandments (such as the Paschal lamb and other commandments related to Passover). But the trust or faithfulness of the married couple is comparable to the *emunah* that is required in the *yod* level. This is the kind of faith the Israelites expressed when they accepted the Torah at Mount Sinai. As the sages explain, when they said *na'aseh ve-nishmah* (we will do, and we will obey) they made a radical commitment that went beyond reason.[30] In other words, they advanced to a higher kind of *emunah* – an *emunah* that was "head over heels" and that went well beyond the evidence of past miracles. As explained earlier, the *yod* level involves a total or "head over heels" commitment to do *everything* that God might want you to do, no matter how puzzling it may seem. This requires not only *ne'emanut* but also *emunah*.

So far, we have said that *emunah* involves a *practical* element, that is, a willingness to do whatever God wants, no matter how difficult or puzzling it may seem. *Emunah* also involves a *cognitive* aspect, namely, accepting certain traditional Jewish teachings that may be impossible to prove or rationally know. These include the doctrines of the world to come and the resurrection of the dead.[31] According to Jewish tradition, *emunah*, or faith, in these doctrines is mandatory.

Why are these doctrines so important? One reason is that they are related to the belief in God's justice. In this world it seems clear that the righteous are not (always) rewarded nor are the wicked (always)

---

30. *Tractate Shabbat* 88a.

31. Some Jewish philosophers have argued that such doctrines are rationally provable, or at least that it follows from other doctrines about God. Some Kabbalists might argue that the belief in an afterlife is supported by experience of communication with dead souls. However, we should distinguish the belief in an *afterlife* from the belief in the *resurrection* of the dead. Moreover, even if one accepts such approaches, it remains the case that, at least relative to other Jewish doctrines, these teachings are more a matter of faith than reason.

punished for their deeds. If God is supremely just, there *must* be a reckoning in the next world. Yet, this alone would not seem to require a resurrection of the dead. For, if there is a world where the souls go up to after death, reward and punishment could take place there, without the need for a bodily resurrection. Instead, we can relate the doctrine of bodily resurrection to the concept of *dirah batachtonim*, which we have already noted is associated with the level of the *yod*. God seeks a dwelling place in the "lower realms" – that means the physical realm. This process will only take place in the context of bodily resurrection. Hence, the belief in a bodily resurrection is connected with a belief in the divine project of *dirah batachtonim*.

We have explained why a certain kind of *emunah* is necessary for the total commitment involved in the *devekut* and *hitbatlut* of the will. We have also seen that *emunah* in the resurrection plays a role in the commitment to the project of bringing about *dirah batachtonim*. Next, we move on to *chochmah*.

THE VIRTUE OF WISDOM (*CHOCHMAH*)

EARLIER WE SAID that one aspect of *devekut/hitbatlut* is that one not only does the *mitzvot*, but also seeks to do what God would want us to do – even without being told. We had pushed off the obvious question, how can one possibly know what God would want without being told what to do or avoid? The answer has to do with yet another *middah* associated with the *yod*, namely, *chochmah*, or wisdom.

In the previous chapter, we noted that learning and study of Torah is a crucial part of the upper *heh*. In order to do the *mitzvot* one must learn what they are; and in accepting God's *mitzvot*, we implicitly accept upon ourselves to learn the Torah so we can know the *mitzvot*. However, learning Torah also plays a key role in attaining *devekut/hitbatlut* (understood as bonding with God's will). In fact, we may say that there are two modes of Torah study. There is a *heh* mode of learning and a *yod* mode of learning. In the *heh* mode, one studies Torah in order to know and understand the *mitzvot* so that one can fulfill them. In other words, one studies *al menat laasot*, that is, in order to fulfill the Torah. This is connected with *binah*, or comprehension, or understanding. But at the *yod* level, studying Torah is done not only *al menat laasot* but rather as way of *attaining a bond with God's will*. As explained above, the Torah is an expression of God's will. At the *yod* level, a person learns not just in order to know *what to do*, but in order to conform or *bond one's will with God's will*.[32] This does not mean one has abandoned the mode of *al menat laasot*. For if I intend to bond my will with God's will through learning, I still intend also to do God's will; it's just that now something

---

32. See *Tanya*, end of chapter. 5.

else is going on as well. This is a higher, more advanced type of learning. It involves not only *binah* but also *chochmah*.

Again, we may use the analogy of the married couple to explain this. A good husband wants to know what his wife needs or wants him to do, in order that he may do those things. He will listen to his wife, so that he may know what she needs him to do. However, a good husband also wishes to bond with his wife by knowing what is on her mind and what her desires are. There may even be things the wife wants or thinks about that he can't do because of some extenuating circumstance, but if they are the wife's dreams and hopes – he is interested to hear them. Something similar applies to Torah study. One reason we learn Torah is to know what God wants us to do. The other reason is that, even if we can't do all of of the commandments, we still need to learn what God wants, as a way of bonding our will with God's will.[33]

There is another dimension to *chochmah*. A person who engages in fulfilling the *mitzvot* diligently with the proper intent, and who engages in this *yod* type of learning is eventually able to originate *chidushei Torah*, that is, novel Torah thoughts. A *chidush* is a creative gem. It is based on tradition but it goes farther than what has been said before. Notoriously, in rabbinic and Talmudic discussions, there are many disagreements. What one *chacham* sees as a wondrous innovation, another *chacham* might see as a mistake or a distortion. Thus, the tradition is filled with disagreements among the *chachamim*. For practical purposes, there is a method for settling disputes. Nevertheless, these disagreements are still studied and valued as an integral part of the tradition.[34]

To the degree that a person attains *devekut* with God's will, and develops the *middah* of *chochmah*, one is like a person who is so close to their beloved that *they are able to figure out what their beloved would wish even without being told.* Again, the analogy of the married couple is helpful. A good wife will be able to know without being told what her husband might want. Of course, this doesn't just happen by itself. It comes with patient study and with a bonding of the will through practice. After some time of living together, one is able to surmise what is the will of one's partner without actually being told. This is similar to the

---

33. This does not mean that while one is learning one needs to have deep mystical thoughts or feelings flowing through one's head at the time of learning. See *Nefesh Hachaim* 4:1–3. In learning the plain meaning of the Torah, one is thereby binding one's will with God's will.

34. See *Tractate Eruvin* 13b: "*Elu ve-elu divrei elokim chayim.*" Translation: These (words) and (the words) of those (who disagree) are both words of the living God!"

level attained by *talmidei chachamim* (wise students or Torah sages). The *talmid chacham* is not simply a person who knows a great deal of Torah. Rather, the *talmid chacham* is able to innovate *chidushei torah* by using *chochmah,* or creative wisdom. In this way, the *talmid chacham* figures out what God wants, even without being told. The massive tradition of halachic, aggadic, liturgical, Kabbalistic, Chassidic, and Jewish philosophical literature is a wealth of creative thought. Even someone who studies this literature superficially can get a sense of the remarkable creativity in this tradition. With patience and diligence, such study sinks in to a person and becomes part of him, so that he is eventually able to produce his own *chidushim* as well.

The *talmid chacham* innovates not only for himself, but for the Congregation of Israel. The Congregation relies on the wisdom of the sages for guidance not only in keeping the Torah but also for the pursuit of *devekut/hitbatlut.* This includes specifically the *mitzvot derabannan* (rabbinic commandments). One of these is *tefillah,* or prayer, and specifically the *Amidah,* which was composed with great creative wisdom.[35] As we shall see later, *tefillah* plays a crucial role in cultivating the *devekut/hitbatlut* and its associated *middot,* namely, *emunah* and *chochmah.*

There is a tension between *emunah* and *chochmah,* which parallels the tension between *yirah* and *ahavah. Chochmah* is a right-sided virtue; *emunah* is a left-sided virtue. With *emunah,* one recognizes that one *cannot* always understand or predict what God might want. *Emunah* involves an abnegation of one's reason. Yet, with *chochmah,* a person uses one's ingenuity to come up with novel thoughts about what God would want, even without being told. In a way, they seem like direct opposites. The truth is that they go hand in hand. Like *ahavah* and *yirah,* they are two sides of the same coin.

---

35. There is a dispute about whether daily prayer is a divine or rabbinic commandment. See Maimonides, *Hilchot Tefillah* 1:1 and *Kesef Mishneh,* ad loc. However, all agree that the text of the *Amidah* was composed by the Rabbis.

A HIGHER KIND OF *DEVEKUT*
AND *HITBATLUT*: BEING WITH GOD

SO FAR, WE HAVE TALKED about *hitbatlut* and *devekut* as a matter that involves one's *ratzon,* or will. We have also discussed *emunah* and *chochmah*. Have we reached the pinnacle of the Jewish spiritual path? Can one go any further beyond *hitbatlut* and *devekut* of the will, and its associated *middot*?

Just as God's *atzmut,* or essence, is not identical with his will, nor with his capacity for wisdom, so too, in the human person, one's *being* is not identical with one's will, nor with one's capacity for wisdom. Indeed, beyond the five aspects of the soul there is the very core of the being of the person. Hence, if there is a higher kind of *devekut* and *hitbatlut* it would involve relating to God not just with one's will, nor with one's capacity for wisdom, nor with any of the other powers of the soul, but *with one's very being.* In order to bridge the gap between oneself and God, one must bond *one's very being* to God. Such a relationship would not be mediated by some specific activity or thought process that is associated with a specific power or ability of the person. It would be a direct "existential" connection between the very being of a person and God. Is such a relationship with God possible?

It seems there is an obvious problem here. The *ein sof,* or essence, of God is beyond all the manifestations and expressions of God. So, how can a person possibly "connect" directly with God's essence? And, if we understand God's essence as Being itself, how might we understand the notion of "*devekut/hitbatlut*" with Being itself? Here we are treading on very difficult and sacred ground. Mystics in many traditions have tried to articulate this very pinnacle of spiritual experience of union with God, and not always with much success or logical clarity. Indeed, there is a worry here that we might be going dangerously too far. Kabbalah

221

teaches that it is not only impossible, but also forbidden, to grasp the divine essence.[36] Yet we seem to be trying to do just that. On the other hand, perhaps there is a more direct way of connecting with God's essence than anything spoken of so far – but without grasping the essence.

If there is such a higher kind of *devekut/hitbatlut*, it is not mediated by thought or will. It can't be just *thinking about God* or even *doing what God wants*. There is only one alternative left. If it involves our *being*, it must involve "being with" God in some way.[37] Let us explore this possibility. We may think of *being with God* as an event that can occur. As an event, it would have a duration, and it would come to an end. It may then recur later. We may also think of *being with God* as a character trait, or *middah*. As a *middah*, it would involve a certain way of being, perhaps a set of practices, that one can cultivate, sustain over time, and improve on.

The notion of "being with" someone is found in human relationships. Consider two people who are in love or are close friends. Even without speaking or doing something together or enjoying some activity together, just "being with" one's beloved can *itself* be part of a close relationship. There is a kind of union or "*devekut*" event that takes place here, which goes beyond what a person is doing or saying or even thinking at that time. There is also a kind of exclusivity or "*hitbatlut*" here, for "being with" the beloved requires turning away or "emptying oneself" from other things, activities, and indeed, other people. In that moment, it is as if nothing else matters other than the beloved. In this sense, "being with someone" is an *event* that occurs; it takes place at a certain time, it has a duration that lasts for a certain time, and then it comes to an end. It may then of course recur later.

Exactly what happens in this event of "being with" one's beloved is hard to describe. There is not too much one can say about the content

---

36. *Leit machshavah tefisah beh klal* (No thought can grasp him). *Tikunei Zohar* 17a. See also R. Ashlag, *Hakdamah Le'sefer Hazohar* 2. Maimonides also writes that it is impossible to have positive knowledge of God's essence. This is a major theme of the *Guide to the Perplexed*. See I:54. Many Kabbalists discourage any attempt to think directly about God's essence.

37. This notion dovetails with the proposal by the scholar Amos Chacham that the very meaning of the name י-ה-ו-ה signifies *being-with*, in the sense of *being together with* another person or group of persons. Chacham integrates this interpretation of the Tetragrammaton with the Scriptural account of God's command to Moshe to lead the Israelites from slavery to freedom. God tells Moshe that his Name is י-ה-ו-ה, which connotes *being with another*, in this case, *being with the Israelites* who are suffering. See his commentary on *Parshat Vaera*, (*Shmot, Da'at Mikra*, p. 109).

of the event itself, without waxing poetic. It is a kind of union, but it is surely not a literal "becoming identical with." It is not primarily an intellectual or cognitive event, even if it involves the mind in some way. It is more of an "existential" relationship – a relationship that involves one's being. Also, it is an event that one can promote (or discourage). That is, one can do certain things (and avoid certain other things) to promote the occurrence of this event on a regular basis. For example, spending "quality time" with one's beloved will tend to promote the occurrence of this type of event. Conversely, doing certain other things – such as allowing oneself to be focused more regularly on someone or something else – will minimize this event. For example, if a husband comes home from work and plops down in front of the TV for the evening – this is not likely to cultivate the event of "being with" his wife. Similarly, if the wife is constantly texting on her cell phone during dinner, this is not conducive to cultivating the event of "being with" her husband. In this way, we may regard "being with" as a character trait – not just as an event. As a character trait, it involves regularly doing those things that will allow or cause one to "be with" one's beloved (and avoiding those things that are detrimental to this event).

Thus far, we have discussed the notion of "being with" another human person, both as an event, and as a character trait. The notion not only makes sense, but also is something with which we are quite familiar. Is it possible for a person to have such a relationship of "being with" God?

Judaism teaches not only that such an event is possible, but that it has happened, and can happen again. As explained earlier, the *yod* represents the notion that God seeks a dwelling place in the lower realms, or *dirah batachtonim*. At Sinai, God "came down upon the mountain" and revealed Himself to the people of Israel. The purpose of that event was not only to give the Law or Torah. God could have given the Torah to Moshe without the revelation of Himself at Sinai. As noted earlier, several *mitzvot* were already communicated to Israel before the giving of the Torah at Sinai. In fact, most of the Law was communicated to Moshe alone and only thereafter to Israel. Hence, the purpose of that event was not only for God to reveal his *ratzon*, or will, as expressed in the Torah. Rather, the awesome event at Sinai was the foundational *devekut/hitbatlut* event. It was a *devekut* event in that it was a profound direct "meeting" between God Himself and Israel. This is the significance of the divine statement, "*Anochi Hashem elokecha*" – "I am the Lord your God." It was also a *hitbatlut* event in the sense that it was profoundly exclusive; there was no room for Israel to focus on anything else but God. This is the significance of "Thou shalt have no other gods before me."

Moreover, as the *midrash* teaches, during that event, the souls of the Israelites fled from their bodies in momentary death.[38] For that moment, it was as if nothing else exists, other than God. The fact that it took place in an isolated wilderness is also connected with the notion of seclusion or *hitbodedut*. In order to achieve the intimate bond with God, all other interests must be cleared away or nullified. Finally, the *korbanot*, or sacrifices, that were given at Sinai[39] also represent *devekut/hitbatlut*.

The event of God's revelation at Sinai was a one-time only event. Yet, as noted earlier, something similar occurred on a more sustained and regular basis, when God rested in the Tabernacle and later, in the Temple. The Temple was the true place for God to have a *"dirah batachtonim."* During the time of the Temple, one could visit the House of God – and "be together with God."[40] Of course, the typical thing to do when coming to the Temple would be to offer a *korban*, or sacrifice. Earlier we explained how the bringing of a *korban*, or sacrifice, cultivates *devekut/hitbatlut* of the will. By sacrificing something of value and creating a *"re'ach nicho'ach"* one exhibits abnegation, or *bittul*, of one's will to God's will. Yet, there is another aspect of sacrifices. It also expresses the higher kind of *devekut/hitbatlut*.

Through the act of immolation, one expresses *hitbatlut*, or nullification, of everything other than God. One thereby represents the fact that, in comparison to God, it is as if nothing else exists – including oneself. [41] At the same time, through its slaughter, the soul of the animal is brought back to God. Indeed, the root of the word *korban* is *karov*, which means *come close*. The purpose of the sacrifice is not mere destruction as an end in itself; it is rather a nullification or abnegation for the purpose of bonding with God. In this way, the bringing of a *korban* in God's Temple ritually enacts this higher kind of *devekut/hitbatlut*; that is, *being exclusively with God*. Indeed, the Torah explicitly connects the command to bring the *korban tamid* (daily offering) with the original offering at Sinai.[42] This implies that the daily service in the Temple is a reenactment of the offering at Sinai. The *devekut/hitbatlut* achieved through the daily offering is a re-living of the *devekut/hitbatlut* that was achieved at Sinai.

---

38. *Tractate Shabbat* 88b. See also *Tanya*, chapter 36.

39. Exodus 24:5.

40. This was David's prayer in Psalms 27:4: *May I dwell in the house of Hashem, all the days of my life, to see the sweetness of Hashem, and to visit in his palace.*

41. In this way, one may view *hitbatlut* as an advanced form of *anavah*, or humility. This counteracts the "pride" or *gaiut* that one experiences in the upper *heh*. See Chapter 3, note 35.

42. Numbers 28:6.

One might be tempted to say that until the Temple is rebuilt there is no way to achieve the event of "being with God." Happily, the Sages (especially the Kabbalists and Chassidic masters) teach that there is something analogous that the individual Israelite may achieve, even now, and on a regular basis.[43] There is a kind of *devekut/hitbatlut* which is an event of "being with" God that an individual can have in this world. Metaphorically, it may be referred to as "basking in the presence of God's face."[44] This kind of *devekut/hitbatlut* is a condition of one's *very being*, not just one's will or one's thoughts. Surely, it *involves* having certain thoughts and dispositions, and it has an *effect* on one's will, thoughts, actions, etc.; but that is a separate matter. In this sense, *devekut* involves a bond with God or Being that goes beyond thought and will, and certainly beyond any bodily performance of *mitzvot*. The same goes for *hitbatlut* at this level. Just as this higher kind of *devekut* involves connecting one's very being with God himself, so too, this higher kind of *hitbatlut* involves not merely not wanting what God doesn't want, but rather something more extreme, namely, a nullification of all else before God.

We have explained the idea of "being with God" along the lines analogous to what is involved in "being with" another person. In the case of a human being, the person is physical, so "being with" him or her (usually) involves being physically in the same location. In the case of God, it can't mean just that, for God is not a physical being. What then might it mean to "be with God"? Of course, it presupposes a commitment to fulfill and uphold God's commands and plans, but that is *devekut* of the will to God's will. The question here is, what can it possibly mean to be "with

---

43. According to the Baal Shem Tov, even the joy (*ta'anug*) of the next world can be attained, to some degree, in this world. See *Netivot Shalom* Vol. 2 on *Shabbat*, p. 53. On this view, the verse quoted in note 40 above may be interpreted homiletically. The sought after condition of "dwelling in the house of Hashem" is a condition of one's being, and does not necessarily require the physical presence of the Temple.

44. Thus, *he'arat panim* (shining of God's face) is another way of talking about *devekut*. See Maharal, *Drush Le'Shavuot*, 37; *Sefat Emet, Ki Tissa* 26. See Ramchal, *Derech Hashem*, Part I: Chapter 2:3, and *Da'at Tevunot* (Goldblatt ed., pages 351–352). For Ramchal, the metaphor of *devekut* as looking in God's face beautifully expresses the notion that *devekut* represents the ultimate triumph over existential shame. Recall Ramchal's metaphor of the poor man who "ate from that which is not his" and was embarrassed to look in "the face of the giver." By doing *mitzvot* (achieving the upper *heh* level) we absolve ourselves of existential shame, and we can truly enjoy God's gifts to us. By attaining *devekut* (achieving the *yod* level) we gain something even better – namely, looking directly at "the face of the giver" – in this case, God!

God's essence"? This is not an easy question to answer, but we shall do our best.

In this book, we have attempted to understand God's essence as *Being itself*. To be together with God would mean to "be with Being itself." At first blush, this may sound almost nonsensical. It may be explained as follows. For a person to be with God or with Being involves a condition of "*just being* in the presence of Being." It is a condition of not doing anything specific – not thinking, not moving, not walking, not talking, but simply, *just being*. It involves a kind of shutdown of all activity, at least temporarily. To "be with Being itself," one has come to a state of utter stillness and quietude; we may call this *menuchah* (repose). On the other hand, it is not simply a state of mindless relaxation, either. There is something positive going on. Perhaps the best way to describe it is to say that it involves *repose in God*. We shall return to this notion later in our discussion of the *Amidah*.

Even though it is difficult to talk much about the *content* of the event of *devekut /hitbatlut* itself, much can be said about how to get there. As noted above, there are actions one can *do* (or *avoid*) to cultivate the relationship of "being with" another person. The same thing is true in the case of developing this relationship with God. As stated earlier, every *mitzvah* is an opportunity for cultivating *devekut/hitbatlut*.[45] But, there are specific *mitzvot* that especially give us the opportunity to "be with God."[46] One such *mitzvah* is Shabbat – if observed with the proper intent. On *Shabbat*, the refraining from work is a form of *hitbatlut*, or "clearing away," from the mundane. The positive *mitzvot* of *Shabbat* include *kiddush* (sanctification), *kibbud* (honoring with fine clothing), and *oneg* (enjoying with fine food, wine, song, etc.) and special *tefillot* (prayers). *Shabbat* is also an especially good time for Torah study, and especially study of Kabbalah. These are all ways of achieving *devekut*. When both the negative and positive commandments and customs are observed with the proper intent, *Shabbat* becomes a day of *menuchah* (repose) that is "fulfilling and peaceful, quiet and secure" (*menuchat shalom ve-shalva, hashket va-vetach*).[47] In sum, *Shabbat* is a day of *devekut/hitbatlut*, or being with God.

---

45. See Introduction, note 20.

46. On the unique nature of *Shabbat*, see *Netivot Shalom* Vol. 2, pages 20ff; *Netivot Shalom* on *Parshat Vaera*. *Shabbat* is the day for *devekut* and *hashraat shekhinah* (the indwelling of the divine presence). This is also reflected in the special nature of the *Shabbat* prayers, in which we ask not for our mundane needs but for *devekut* and *menuchah*.

47. This phrase comes from the afternoon, or *Mincha*, prayer of *Shabbat*. In this

Like *Shabbat*, the Holy Days are also set aside for the congregation of Israel to "be with God." *Shavuot* also has this character, for there is no focus on any specific *mitzvah* but rather a focus on the Torah as a whole. The celebration of *Shavuot* also involves a reenactment of the foundational *devekut/hitbatlut* event at Sinai. In some measure, the *mitzvah* of dwelling in the *sukkah* fits in with the theme of promoting *devekut*; dwelling in the *sukkah* is like dwelling in God's house. Most of all, the celebration of *Shmini Atzeret* is a day which Israel "spends with God." On this holiday, as on *Shabbat*, there are no *mitzvot* that involve the use of a specific object, such as a *shofar* or *matzoh*. It is important to bear in mind that the *keeping* of these *mitzvot* and practices should not be confused with *devekut/hitbatlut* itself. One can keep the *mitzvot* scrupulously – with love and reverence – but still fail to have the proper intent necessary to promote the higher kind of *devekut/hitbatlut*. Still, with the proper intent, they contribute toward its cultivation.

In addition to what has been said so far, two spiritual practices cultivate "being with God." These are *hitbodedut* (seclusion) and *hitbonenut* (meditation).[48] Like *devekut* and *hitbatlut*, *hitbodedut* and *hitbonenut* go hand in hand. One is the negative and one is the positive side of the same coin. *Hitbodedut* is the practice of secluding oneself or being alone. It involves removing oneself from interaction with the various things of this world, especially other people. Through this process, a person may cultivate the higher kind of *hitbatlut* – clearing everything out of one's life except for God. One engages in *hitbodedut* not to escape from society, nor to meditate on oneself or on Nothingness. Rather, one engages in *hitbodedut* in order to engage in *hitbonenut*, or meditation, on God. One may thereby approach the state of stillness or repose in God.

Hitbonenut, or meditation, is a focused, intense, concentration or contemplation on God, that is, on God's essence, and/or on God as He is manifest in the world. The notion that one may contemplate God's essence may seem problematic, and we shall return to discuss this point shortly. First, let us clarify the difference between *hitbonenut* and other

prayer, some form of the word *menucha* occurs *ten* times. (It occurs at least twice in every *tefillah* for *Shabbat*, but eight extra times in the afternoon prayer.) Clearly, the sages who constructed the prayers went out of their way to emphasize the significance of *menuchah* at this point of *Shabbat*. In Kabbalah, the *mincha* of *Shabbat* is considered the climax of the *Shabbat* (see *Zohar* 2:89a). It represents the time for achieving the highest level of *devekut/hitabatlut*. No wonder, then, that we pray for *menuchah* especially during the *Mincha* of *Shabbat*.

48. On *hitbodedut*, see Ramchal, *Mesilat Yesharim*, in his discussion of *kedushah*. On the importance of *hitbodedut* for achieving *hitbatlut* see *Likutei Moharan* 52.

forms of reflection on God as He is manifest in the world. *Hitbonenut* is not the common type of thinking about God that one employs during recitation of Psalms and most blessings. Whereas the latter type of thinking about God is charged with poetical enthusiasm and song, *hitbonenut* is more purely cerebral and dispassionate. Nor is *hitbonenut* the same thing as learning or studying Torah or even Kabbalistic teachings. We must distinguish *hitbonenut* from *havanah*, or *ratiocination*, which involves "dialectical" thinking about God. Dialectical thinking involves asking questions and trying to figure out answers about God's nature, attributes, etc., or using analytical thinking in application to the idea of God, the Torah, and related issues. The latter is a process that is associated more with *binah*. Important as such a process is, it is not *hitbonenut*. Perhaps the simplest way to put it is to say that whereas *binah* involves thinking *about* God, *hitbonenut* involves thinking *of* God.

We have said that one may engage in *hitbonenut* not only on God as manifest in the world, but also on *God's essence itself*. The notion that one can and should meditate or dwell on God's essence may seem problematic, for as mentioned above, it is impossible to grasp the essence, and that indeed, one is forbidden even to try to do so. Yet, we may and must distinguish *grasping* the essence from *thinking of* it. To grasp the essence would be to *comprehend* or *fully understand* the essence of God; that is impossible. But, to *think* of the essence is quite possible; indeed, we must be able to think of God's essence in some way, otherwise we thereby detach the essence from its expressions. Moreover, if we could not think of God's essence in some way, the prohibition against trying to comprehend God's essence would be unintelligible to us. Surely, there is a danger involved in thinking of the essence for *too long*, lest one comes to particularize or "finitize" Being itself, which would be problematic. As long as one bears in mind that Being itself is infinite, one may and must meditate at least occasionally on God's essence. Naturally, such *hitbonenut* on God's essence involves a *silent* and *wordless* meditation. There is little or no verbal content to this meditation, for there is nothing specific to say or even think of, if one is focusing purely on God's infinite essence (Being itself). We shall return to this issue later when we discuss the *Amidah*.

Earlier we mentioned that an ideal place to "be with God" is in the Temple, or *Beit Mikdash*, also known as "God's house." The sages teach that in some measure God's presence rests in a synagogue. Hence, an ideal place for *hitbodedut* and *hitbonenut* would be in a synagogue. Indeed, the most common and perhaps the primary way in which we may cultivate the higher kind of *devekut/hitbatlut* is through *tefillah*, or prayer, especially the *Amidah*, which is best done in a synagogue. There is a strong parallel between the *Amidah* and the *devekut* event that occurred at Mount Sinai. The Sages often refer to the event at Sinai as *Ma'amad Har Sinai* (the *standing* at Mount Sinai). This phrase itself alludes to a link between the event at Sinai and the *Amidah* (the *standing* prayer). Earlier we noted that the Torah makes an explicit connection between the *korban tamid* (daily sacrifice) and the communal sacrifice at Sinai. As noted earlier, the *Amidah* stands in for the *korban tamid*, or daily sacrifice. It follows that the *Amidah* also constitutes a reliving of that foundational *devekut/hitbatlut* event that took place at Sinai. Soon, we shall see in more detail how the *Amidah* helps us cultivate both the lower and higher kinds of *devekut/hitbatlut* with God.[49]

---

49. We said above that one of the main vehicles for *devekut/hitbatlut* is through keeping *Shabbat* and the Holidays. It is no accident that there is an extra sacrifice (*korban musaf*) on those days. On holy days, there is an opportunity for achieving a greater level of *devekut*. Therefore there is an additional sacrifice – and in our day, an additional *tefillah*. Moreover, on *Shabbat* and especially *Shavuot* (the festival that commemorates the revelation at Sinai) a reliving of the experience of the revelation of the Torah is achieved through the public reading of the Torah in the synagogue. It is taught that the Torah was given on *Shabbat* (*Tractate Shabbat* 86b).

KNOWLEDGE OF GOD
(*DA'AT HASHEM*)

THERE IS ONE MORE COGNITIVE VIRTUE associated with the *yod*, namely, the *middah* of *da'at Hashem* or knowledge of God. The term *da* in Hebrew often connotes a *chibur* or connection.[50] *Da'at Hashem* is a kind of experiential knowledge or conscious awareness of God. A person who has such an experience literally feels God's presence. This requires careful explanation.

First, we must distinguish *da'at* from *hitbonenut*. *Hitbonenut* is the activity of meditation or contemplation; *da'at* is an experience. *Da'at Hashem* is an experiential knowledge of God. It is possible that the effort of meditation may bring about an experience of *da'at Hashem*. But not every effort of *hitbonenut* successfully brings about *da'at*. It is also theoretically possible that an experience of *da'at Hashem* could come upon a person spontaneously, without *hitbonenut*. In this case, one is "surprised by God." However, it is more likely to occur, and it is more likely to last longer, if the *da'at* is achieved through the effort of *hitbonenut*.

We must also distinguish *da'at* from *binah*, or *understanding*, which is associated with the upper *heh*. Both are forms of cognition or knowing. However, whereas *binah* is rational comprehension or understanding of God, *da'at* is an experiential connection or conscious awareness of God. For example, it is one thing to know and understand that there is a King who lives in a palace; it is quite another to be in the palace and to experience the presence of the King.[51] A person who has *binah* is like

---

50. The verb *da* is used to connote a coupling, or *zivug*, of male and female. (Genesis 4:1). Also, see *Tanya*, chapter 3. *Da'at* stabilizes and fixes the remaining lower *middot*. We also find that *da'at* connotes feeling, or *hargasha*. See *Tanya*, chapter 46.

51. Philosophers have drawn a distinction between *knowledge about* and

the former; a person who has *da'at,* or knowledge, of *Hashem* is like the latter. *Binah* involves recognition of God that is based on reasons – such as learning about God from Scripture, or coming to a recognition of God based on reflection on the orderliness of nature. *Da'at* involves a conscious knowledge or immediate experience of God.

Da'at Hashem, or experiential knowledge of God, is a very lofty level, and it may seem to some readers that this is rather too lofty for ordinary Jews to achieve. Can we really attain experiential knowledge of God? Isn't that something reserved for saints, prophets, and mystics? Indeed, does anyone in this day and age really have such "knowledge" of God? For, if someone had such knowledge, wouldn't that mean that God's existence would be provable or demonstrable?

Several things must be said. First, *da'at,* or knowledge, of *Hashem* is *not* an indirect or unmediated experiential knowledge of the essence of God, or *ein sof.* That is not possible, even for a great *tsaddik* (saint). Just as it is impossible to comprehend God's essence, it is also impossible to have an unmediated awareness or experience of God or Being itself. A conscious experience occurs *in time,* and Being itself is "atemporal" or beyond time. The attempt to gain such a state is forbidden; it would be an attempt to "grasp" the essence. Such an attempt can only result in *hagshamah* – that is, a limitation or "finitization" of the Infinite.

If *da'at* is not an experience of God's essence directly, what is it then? We have said that *da'at Hashem* is an experience of some sort in which a person feels that God is present in some palpable way. Presumably, this is something that occurs relatively rarely, during prayer or during moments of great inspiration. The following question arises. As explained in the very first chapter of this book, God is present everywhere and all the time. This is especially so if we understand God's essence as Being itself. Being is manifest at every moment without fail. At every moment, a person can be aware of Being itself, if only indirectly. It follows that one should always be able, in some sense, to experience the presence of God. This seems to undermine the notion that *da'at Hashem* is a special experience that occurs relatively rarely. How can this be?

A distinction must be made. The awareness of *being itself* is common and relatively easy to attain. It is the first stage of the spiritual path. It is available to anyone without much effort. But, that is not what is meant here by "*da'at Hashem.*" In most cases, "*da'at Hashem*" takes a great deal

---

knowledge of something or someone. A related distinction is between *knowledge by acquaintance* and *knowledge by description.*

of effort.[52] It has to do with experiencing God or Being *under a certain description*. One might experience the very same thing under one description, or experience it under another description. Even though the object of the experience is the same, the experience may be very different. This notion, and its application to our case, may be explained by means of example.

Suppose that I happen to be a great enthusiast of classical piano music. One day I walk out of my house, and I pass by a stranger in the street. Unbeknownst to me, that stranger was actually the world's greatest concert pianist. In that case, my experience of the fellow was rather ordinary. On the other hand, suppose I am told in advance that the world's greatest concert pianist is about to walk down my street. Knowing this, I rush out to experience being in his presence. When he walks by, my experience is charged with excitement and pride. Now, in both cases, my own visual experience is exactly the same. Also, an outside observer looking at both events might not notice any difference. But, the inner quality of the two experiences is very different. For, in the first case I experience the man's presence under the description, "ordinary stranger." In the second case, I experience the presence of the very same man under the description, "world's greatest concert pianist." The two experiences are vastly different. Also, knowing more about the pianist and about classical music will enhance the quality and richness of the experience.

Using this analogy, we can explain what is meant by *da'at Hashem*. *Da'at Hashem* is not merely an awareness of Being itself as manifested in beings. That is an experience that almost anyone can have. In the example above, it would be like experiencing the presence of the great pianist under the description, *ordinary stranger*. Rather, *da'at Hashem* occurs when a person experiences God or Being *under the description of Hashem* or י-ה-ו-ה. In the example given above, this would be like experiencing the presence of the very same man under the description, *world's greatest pianist*. Similarly, just as the quality of the experience of the great pianist will be influenced by how much one knows about him, so too, *da'at Hashem* is an experience that will be influenced by how much one knows about *Hashem*. Indeed, one needs to have gone through all the stages of the spiritual path before one can experience God or Being as י-ה-ו-ה. All the steps one has taken – all the *middot* one has developed – to build up to the point where one is able to experience

---

52. As the sources quoted below (note 249) indicate, *ruach hakodesh* is available to anyone – *according to his or her deeds*.

Being as י-ה-ו-ה will inform the quality of this experience. The more one has developed those *middot*, the more intense will that experience be.

On the approach taken here, *da'at* is a potential *result* of *devekut/ hitbatlut*, which itself is at the pinnacle of the entire Jewish spiritual path. In particular, it is a result of the *higher* kind of *devekut/hitbatlut*. By "being with God" a person may achieve the experience of God as *Hashem*. Yet, there is no guarantee that such an experience will occur. In a sense, *da'at* is a reward or a gift from God, which comes to a person to the extent that he or she has attained *devekut/hitbatlut*.[53] Earlier we discussed the issue of whether it is rational to believe in *keter* and *chochmah*. If one is fortunate to have it, the experience of *da'at Hashem* adds strength and power to one's conviction or belief in God as *Hashem*. Yet, one must bear in mind that, just because a person has *da'at Hashem* does not mean he is cognitively certain of what he has experienced, nor does it mean he can "prove" God's existence to another person. If one has *da'at*, one has an "inner knowledge" that God is *Hashem*. Such an experience strengthens one's own conviction – but it does not necessarily provide cognitive certainty or a proof that would convince *someone else* that God is *Hashem*.[54]

Our experiences affect our character. If a person has experienced *da'at Hashem*, it becomes part of that person's makeup. In some cases, an experience of *da'at Hashem* may bring with it some fresh insight or realization.[55] For example, a person might realize that he has been doing

---

53. In *Mesilat Yesharim*, Ramchal expresses a similar notion about the attainment of *kedushah*. Namely, *techilato hishtadlut; sofo matanah* (it starts with effort, but in the end, it is a gift). This may seem to undermine the notion that we can escape existential shame at the last stage. However, this needs to be understood properly. Since it is preceded by effort, the "gift" is in some way earned after all. In saying that it is a gift, Ramchal does not mean it is unearned. Rather he means that it is not something a person can manufacture on one's own.

54. The philosopher and psychologist William James comes to a similar conclusion in his classic work, *The Varieties of Religious Experience*.

55. Such an insight should not be confused with an innovation, or *chidush*, achieved through *chochmah* (as discussed above). When a person comes up with his own original idea, then that is *chochmah* at work. It is something a person achieves on his own. But when a person has an experience of God in real time, and is thereby enriched with an insight, that is not quite the same thing. The great sages and mystics distinguished their own output of *chochmah*, from those insights that they might receive through visitations from spirits or angels. Both require effort, but still one is a gift from on high while the other is a result of creative genius. The Gaon of Vilna preferred that Torah insights should *not* be granted to him as a gift; he preferred to come to them using his own effort. (See R.Chaim of Volozhin's introduction to the Gaon of Vilna's commentary on *Sifra Detzniyuta*.)

something wrong, or that he ought to be focusing on some particular area of good deeds. A person who experiences this is able to use the insight to grow further in his lower *middot*, which then allow him to reach a higher level of *devekut*. This in turn may lead to yet fresh insights that again lead to further spiritual growth. And the cycle goes on.

It is important to note that there are *degrees* of *da'at*. One can have a mild sense of *da'at Hashem*; or one can have an extremely intense experience of *da'at Hashem*. In its extreme form, it involves *nevuah* (prophecy). In its milder form, it may involve *ruach hakodesh* (holy spirit).[56] There are various kinds and degrees of *ruach hakodesh*. At a very high level of *ruach hakodesh*, a person might have some insight about the future. It could be about some difficult matter in Jewish Law. A high level of *ruach hakodesh* is likely to befall only a very devout and learned individual. However, a lower level of *ruach hakodesh* is also possible for people who are on a lower spiritual level. More commonly, the insight would be some kind of guidance or direction – a piece of advice, or *etzah*, about how one might improve in one's spiritual progress.

The effort to achieve *da'at Hashem* and some measure of *ruach hakodesh* is an integral part of the Jewish spiritual path. In *Mesilat Yesharim*, Rabbi Moshe Chaim Luzzatto wrote that the spiritual path ultimately leads to *kedushah* and then *ruach hakodesh*. It is a legitimate goal to strive for, even if one knows one is unlikely to succeed fully. With diligent effort, progress can be made. This is especially true if we accept the notion that there are degrees of *da'at* and *ruach hakodesh*. Arguably, many ordinary religious Jews experience *da'at Hashem* in some degree on *Shabbat*. They feel a palpable sense of God's holiness. To the degree that a person keeps *Shabbat* both in the negative and positive *mitzvot*, he

---

56. The nature of *ruach hakodesh* is a vast topic. Some sources seem to imply that *ruach hakodesh* is no longer available in our day (*Yoma* 9b). Other sources indicate that it is possible for anyone to attain some degree of *ruach hakodesh*. See *Seder Eliahu Rabbah*, chapter 9: "The school of Eliahu taught, *I call heaven and earth as witnesses to the fact that for any man or woman, slave or maidservant – ruach hakodesh rests upon a person in accord with his or her deeds*." In the liturgy for festivals (in the *Ribbono shel olam* prayer said when taking out the Torah) we explicitly ask for *ruach hakodesh*. For a relatively recent writer who claimed that all Jews can reach and should strive for *ruach hakodesh* – "each according to his measure," see R. Pinchas Meir ben Eliayhu of Vilna, *Sefer Habrit* p. 7. He writes that one of the purposes of his book is to help people reach this level. The only way to resolve this contradiction is to say that there are different types of *ruach hakodesh*. Indeed, even the source (*Yoma* 9b) referred to above that indicates *ruach hakodesh* is no longer available suggests that some form of divine communication is still available (namely, *bat kol*, a heavenly voice).

or she may actually experience "God as *Hashem*" on *Shabbat*. Another possibility is that one may have this experience at a holy place such as the *Kotel*. Another place this is achieved is during the *tefillah* of the Amidah. We shall return to this point later. The point here is that *ruach hakodesh* is a legitimate goal for every Jew, not just the saint.

Earlier we discussed the connection between the *korban tamid* (daily sacrifice) and *devekut/hitbatlut*. Here we may note a connection between the *ketoret hasamim* (burning of the incense) and the experience of *da'at Hashem*. The incense was burned every day after the daily sacrifice had been brought. Whereas the animal sacrifice is made on the outer altar, the incense is burned on the inner altar, which is placed directly opposite the ark that sat inside the Holy of Holies. Thus, the incense offering represents an even more intimate connection with God than does the daily animal sacrifice.[57] It is with the cloud of incense that the High Priest enters the Holy of Holies once a year on Yom Kippur, and God says that it is "with the cloud of incense that I will appear over the covering" of the ark (Leviticus, 16:2.). Thus, the incense offering is connected with the experience of God. The incense prevents death while the High Priest enters the innermost chamber of the divine indwelling, from which the divine presence makes itself known or experienced. The worry about death in connection with the incense reminds us of the danger inherent in seeking an intimate relationship with God. If one comes too close too fast, or in an inappropriate fashion, one is liable to make a costly mistake.[58] Nevertheless, the incense offering on the small altar reminds us that despite the difficulties and the dangers, it is possible to have this kind of experience of God as *Hashem*.

We may now complete the chart of *middot* that we started in the first chapter, and continued to build in subsequent chapters. *Ahavah* and *yirah*, taken to their natural conclusion, develop into *devekut/hitbatlut*. However, one can reach *devekut/hitbatlut* only with the right-sided virtue of *chochmah* and the left-sided virtue of *emunah*. *Devekut/hitbatlut* stands at the culmination of the spiritual path. *Da'at* is an offspring or consequence of *hitbatlut/devekut*. *Da'at*, or knowledge of God leads to

---

57. Perhaps it is no accident that one of the main fragrant ingredients of the incense mixture (Exodus 30:34) was frankincense, or *levonah*, which is related to the Hebrew word *lavan*, or white. As discussed above, white is the color associated with *keter*. It is also noteworthy that frankincense is called *levonah zakkah*, that is, "pure" frankincense.

58. Consider the episode of Aaron's sons, Nadav and Avihu, which also involved an incense offering of some sort, but was offered improperly, with devastating consequences. See Leviticus 10:1.

yet a deeper commitment of *kabbalat ol malchut shamayim* and *mitz-vot*; the more one knows God, the better one can fulfill the commitment to accept God as King and fulfill the commandments.

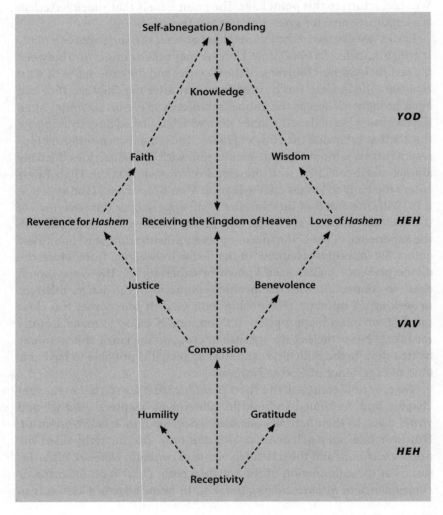

Earlier in this book, we discussed whether an agnostic can pursue and possibly even attain certain levels of the Jewish spiritual path. We had said that an agnostic could attain the lower virtues of receptivity and humility, as well as the esthetic, creative, and moral virtues. We also said that one who rejects the belief that God is King or that God has given *mitzvot* cannot reach the level of the upper *heh*. All the more so, an agnostic cannot possibly reach the *middot* of the *yod*. To reach *devekut, hitbatlut, emunah* and *chochmah,* one cannot remain an agnostic. Moreover, if one experiences *da'at Hashem,* one has a strengthened conviction in God, for at that point one actually knows God as *Hashem.*

The *middot* of the *yod* are very lofty. They stand at the pinnacle of the Jewish spiritual path. How can we cultivate them? They take hard work, and we can only reach them if we have first built up the lower *middot.* One of the essential keys to cultivating the *middot* of the *yod* lies in the final stage of *Shacharit,* the *Amidah.* This is the subject of the next and final section.

THE FOURTH STAGE OF *SHACHARIT*: THE STANDING PRAYER

Approaching the *Amidah*

The fourth stage of *Shacharit* corresponds to the *yod* of the divine Name.[59] The sages refer to this stage as *tefillah* (prayer) and as "*avodah she-balev*," or "worship of the heart," or more literally "worship that is *in* the heart." It is also referred to as the *Amidah* (standing prayer) and as the *Shemonah Esrei Brachot* (Eighteen Blessings).[60] In what follows, our aim is to show how the *Amidah* serves as a vehicle to cultivate the *middot* associated with the *yod*.

First, let us discuss the significance of the number eighteen in this context. It is no accident that the most common name for the *Amidah* is *Shemonah Esrei*, which simply means, "Eighteen." Many Jews refer to the *Amidah* as *Shemonah Esrei* – even during the *Shabbat* when there are only seven blessings. The Talmud gives various reasons for why there are precisely eighteen blessings.[61] One opinion is that the eighteen blessings

---

59. In note 21 in the Introduction, we noted that Ramchal divided his book, *Derech Hashem*, into four parts. We are now in position to suggest a correspondence between these four parts and the four aspects of the Name, as explained in this book. (1) *Yesodot* (Fundamentals) corresponds to the lower *heh* or foundational stage. (2) *Hashgachah* (Divine Providence) corresponds to the *vav*, which represents the moral *middot* with which God manages the world. (3) *Nevuah* (Prophecy) corresponds to the upper *heh*, which represents the notion that God communicates in speech and reveals his will in commandments. (4) *Avodah* (Worship) corresponds to the *yod*, which represents *tefillah*, or prayer.

60. At some point, an additional blessing was added, so there are actually nineteen blessings. See *Tractate Brachot* 28b. However, it is still referred to as the "*Shemonah Esrei.*"

61. Ibid.

correspond to the number of times God's name is mentioned in some form in the *Shema*. Another opinion is that the eighteen blessings correspond to the number of times God's name is mentioned in Psalm 29. It is also said to correspond to the number of small bones that make up the human spine. Another possible allusion (not mentioned in the Talmud) is that the number eighteen is the *gematria,* or numerical value, of the Hebrew word *chai,* or life.

The first opinion above suggests an equation of sorts between the *Shema* and the *Amidah*. The other opinions hint at a contrast between the *Shema* and the *Amidah* (and a corresponding contrast between the *middot* of the upper *heh* and the *middot* of the *yod*). The *Shema* has 248 words that correspond to the limbs of the human. But the *Amidah* corresponds to the *chai,* or life, that courses through those limbs. The word *chai* is related to *chayah,* which is the part of the soul that corresponds to the *yod* (along with *yechidah*). *Chai* is also connected with *chayim,* which is the numerical value of *chacham* (thus hinting at *chochmah,* which is associated with the *yod*). Proverbs (4:11–22) teaches that *chochmah* (wisdom) gives *chayim* (life). Moreover, an important aspect of the *Amidah* is *hitbatlut,* which is represented by the *bowing* that is done at certain points during the *Amidah*. The halacha is that one is supposed to bow *until all of the bones of the spine protrude*. In this way, the number eighteen alludes to *hitbatlut*. Finally, the correspondence to the number of times the Name is mentioned in Psalm 29 suggests that the *Amidah* has a higher purpose than the *Shema*. Whereas the purpose of the *Shema* is to accept God's kingdom upon all the limbs of one's body, the purpose of the Amidah is to achieve *devekeut/hitbatlut*.[62]

Before turning to the *Amidah* itself, let us consider the transition from the third section of *Shacharit* to this fourth stage. In earlier chapters, we noted that in the transition from one level to the next, one has to realize there is something flawed or missing in the lower stage, which prompts the need to advance to the higher stage. For example, one is motivated to move from the lower *heh* to the *vav* because of the disturbing experience of existential shame. Next, to get from the *vav* to the upper *heh* one needs to recognize that the *middot* of the *vav* only alleviate existential shame but do not really banish it; this leads to existential despair, and one comes to realize that the only way to escape existential despair is by committing oneself to *mitzvot*. Similarly, in the liturgy of *Shacharit* the

---

62. We also find the notion that the *chut hashidra* (the spine) is considered distinct from the 248 limbs. See R. Schneur Zalman, *Likutei Torah: Parshat Balak,* p. 140.

transition between the first and second stage of *Shacharit* is marked by *Kaddish Yatom*. The transition between the second and the third stage is marked by *Kaddish* and *Borchu*.

However, earlier in this chapter, we saw that the transition from the *middot* of the upper *heh* to the *middot* of the *yod* works somewhat differently. At one point, we suggested that one can look at the *middot* of the *yod* as a natural outgrowth of the *middot* of the upper *heh*. Similarly, the transition from the third stage of *Shacharit* to the fourth stage is unique when compared to the other transitions. After reciting the blessing on *geulah* (redemption) which precedes the *Amidah*, one proceeds without hesitation to the beginning of the *Amidah*.[63] There is no *Kaddish* here. The reason is that the spiritual seeker wants to go *immediately* from the upper *heh* to the *yod*. As explained above, the *middot* of *devekut* and *hitbatlut* and *chochmah* are natural consequences of the *middot* of *ahavah* and *yirah*. When taken to their logical extremes, they result in *devekut* and *hitbatlut*. Nevertheless, the fact remains that in moving to the *Amidah*, we are moving on to a new and higher level.

The transition to the higher level is exhibited in several ways. Earlier we discussed the role of the *tzitzit* in the upper *heh*. As explained earlier, one of the reasons for why we read the portion of *tzitzit* is that even if we truly love and fear God, we know that we must find ways to help ourselves overcome those inclinations that tempt us to violate the commandments.[64]

The battle with our inclinations, or *hirhurim*, is very much a part of the service associated with the upper *heh*, and the *tzitzit* are a reminder for us to keep the commandments and "not stray after our hearts and eyes." Shortly after we have concluded the portion of *tzitzit*, as we approach the *Amidah*, the custom is that *we purposefully release the tzitzit*.[65] For,

---

63. Halachically, this is known as the concept of *Smichat Geulah le'tfillah*. See *Tractate Brachot* 9b; *SA:OC:* 66:9.

64. See *Tanya*, chapter 27. It seems that the main function of *parshat tzitzit* (helping a person not to go astray) is for the *beinoni*, not the *tzaddik*. See above, note 24.

65. The custom (cited by *Magen Avraham* on *SA:OC:* 24 and based on the Ari) is to release the *tzitzit* precisely in between the words *la'ad* (forever) and *u-le'olmay olamim* (for eternity). See *Sha'ar Hakavanot* p. 178. His explanation is beyond the level of this book. I suggest an explanation as follows: (Those who follow his explanation may regard mine as a simplistic version of his.) Both phrases "*la-ad*" and "*le-olmay olamim*" seem to mean the same thing, namely, *forevermore*. But there are two kinds of "forever." One is that throughout the generations, the people of Israel last forever. Although one generation dies out, another generation continues in its place. This is a physical kind of everlastingness, and this is referred to by the term *la'ad*.

as we near the final stage of *Shacharit*, we are advancing toward *devekut/ hitbatlut*. In the *Amidah* there is not a single place where we touch the *tzitzit* (or *tefillin*, for that matter). In fact, one is decidedly *not* supposed to do this during the *Amidah*. This is different from all the other three stages. Here we have entered a special zone, where touching and seeing the *tefillin* and *tzitzit* would actually be a hindrance rather than a help. If we reach mastery of temptation, as we should in the *hitbatlut* and *devekut* of the *yod*, then the *tzitzit* are no longer necessary to focus on. (One *wears* them while saying the *Amidah*. But one shouldn't be focusing on them directly.)

Before moving to the content of the *Amidah*, let us discuss a few *halachot* and customs about the manner in which the *Amidah* should be said. To cultivate the *middot* of the *yod*, the manner in which the *Amidah* is said is almost as important as the content of the *Amidah*. First, relevant here is the halacha that we are supposed to approach the *Amidah* with a somber mood of *aimah* and *hachnaa* (trepidation and submission).[66] This is similar to how the Sages understood the mood of the Israelites during the event of the giving of the Torah, namely, fear and trepidation. Note the contrast between this approach and how one is supposed to approach the *Shema*. The entry into *Shema* is with love and awe. The entry into the *Amidah* is not just with love and awe, but rather something more intense. Interestingly, while the Amidah contains several references to God's love for Israel, it does not contain a single reference to the love of Israel for God! This otherwise astonishing fact may be explained in light of the fact that whereas the purpose of the *Shema* is to cultivate a loving /respectful relationship with God, the purpose of the *Amidah* is to cultivate something more advanced, namely, *hitbatlut/ devekut*. This also relates to the fact that the *Shema* is generally said in

---

Another kind of everlastingness is the eternity of the soul, which is a non-physical everlastingness. This is referred to as *le'olmay olamim*. Now, the *tzitzit* are worn on the body. The soul itself does not need the *tzitzit*. Hence, as we make the transition from thinking about the everlastingness of the Jewish body to the everlastingness of the Jewish soul, we purposefully release the *tzitzit*. This ties into the point made here regarding the transition from the upper *heh* to the *yod*. The upper *heh* is associated more with the physical *mitzvot* and the physical redemption from Egypt. The *yod* is associated more with the purely spiritual *middot* of *devekut* and *hitbatlut*, and the spiritual redemption of the soul from the mundane.

66. See *SA:OC*: 93. Some suggest that we should go into the *Amidah* out of *simcha shel mitzvah* (the joy of doing commandments) or out of *divrei Torah* (words of Torah). However, see the commentary of Ba"ch, ad loc. He explains that those suggestions are fallback alternatives for those who cannot muster up the proper *aimah* and *hachnaa*. They are fallbacks to avoid lightheadedness and frivolity.

the relaxed pose of sitting, whereas the *Amidah* is supposed to be said standing.

The implication should not be drawn that love and awe are *abandoned* once a person reaches the *Amidah*. We made a similar point earlier that in moving to love and awe of the upper *heh*, we do not abandon the *mid-dot* of the *vav*, but rather build on them. Similarly, the love and reverence that one cultivates in the upper *heh* level while saying *Shema* are the building blocks or stepping stones to the "trepidation and submission" that are necessary for achieving *devekut/hitbatlut* in the *Amidah*.

Another well-accepted custom is that of taking three steps forward just as one goes into the *Amidah*.[67] There are a number of reasons given for this. The basic idea is that it represents preparation for coming close to something important, such as standing before the King. Another association is the following. Earlier we explained that whereas the upper *heh* is associated with the receiving of *commandments*, the *yod* is associated with receiving the *Torah*. The three steps hint at the three camps that Moshe made at Mount Sinai and the three days of *hagbala*, or preparation, that the people of Israel needed before the revelation of God. It is also taught that Moshe had to penetrate three levels of darkness before he could reach the state of prophecy in which he received the Torah. In either case, the three steps which we take before the *Amidah* illustrate a parallelism between the *Amidah* and *Ma'amad Har Sinai*. Perhaps it also hints at the three stages of the spiritual journey that one needs to pass through before one reaches the level of the *yod*.

The sages were very demanding in prescribing the precise manner in which the *Amidah* should be said. The *Amidah* must be said with feet together and in a whispering voice that only the individual may hear but is not audible to others around him.[68] One opinion goes so far as to say

---

67. Rama on *SA:OC*: 95:1. *Kaf Hachayim* (ad loc.) cites explanations that connect the three steps with the event of the revelation at Sinai. Also, see *SA:OC*: 141, for more parallels between how one is supposed to conduct oneself during the *Amidah* and how one should comport oneself during the reading of the Torah. This drives home the parallel between the *Amidah* and the event of *Ma'amad har Sinai*.

68. *SA:OC*: 101:2. As noted earlier, certain syllables in Hebrew (as in almost any language) are impossible to pronounce correctly in a whisper. For example, it is impossible to distinguish a *z* from an *s* without saying aloud the syllable *z*. Given the halacha that the *Amidah* must be said silently, it follows that one is *compelled* to mispronounce some of the syllables! This is unlike the *Shema*, which is supposed to be chanted aloud and enunciated clearly. (See the discussion above, 177ff.) Unlike the *Shema*, the inner meaning of the *Amidah* is more important than the actual saying of the words.

that one is not even supposed to hear oneself praying.[69] As noted, the *Amidah* must be said standing, but it also involves bowing. None of the other three stages of prayer involves such rigorous requirements. Unlike any other stage, absolutely no interruptions (*hafsakot*) are allowed during the middle of the *Amidah*. Also, the halachic authorities debate whether one should sway (*shuckle*) during the *Amidah*. Some say it is permissible, but others discourage any unnecessary motion of the body during the *Amidah*.[70] Similarly, there is discussion about whether one should pray the *Amidah* from a prayer book or by heart with eyes closed. Interestingly, no authority says one should cover one's eyes with one's hand, as one does during the *Shema*. Some say it is permissible to read the prayer from a book; others say that if one can do so without losing concentration it is best to recite the prayer by heart.[71]

In sum, the rules for saying the *Amidah* are far more stringent than any other part of *Shacharit*, including the *Shema*. One might think this is odd given that the recitation of *Shema* is a divinely ordained commandment whereas the *Amidah* is a rabbinic commandment. Yet, that is precisely the point. The *Amidah* is a spiritual vehicle that is designed by the Rabbis to take us *beyond* the *ahavah* and *yirah* associated with the *Shema*. Indeed, earlier we noted the tactile nature of the *Shema*. In reciting the *Shema*, one accepts God's kingdom and God's commandments *on one's body*. One says it aloud, preferably with a cantillation tune, from a *siddur*, holding and looking at one's *tzitzit*, touching one's *tefillin*, while thinking of the 248 limbs of the body. During the *Amidah*, the role of the body is diminished. It is as if we are angels standing before God without a body. During the *Amidah* one is supposed to focus on achieving the *inward* relationship with God of *devekut* and *hitbatlut*. The less we focus on our body, the more we can focus on connecting our *ratzon*, or will, with God's will. All the *halachot* and customs of the manner in which the *Amidah* is recited are directed toward achieving *hitbatlut* and *devekut*.

---

69. See *Tur, OC*: 101. This view is not generally accepted.

70. *Rama* endorses swaying during *tefillah* (*SA:OC*: 48:1). However, *Shalah* (Part 2, 79) and *Kitzur Shalah* (on *Tefillah*, p. 70) strongly criticize this view and insist that one should be motionless. Menahem Azariah di Fano (a great Kabbalist) also opposed swaying during the *Amidah* (See "*Asarah Ma'amarot: Em Kol Chai*," § 33, Amsterdam, 1649; *idem*, Responsa, No. 113, Venice, 1600). *Mishnah Berurah* (48: *s.k.*5) writes that, as there is a dispute about this, each person should do what helps his own concentration (*kavvanah*).

71. The Zohar strongly emphasizes saying the Amidah with closed eyes, or at the least with eyes cast downward. *Zohar* 3:261a. *Piskei Tshuvot* on *SA:OC*:94 cites the Baal Shem Tov that if possible, it is best to pray by heart.

244   THE WAY OF THE NAME: YOD

The Purpose of Petitionary Prayer

Let us now turn to the content of the *Amidah*. A brief overview will be helpful. The *Amidah* begins with three blessings that form the introduction, which involve praise of God and the affirmation of God's *kedushah*, or holiness. The bulk of the *Amidah* is petitionary prayer, in which we ask for various things including, knowledge, forgiveness, national redemption, health, material blessing, the ingathering of the exiles, and so forth. The last three blessings include a prayer that our service should be accepted, a blessing that includes thanksgiving, and finally, a blessing in which we ask for *shalom* (peace, fulfillment, or completion).[72]

The *Amidah* is entirely composed by the Rabbis. It is made up entirely of blessings, and in this way, it is somewhat like the initial stages of the lower *heh* (the Morning Blessings).Yet, the *Amidah* is unlike any other stage in that there are virtually no scriptural verses except for the introductory verse (*Adonai, sefatay tiftach*) and the final verse (*Yihyu leratzon imrei fi*).[73] Unlike any other stage of the prayer, there is virtually no rabbinic poetry in the *Amidah*. Finally, unlike any other section of the *Shacharit*, innovations by the individual are allowed in the *Amidah*; indeed, they are encouraged in many blessings (especially in *Shema kolenu* and *Elokai netzor*). As we shall explain later, the fact that innovations are allowed and encouraged conveys profound lessons regarding *devekut/hitbatlut*. In this section, we shall focus on those aspects of the *Amidah* which cultivate *devekut* and *hitbatlut* of the will. In subsequent sections, we shall explain how through the *Amidah* a person may cultivate the other *middot* of the *yod*.

At the very beginning of the *Amidah* one is supposed to bow. As mentioned above, one is supposed to bow to the point where all of the bones in the spine protrude. A person who does this extreme kind of bowing will find that when all the bones protrude, the sinews in the spine are relaxed. When a person bows over completely in this way, one can literally feel a sense of utter submission and "giving in" to God's will.

The blessing at the opening of the *Amidah* is unique. It does not begin with the customary formulation, "Blessed are you *Hashem*, our God,

---

72. See *Tractate Brachot* 34a. The person who prays is like a servant who comes before his master to make requests. The first three blessings are praise, the middle blessings are requests, and the last three blessings are praise and thanksgiving before departing.

73. This is the exact opposite or "mirror image" of *PZ*, which begins and ends with a blessing, but is made up of Scriptural verses.

King of the universe. . . ." Rather, it begins "Blessed are You *Hashem* our God, the God of Abraham, the God of Isaac, and the God of Jacob. . . ." No other blessing in the entire Jewish liturgy is like this. Why the switch from the regular "King of the universe"? Furthermore, once we have said God of our fathers, why do we need to mention their names? And, if we must mention their names, why not say more simply, "the God of Abraham, Isaac, and Jacob"? Why do we need to say "the *God* of Abraham, the *God* of Isaac, and the *God* of Jacob"?

Clearly, this formulation underscores the intimate relationship between God and individual persons, namely, our ancestors. The formulation "God of Abraham, God of Isaac, God of Jacob" is far more personal than the usual phrase, "King of the universe." To emphasize this point, the text indicates that each patriarch had his own relationship with God, tailored to his individual personality. There is an emphasis on God's love here, and on God's intimacy with individuals. The difference between the *Amidah* and the Blessings of the *Shema* here is striking. In the upper *heh*, God is recognized as intervening in the natural order, as the redeemer of Israel from Egypt, and as the Giver of commandments. In that stage, we mention the *people* of Israel frequently, but never once do we mention the individuals, Abraham and Isaac.[74] In the upper *heh* we make reference to the Chosenness of Israel, but here in the *yod* there is a heightened emphasis on God as one who relates to specific individuals. It is only in the *yod* that we focus on *Hashem* as our God and the God of our fathers, Abraham, Isaac, and Jacob. The lesson is that the *Amidah* affords the individual Jew an opportunity to carve out a unique relationship with God that is personalized or tailored to one's individuality.

There is another reason for why the first blessing refers to the patriarchs. Kabbalah teaches that *"Ha-avot, hen hen hamerkavah"* – the patriarchs were "the divine chariot." Like a team of obedient horses, whose wills are completely subservient to the direction of the charioteer, all three patriarchs were completely subservient to God's will. *Tanya*[75] explains that this means the patriarchs achieved *devekut* and *hitbatlut*.

---

74. The name of Jacob is mentioned once in the last blessing of *Shema*; it refers to the children of Jacob (people of Israel) and not the individual man, Jacob. It is also worth noting that the first blessing of the *Amidah* concludes with *magen Avraham* (shield of Avraham). One might have expected the blessing to conclude rather with something like *magen avot* (shield of the fathers). This too is a reflection of God's particularization of his relationship with the individual, in this case, Avraham. It serves as an inspiration for each individual to develop a unique relationship with God.

75. *Tanya* Chapters 18, 34, 37, 39.

Tanya also teaches that since we are descendants of the patriarchs, we too have the ability to reach *devekut/hitbatlut*, even if we are not the greatest spiritual giants ourselves. Since the purpose of the *Amidah* is to help us develop the *middot* of *devekut/hitbatlut*, it makes sense that we refer to the patriarchs in this first blessing.

Let us move on to the second blessing, *mechayeh hameytim* ("Who revives the dead"). A major theme of this blessing is God's omnipotence. God holds life and death in his hands. In other words, one must recognize one's utter dependence on God. In a sense, the second blessing is a highly advanced version of the *Modeh ani* which was uttered at the first moment of waking. However, whereas the point of *Modeh ani* was simply to express thanks, the point of this blessing in the *Amidah* is to motivate utter devotion and submission of the will to God. There is something else in this blessing, namely, the affirmation of our faith that God will resurrect the dead. We shall return to that point later.

Next, in the third blessing we affirm God's *Kedushah*, or holiness. This is the culmination of the three first blessings. We have seen this pattern in the liturgy before, where the affirmation of God's holiness comes toward the end of a section or subsection. Having affirmed that God is the God of the Patriarchs, and that God holds life and death in his hands, we affirm that ultimately God himself is beyond any expression or manifestation of Himself in the world. During the repetition of the *Amidah*, we say the *Kedushah*. Note the contrast between the earlier *Kedushah* recited during the Blessings of *Shema* and the *Kedushah* recited in the repetition of the *Amidah*. In the upper *heh*, we merely *describe* what the angels do. At that point, we say it while seated, and even without a *minyan*. In the *yod*, we *ourselves* sanctify God. Here we stand with feet together like angels, and we say it only if there is a *minyan*. This alone speaks volumes about the difference between the level of the *yod* as opposed to the upper *heh*. Clearly, the bond with God in the *yod* is much higher than that of the upper *heh*.

After the first three blessings, the bulk of the *Amidah* engages in petitionary prayer or *bakashah* (petitioning) of God for various things. The notion of petitionary prayer raises a philosophical conundrum. Does it really make sense that we should ask God for anything? If it is good and proper for us to have that thing, surely God would give it to us without our prayers; if it is not good or proper that we have it, God shouldn't give it to us even if we do pray for it. What then is the aim of petitionary prayer?

One classic answer is that the purpose of petitionary prayer is not really to have any impact on God, but rather to remind ourselves of our utter dependence on God. We shall return to that notion shortly. Another, related answer is that although God does want to do good things for us, he wants us to pray for them as well. Some things he will give us whether we pray or not; but there are some things that will be good for him to give us, *only if we pray for them*. The purpose of petitionary prayer is to work on oneself, to become the kind of person who longs for what is good. We cultivate that longing by praying. In asking God for things, we not only seek that God should change the world, but we also seek to change ourselves. By praying for those things which we should pray for, we slowly but surely *conform our will to God's will*. In this way, we advance beyond the *ahavah* and *yirah* of the upper *heh* and cultivate *devekut* and *hitbatlut* of the will.

The main body of the *Amidah* is concerned with communal goods such as, forgiveness, redemption, the ingathering of the exiles, rebuilding of Jerusalem, and so on. The last blessing is the blessing for *shalom*, or peace. We shall discuss that blessing later. The halacha is that the prayer is not completely finished until and unless one says the verse, *Yehyu leratzon imrei fi ve-hegyon libi lefanecha, Hashem tzuri ve-goali*. Translation: *May the words of my mouth and the thoughts of my heart be in accord with your will, O Hashem, my rock and redeemer*. The reference to God's *ratzon* is not accidental. This final prayer is in a way the whole point of the petitions of the *Amidah*. For here, one asks God to conform our will to His will. This is an explicit prayer for *devekut/ hitbatlut* of the will.

After the blessing for *shalom*, there is the appended prayer, *Elokai netzor*. Actually, the Talmud says that different rabbis would say different prayers at this point.[76] For at this point, personal prayers of one's own composition are not only appropriate but encouraged. Over time, the prayer that was selected for inclusion is *Elokai netzor*. Not surprisingly, the main theme of this prayer is that God should conform one's will to God's will. At the culmination of the *Amidah*, it is especially proper to pray for divine aid in one's spiritual life, rather than material goods – which would perhaps be more appropriate to add into the earlier *Shema Kolenu* prayer.

In summary, the *Amidah* cultivates both *devekut* and *hitbatlut* of the will. It is through petitionary prayer that we seek to effect a change in the world – by changing ourselves. The quest for *devekut* of the will has an active character. In Kabbalistic terms, this active aspect is masculine, and it is connected with the requirement to stand upright

---

76. *Tractate Brachot* 17a.

during the prayer. This contrasts with the receptive nature of the *Shema* which is generally said while seated. On the other hand, a major theme of the *Amidah* is also *hitbatlut,* and this is expressed through *bowing,* which is the direct opposite of standing upright. It is through the bowing and standing of the *Amidah* that we aim to achieve *devekut/hitbatlut.*

Utter Dependence and Total Faith

So far we have seen how the *Amidah* cultivates *devekut* and *hitbatlut* of the will. It is equally the case that the *Amidah* helps us cultivate *emunah* and *chochmah.* Let us discuss these points in turn.

Recall that *emunah,* or faith, involves a total "head over heels" commitment to do whatever God commands, even if it is difficult or doesn't seem to make sense. One way in which the *Amidah* cultivates this faith is by reminding us that everything that we have comes from God. Most importantly, life and death are in God's hands. While the first blessing focuses on the intimate or personal relationship that God had with each of the patriarchs, the second blessing focuses on God's omnipotence in general, and in particular on the fact that God is *Melech maymit umechayeh* (the King who causes death and life). If we can genuinely affirm that we are totally in God's hands, a total commitment to God comes naturally.

Indeed, almost all of the *Amidah* – all petitionary prayer – expresses the fact that we are utterly dependent on God. Each petition concludes with a blessing, which is in effect a recognition that God is the source of some particular kind of good (wisdom, forgiveness, health, wealth, etc.). There is a paradox here. On the one hand, by praying, we indicate that, by God's grace, we have the power to change the world through speech. How proud must we feel as we stand before God, asking the Omnipotent to do what we wish! On the other hand, by praying we also indicate our utter dependence on God. How humble must we feel, as we acknowledge through prayer that everything we have or ever will have comes from God!

The second blessing is connected to the theme of faith, or *emunah,* in another way. In this blessing, we affirm that God is *mekayem emunato lisheinei afar* – "he upholds his faithfulness to those who sleep in the dust." We also say *ve-ne'eman atah lehachayot metim* – "and you are faithful to revive the dead." The faith we have in the resurrection of the dead is rather different from the faith that we have in the redemption of Israel, which we had expressed in the previous section (the last blessing of *Shema*).[77] As explained earlier, there is a difference between these two sorts of faith. We have experienced national redemption over and again. Hence, the faith in national redemption is a rational sort of faith. We have reason based on past experience to believe that God will redeem us once again. But, we have never experienced the resurrection of the dead. Hence, this latter faith falls into the category of *emunah*, a faith that goes beyond reason.

The Power of Innovation

In this section, we shall see how the *Amidah* cultivates *chochmah*, or creative wisdom, in the worship of God. Recall that *chochmah* involves innovation, or the power to originate *chidushim*. The power of *chochmah* is closely linked with *yechidah*, or the capacity of free will. We find that innovation plays a very strong role in the *Amidah*. Indeed, the *Amidah* itself is a great human innovation. As noted earlier, Judaism teaches that it is a divine commandment to recite the *Shema*, but human beings (i.e., the rabbis) instituted and composed the *Amidah*. This contrasts sharply with the other stages of *Shacharit*. In all the other three stages, major sections are drawn directly from the Scriptures. The content of the *Amidah* is entirely rabbinic. It is by far the most creative section of the *Shacharit*.

Another way in which the *Amidah* exhibits innovation or spontaneity is that it is much more flexible than the three previous stages of *Shacharit*. Depending on the day or time of year, different things are said. There are numerous seasonal insertions and deletions. This is completely unlike any other stage in the *Shacharit*.[78]

---

77. No mention is made of the exodus from Egypt in the entire *Amidah*. This is somewhat remarkable, given the importance of this event in Jewish tradition and in other parts of the liturgy. Its conspicuous absence underscores a sharp difference between the *Amidah* and *Shema*. Whereas the *Shema* and its blessings focus more on the past, the *Amidah* focuses more on the present and the future. This difference is expressed keenly in the fact that whereas the last blessing of *Shema* ends with the past tense, *"ga'al Yisrael"* (he *redeemed* Israel), one of the middle blessings of the *Amidah* is the present tense *"goel Yisrael"* (he *redeems* Israel).

78. For example, depending on the season, we say *morid hatal* or *mashiv haruach*, *veten tal umatar*, or *veten brachah*. During the ten days of repentance, we say *Hamelech Hakadosh* instead of *Ha-el Hakadosh*; on fast days we say *Anenu*; on Rosh Chodesh and the intermediate days of Pesach or Sukkot we say *Yaaleh veyavo*; on Chanukah and Purim we say *Al hanissim*, etc. On *Shabbat* and holidays, the middle section of the *Amidah* is entirely different. There are some changes and additions in the other sections of *Shacharit* during *Shabbat* and holidays, but they are minor

Once again, we note a sharp contrast between the *Amidah* and the *Shema*. Recall that the upper *heh* represents *binah*, that is, comprehension or understanding of that which is the case. It also represents *kabbalat ol malchut shamayim*. Judaism teaches that certain things are the case and never change. The *Shema* is fixed or set in stone; no innovations are appropriate. The *Shema* is exactly the same, without change, every single day of the year. On the other hand, the *Amidah* corresponds to the *yod*, which represents the freedom of *chochmah*, or creativity. Hence, the *Amidah* is very much subject to change.

In fact, the Amidah had better *not* be fixed — for otherwise, it is not genuine prayer. It is taught that a *tefillah* that is *keva* (fixed) is not a genuine prayer. The Talmud discusses different interpretations of what it means for a prayer to be "fixed."[79] One is that a person should not pray by rote or in a robotic fashion. Another is that one should not pray as if one is relieving oneself of a burden. Another interpretation is that one should be able to *innovate* something different depending on the circumstances of the prayer. A simple interpretation of this would be that one's prayer should vary depending on the circumstances. Thus, for example, a person should pray for rain when appropriate and not pray for rain when not appropriate. This is exactly what we do. Another more demanding interpretation is that one should be able to innovate something of a personal nature in every prayer. The halacha is that we do not actually need to do this,[80] but it is certainly a good thing to be able to pray in such a manner that one *could* innovate if one had the need.

We have already spoken of the parallelism between the *Amidah* and the morning sacrifice of the *korban tamid*. During the times of the Temple, an individual could bring a free will offering if he so wished. This concept is paralleled by the notion that one can make a *tefillat nedavah*, or voluntary prayer offering. Although it is uncommon in our day for anyone to do this, the halacha provides for a person to recite the entire *Amidah* outside the boundaries of the regular, mandatory daily services. Various rules pertain to this *tefillat nedavah*, including the requirement that the person must insert some innovation, to distinguish it from the required prayers. No other section of the *Shacharit* may be repeated

---

compared to the changes in the *Amidah*. For example, on *Shabbat* we say more Psalms during *PZ*, but the main Psalms are still the same — *Ashrei* and the *Halleluyahs*. The only major change is the addition of *Nishmat* (see footnote 57 in Chapter 3). On *Shabbat* the first blessing of *Shema* is somewhat different, but the *Shema* itself and the other two blessings are the same as on the weekdays.

79. *Tractate Brachot* 28b–29a.
80. *SA:OC*: 98:3.

(in its entirety) even with an innovation. Again, this reflects the unique nature of the *Amidah* and its special link with individual autonomy.

Unlike any of the other three stages, there is much room for personal innovation especially in *Shema kolenu* and in *Elokai netzor*. What a person asks for here in these sections depends on the needs and circumstances of the individual. This is not a simple matter and should not be taken lightly. Perhaps one should think carefully about what one wants to say and even write a draft of one's prayers, and then refine the draft. Perhaps one should not just extemporize a prayer. It's a craft or an art, and it takes *chochmah* to do it well. Nevertheless, the bottom line is that innovation is appropriate and encouraged and even in some measure required. Perhaps a spontaneous prayer that comes from the heart is not inappropriate after all.

At first glance, it may seem paradoxical that the highest level of *Shacharit* is the one in which there is the greatest room for innovation. This teaches us a profound lesson about the significance of the individual in the Jewish spiritual path. The *Amidah* is the highest part of the prayer. Yet not everyone's *tefillah* should be identical. Although we can and should pray for certain things in common, there should be differences in our prayers that reflect our differing individual circumstances. Even if we do not always introduce a *chidush*, or novelty, the *manner* in which we pray should be such that we *could* introduce a novelty. At its highest level, the spiritual path is associated with *yechidah*, the will, which is free. The deepest and most intimate bond with God – *devekut/hitbatlut* – has an intensely personal dimension that is tailored to the unique individuality of every spiritual seeker.

Being with God, in the *Amidah*

So far, we have discussed how the *Amidah* cultivates *devekut/hitbatlut* of the will, as well as *emunah* and *chochmah*. Let us now consider how the *Amidah* cultivates the remaining *middot* of the *yod*. These include the higher kind of *devekut/hitbatlut*, or "being with God."

We have already explained that one way a person cultivates the higher kind of *devekut/hitbatlut* is through *hitbodedut* (seclusion) and *hitbonenut* (meditation on God). There are various ways to achieve *hitbodedut*, such as, going off into a wilderness, leaving communal life for a time, or going on a spiritual retreat. But, how likely is the average person to do this, and how often? The *Amidah* gives every ordinary Jew a chance to do this every day, even in a room full of other people. In a remarkable way, a kind of *hitbodedut* happens during the private *Amidah*. This is made possible by the rigorous *halachot* that govern how the *Amidah* should be said. Again, it is the only part of *Shacharit* that must be said silently, with feet together, with no attention paid to visual aids such as *tefillin* or *tzitzit*, and with no interruptions. Even in a room full of people, each individual is, in some sense, in his own world as he says his own private *tefillah*.

Similarly, it is no easy thing for the average person to take up the activity of *hitbonenut*. Yet, because of its halachic structure, the *Amidah* promotes *hitbonenut*. In the *Amidah*, we calmly and methodically meditate on God. In the *Amidah*, we do not engage in learning or study of Torah. We do not engage in "ratiocination" or philosophical thinking about God's nature. Moreover, the *Amidah* constitutes *hitbonenut* not only because of the *content* of the eighteen blessings, but the *manner* in which one focuses on that content. In this way, the eighteen blessings of the *Amidah* are different from the Morning Blessings, during which one also thinks about God, but also about putting on one's shoes, tying one's belt, and so forth. The eighteen blessings are different from the repetitive and songful praises of *PZ*, in that they are concise and devoid of poetry. As explained earlier, *hitbonenut* is more of a cerebral activity than an emotional one. The eighteen blessings are also different from the Reading of *Shema* and it blessings because, during the *Shema*, although one is thinking about God, one is also thinking about accepting the kingdom of heaven and the *mitzvot* upon oneself. One is also busy touching one's *tefillin*, and holding one's *tzitzit*, and so forth. In contrast, the *Amidah* is an exercise in focused, calm concentration. If we do it properly and with the right intent, we thereby achieve the higher kind of *devekut*, namely, being with God.

Earlier, we explained how the bowing done during the *Amidah* is an expression of submission of our will to God's will. The bowing also cultivates the higher kind of *hitbatlut*. In bowing, I am not only submitting my will to God's will. I am also expressing the fact that I am "as nothing" before God. Of course, it's not that I'm *literally* nothing. Rather, by bowing I express the fact that while my existence is *contingent*, God is *necessary*. Since God or Being itself is being *par excellence*, any other being is "as nothing" in comparison. Just as standing connotes activity, bowing connotes ultimate submission in the presence of God.[81] This notion is also expressed toward the very end of the *Amidah* in *Elokai netzor*, when we say *"nafshi ke-afar lakol tihyeh"* – "let my soul be as dust unto all." This expresses *hitbatlut* of the higher sort.

---

81. *Tanya*, chapter 39.

As noted earlier, the bulk of the *Amidah* is petitionary prayer, or *bakashot*. Earlier we explained that whereas the *middot* of the upper *heh* are driven by self-interest, the *middot* of the *yod* are focused more on God himself. At first glance, it may seem that the *Amidah* is an extended exercise in self-interest. So much of it involves asking for things for ourselves.[82] How can this be explained?

Several points must be made. Firstly, it is important to reiterate that, in the *devekut/hitbatlut* of the *yod*, we do not *abandon* the notion of serving God out of self-interest. Rather, we *add another dimension* to our service, such that the thought of self-interest becomes secondary. This means that we are not working "just" for the reward. We are working to serve God because that's what God wants us to do; it also happens to be in our self-interest to do so. Secondly, as explained earlier, the point of asking for things in the *Amidah* is not so much to get those things, but rather to conform our will to God's will. Self-interest may be on our minds, but it is secondary.

Thirdly, a close look at the Eighteen Blessings reveals that in most cases, even when we pray for our own needs, the truth is that we are praying that God should "actualize himself," that is, manifest or express himself more fully. This recalls the point that the *yod* signifies *keter*, or maximal, divine self-expression. In the *Amidah*, we are asking that God should do what we ask *because that's what God really wants to do anyhow.* Now, it happens that among God's projects is that our own material and spiritual welfare should be advanced. (Thus for example, we say, "Heal us . . . *for you are a God of healing;*" "Hear our prayer. . . . *for you hear the prayers of Israel.*") This is also why each petition ends with a *blessing.* As explained earlier, a blessing is not a petition (nor is it a thank-you) but rather an expression of recognition that *something comes from God.* This is why the *Amidah* is known as the *Eighteen Blessings* (and not, the Eighteen Requests!).

In any event, while the middle blessings focus on our requests, the last three blessings focus more on attaining the proper relationship with God. The first of the last three is *Retzeh*. It is worth contrasting this blessing with the immediately preceding blessing, namely, *Shema*

---

82. In particular, the blessing of *Al hatzadikim* seems to be a direct appeal for *schar*, or reward. Yet, note that we do not simply pray for reward for our good deeds, or *mitzvot* – rather we pray for reward for *all those who trust in you in truth*. We then ask that God should "place our lot with them and not cause us embarrassment." We do not directly pray for our own reward; rather, we pray for reward for all those who trust in God. Even though we are praying for what is in our interest, our motivation is that God should do what he really wants to do, namely, reward all the righteous.

kolenu ("Hear our voice"). On the surface, these blessings seem similar. In both blessings, we ask God to accept our prayer, or *tefillah*. But there's a difference. The term *tefillah* has two different meanings. It can mean petitionary prayer (*bakashah*); it can also mean service or worship (*avodah*). In *Shema kolenu*, we ask God to "hear our voice," that is, accept our *bakashot*, or petitionary prayers. Thus we conclude *Shema kolenu* with the phrase, *"Blessed is Hashem who hears prayer."* In *Retzeh*, we ask God to accept our *tefillah* in the sense of our *worship*. In this latter sense, our *tefillah* is something that replaces, or stands in for, the *korban*, or offering, that was made during the time of the Temple. Thus, we conclude *Retzeh* with the phrase, *"Blessed is Hashem who returns his presence to Zion."* In this blessing, we affirm our belief in the return of the divine presence to Zion, which will enable us to "be with God" in the Temple once again. As noted earlier, the purpose of bringing a *korban*, or offering, is to come "close" to God. In this blessing, we affirm that our *tefillah* is a way of coming close to God, and we express our faith that the day will come when once again we will be with God in the Temple.

The next blessing is *Modim Anachnu* ("We give thanks"). On the surface, the function of this blessing is to give thanks to God for our lives and everything we have. However, an interesting feature is that toward the end of the blessing we express the prayer that one day, *all* living things will thank God. As the culminating blessing says, "Blessed are you *Hashem*, for your Name is good, and it is fitting to thank you." Here, we focus not so much on the fact that *we* thank God, but rather on the fact that it is fitting that God be thanked by all creatures. The point is that we are taking a more objective view of the situation than merely focusing on thanking God for *our* gifts. We recognize that God is worthy of being thanked by all creatures – and in light of that recognition, we thank God.[83]

Finally, *acharon acharon chaviv* – the best is saved for last. The quest for *devekut* is expressed in the fullest way in the culminating blessing, *Sim shalom* (Grant fulfillment, etc.). The term *shalom* is usually translated as *peace*. But, *shalom* really means much more than peace; it connotes *completion* or *fulfillment*. Thus, the sages characterize *shalom* as "the vessel that holds all other blessings." Here we pray, "bless us as one our Father with the light of Your face, for in the light of your face you have given us a living Torah, loving benevolence, and charity, blessing, and compassion. . . ." The request for God to shine upon us the "light of

---

83. This is similar to one of the differences noted earlier between *Yishtabach* and *Baruch Sheamar*. See Chapter 3, p. 165.

His face" is another way of asking for the ultimate blessing of "completion." On those occasions when there is a priestly blessing, the *kohanim* (priests) ask God to bless Israel with the shining light of God's face and with *shalom,* or completion. Here we are not asking for some external gift that God may choose to give us, such as health, or wealth, or national protection. Here we are asking for *devekut* with *God Himself.*

In the reference to "light," we see an allusion to the *yod* or *keter.*[84] In no other section of the *Shacharit* do we pray for the "shining of the light" of God's face. In this passage, we also mention that it was "in the light of God's face" that we received the Torah. The Torah itself uses the notion of *panim bepanim*[85] (face to face) to describe the event at Mount Sinai, which constituted the fundamental *devekut/hitbatlut* event between God and Israel. This reinforces the connection between the *Amidah* and the event of *Ma'mad Har Sinai.* Just as Israel achieved *devekut* as a people at that time, so too, at the culmination of the *Amidah,* we seek the highest bond of *devekut,* or *being with God.*

In *Sim shalom,* our focus is on *devekut* between God and the people of Israel. After *Sim shalom,* we say *Elokai netzor.* We have already noted that the main theme of this prayer is that one asks God to conform one's will to God's will. We also mentioned that personal prayers are to be inserted at this point. At the very end of *Elokai netzor,* there is a custom of inserting a verse that alludes to one's own first name.[86] Whereas

---

84. Recall the discussion above regarding the association of light with the *yod*. In the third stage of *Shacharit* we make numerous references to light, but it is to the light of the heavenly luminaries (*meorot*), rather than the light of God's face. In *Ahava Rabbah* we pray that God should "enlighten our eyes" in the Torah. Interestingly, we do not mention the light of God's face in that blessing. This omission underscores the point that there is a difference between *kabbalat ol mitzvot* and *kabbalat ha-Torah.*

85. Deuteronomy 5:4.

86. This custom is mentioned by *Kitzur Shulchan Aruch* 18:15. See *Tzelosah D'Avraham* by Avraham Landau, Vol. 1, p. 327, for more details on this custom. The reason given is that we do not want our name to be forgotten on the Day of Judgment. This is based on a *midrash* that when the wicked reach the Day of Judgment, they "forget their own name." When a person dies and his soul goes up to heaven, the angels ask the person for his name, and if he cannot remember, that shows he is wicked. By securing the remembrance of our name, we are in effect seeking to avoid falling into the category of the wicked. What does this *midrash* really mean, and why should we mention our name specifically at the end of the *Amidah*? Perhaps this may be explained as follows. The wicked "forget their own name" in the sense that they do not live up to their name, which represents the destiny or true purpose for which their souls came into this world. In mentioning our own name, we remind ourselves of our true purpose in life, which is not only to achieve some good relationship with

the *Amidah* begins with reference to the great individuals, Avraham, Yitzchak, and Yaakov, here each person concludes the *Amidah* with his or her own name. It is as if we are signing off our prayer with our own name, as one might do at the end of a letter. This is yet another way of personalizing our *tefillah*, the purpose of which is to achieve an intimate bond with God.

There is another dimension of the *Amidah*, which emerges if we pose the following question. Earlier we explained that the higher kind of *devekut* is an existential relationship that is not mediated by some intellectual activity; it goes beyond words. Yet, the *Amidah* involves speech – petitionary prayer, the *Kedushah*, the blessings, etc. How then can the *Amidah* be a vehicle for this higher kind of *devekut/hitbatlut*? If all we have is the *Amidah*, are we not "stuck" in words?

First, it is crucial to remember that although *devekut* itself is not a verbal matter, that does not rule out the possibility that a verbal activity might promote or bring about *devekut*. Recall the analogy of "being with" another human, whether a friend or a spouse. While it is true that "being with" another human person is an existential relationship that transcends words, it is still the case that one way to achieve that condition is (partly) through intimate conversation. Something similar is true for "being with God." Most of the *Amidah* is an exercise in *hitbonenut*, or focused concentration on God, insofar as he is manifest in the world in eighteen different ways. So, the *Amidah* itself does involve words. Nevertheless, if done with the proper intent, it still promotes the wordless condition of *devekut*.

Second, and perhaps more importantly, one may (and perhaps one should) include during the *Amidah* a period or a "zone" of silent and non-verbal meditation on God. Halachically, even if one is not saying any words, one is still in the middle of the *Amidah* even if one is silent. Until and unless one says the verse "*yihyu leratzon*, etc." one is still considered to be praying, even if one has finished the final blessing of *Sim shalom*.[87] A silent dimension to the *tefillah* is appropriate at any point during the *tefillah*, as long as one doesn't let one's mind wander. It is especially appropriate after one has concluded the words of the *Amidah* but before one "signs off" the prayer with a verse alluding to one's name.

God, but rather to achieve the relationship of *devekut* with God, which each of us can attain in his or her unique way. This is the ultimate purpose of the *Amidah*, so it is fitting that we mention our own name at its conclusion.

87. *SA:OC*: 122.

In this silent meditation, one may achieve that wordless repose in God, or *menuchah*, which constitutes the bond of "being with God."

Some readers may be surprised to learn that Judaism endorses silent meditation. Support for the practice of silent, non-verbal meditation may be found in the following passage from the Talmud:

> It was taught in a *baraita*: One who prays must wait (*lish-hos*) one hour before his prayer and one hour after his prayer. Before his prayer – as it says, "Fortunate are those who dwell in your house." After one's prayer – as it says, "Indeed the righteous shall praise your name, the upright will dwell in the presence of your face."[88]

The Hebrew term in this passage for the practice of waiting is the word *lish-hos* (to wait or tarry). We are supposed to "tarry" in God's house and ultimately in God's presence. The implication is that this waiting period is *silent*.[89] Evidently, the initial period of waiting before *tefillah* is an attempt to establish *hitbodedut*.[90] The verse cited to support the practice brings to mind the notion discussed earlier, namely, that the image of "dwelling in God's house" represents "being with God." The period after the prayer is a non-verbal stillness in the presence of God. The verse cited to support the practice is, *"the upright will dwell in the presence of your face."* Note the switch from the initial waiting period which involves being *in God's house* to the more elevated aftermath waiting period which involves dwelling *in God's presence*. As explained earlier, the term *panim*, or face, connotes God Himself, as opposed to some gift that God may give. The purpose of the waiting during the aftermath is not merely to sit idly with a blank mind, but rather to bask silently in the glow of God's presence. Through the *Amidah* we may reach a state of *devekut/ hitbatlut*, and we are to remain silently in that devotional state for some period of time.[91]

---

88. *Tractate Brachot* 32b.

89. There is indication elsewhere that the term *shohim* connotes some non-verbal period of silence. There is a halacha that a person who goes into a synagogue just to speak to someone about a personal matter should say a verse, to indicate that the synagogue is a holy place. If a person is unlearned and doesn't know how to say a verse, the *Shulchan Aruch* writes that *yasheh me'at* (he should tarry a short while) in the synagogue. Presumably, that must mean, in silence. *SA:OC* 151:1.

90. See Yeruchem Halevi Lebovitz, *Chever Ma'amarim* p. 309.

91. Granted, there are other ways one might interpret the purpose of this "waiting" period. One might say that the initial waiting period is simply to clear

Silent and non-verbal reflection on God is endorsed in the following passage from Maimonides, *Guide*, I:59:

> The idea [of not speaking about God] is best expressed in the book of Psalms (65:2), "Silence (*dumiah*) is praise to Thee." It is a very expressive remark on this subject: for whatever we utter with the intention of extolling and of praising Him contains something that cannot be applied to God, and includes derogatory expressions. It is therefore more becoming to be silent, and to be content with intellectual reflection, as has been recommended by men of the highest culture, in the words "Commune with your own heart upon your bed, and be still (*ve-domu*), *selah*!" (Psalms 4:5).

We may take Maimonides' comment as not only a rejection of inadequate speech about God, but also as an endorsement of *silent reflection*. The *dumiah* here is not *mere silence*. Surely, Maimonides is not claiming that in the face of inadequate speech, the best thing to do is just *avoid* thinking about God! On the contrary, Maimonides alludes here to a kind of reflection that involves some positive content, but cannot and should not be verbalized. This is silent, non-verbal meditation.

Knowing God as Hashem, through the *Amidah*

We have seen that the *Amidah* is an exercise in *hitbodedut* and *hitbonenut*, and that its purpose is to help a person achieve *hitbatlut* and *devekut*. If a person is successful in this endeavor during the *Amidah*, a likely consequence is that he or she will reach some level of *da'at Hashem*. Recall that *da'at Hashem* is not a direct or unmediated experience of God's essence.[92] That is impossible. On the other hand, it is more than just the experience of Being or God as manifest in things, for that is

---

one's mind from one's personal affairs, and that the aftermath waiting period is to demonstrate one's prayer was not a burden. This seems to be the interpretation of *Tur* and *Shulchan Aruch* (*OC*: 93:1). However, the verses cited in support of the practice in the *baraita* seem to count in favor of the interpretation offered here. As noted shortly below, *Shulchan Aruch* explicitly states that the "original pious ones" achieved *devekut* during prayer (OC 98:1). It is unlikely that such people would need to tarry after the prayer in order to "show that it was not a burden." Perhaps this latter reason was added, to give an explanation for why the custom of waiting afterward would still apply even for those who do not achieve *devekut* during the *Amidah*.

92. See the discussion above of *da'at Hashem*.

a common experience which stems from our ordinary ability to see and touch things in this world. Rather, *da'at Hashem* is the much more sophisticated experience of God or Being *as Hashem*, that is, God as manifest in all of the ways that are symbolized by י-ה-ו-ה. In this sense, one cannot directly *see* Hashem in this world, and perhaps this is one reason why the Zohar teaches that one should keep one's eyes closed during the *Amidah*.[93] If one is fortunate to have it, the experience of God as *Hashem* in the Amidah is felt internally.

The quest for *da'at Hashem* is one of the goals of the *Amidah*. It is not accidental that the very first petitionary blessing in the main body of the eighteen blessings is a prayer for *da'at*.[94] It is worth noting what Rav Yosef Karo wrote in the *Shulchan Aruch*. He describes the requirement for anyone who prays to have total concentration during the *Amidah*. He then goes on to write, quoting directly from the *Tur* (*Orach Chaim*, 98:1):

> And thus the pious ones and men of achievement engaged in *hitbodedut*, and had such intent during their *tefillah* that they reached a level of removing themselves from their bodies, and such an overwhelming power of the mind, to the point where they reached close to the level of prophecy . . .

The author of the *Tanya*, R. Schneur Zalman of Liadi, writes something similar in his *Shulchan Aruch HaRav* (*Hilchot Talmud Torah* 4:5):

> Regarding the *Shemonah Esrei* it was said that the original pious ones would wait one hour before the *tefillah*, spend one hour in *tefillah*, and one hour after *tefillah* – three times a day. . . . [During the *tefillah*] they would connect their da'at to the Master of all blessed be he, with reverence and strong love and in true *devekut*, to the point where they transcended their bodily nature. . . .

Note that here R. Schneur Zalman replaces the reference to *nevuah* (prophecy) with something that sounds more modest. Instead of saying

---

93. See above, note 71. One source says that a person who keeps his eyes open or does not look down during the *Amidah* will not merit to see the light of the *Shekhinah* when he dies. The lesson seems to be that the only proper way to experience the *Shekhinah* during the *Amidah* is with one's eyes closed.

94. The prayer is for *da'at* in general, not specifically *da'at Hashem*. However, on Saturday night the text does explicitly refer to *madda toratecha* (knowledge of your Torah).

that they would achieve a level close to prophecy, he writes that during their *tefillah*, they would achieve *da'at* with God. Ideally, then, *da'at Hashem* is one of the goals of the *Amidah*.

Some readers might think this is well beyond what the ordinary religious person might be able to achieve during prayer. After all, these authors are talking about a very devout group of people and not the average person. But these are halachic works, and so there must be a halachic – that is to say – practical, reason for their bringing this point about the "original pious ones." As explained earlier, there are degrees of *devekut*, and there are degrees of *da'at Hashem*. Like *devekut*, *da'at Hashem* is a positive *mitzvah* that is binding on all Israelites, and so we should strive to reach these lofty goals. During the *Amidah*, everyone should have this goal in mind, even if one hopes to be successful only to some modest degree.

Such an experience may not happen every time one prays, and it may be experienced on some occasions more than others. But, if it does occur, it strengthens the conviction of a person's belief in God as *Hashem*. Furthermore, if one is fortunate enough to have the experience of *da'at Hashem*, some particular insight may occur which enlightens a person about how to grow further along the spiritual path. This need not happen every time one prays, and one certainly should not expect it, but it can and does happen. Perhaps this is one reason why on most ordinary days, the *tefillah* is immediately followed (during the weekday) by *tachanun*, which is a prayer of supplication for forgiveness for our sins. During the *Amidah*, a person may be brought to a higher level of *devekut* than before, which entails a higher level of responsibility as well as a higher level of consciousness. While the *Amidah* can and should be an uplifting and positive spiritual experience, one may also become more acutely aware of one's failings, or of some specific area where one might improve. Thus, after the *Amidah* is over, one turns to supplication for forgiveness. This supplication will be useless if it is not accompanied by an effort to change one's behavior in the future.

Earlier we noted the connection between the burning of incense in the Temple and the pursuit of *da'at Hashem*. Although there is no explicit reference to the incense offering in the *Amidah*, the very last phrase said at the end of the *Amidah* is the following: "May the offering (*minchah*) of Judah and Jerusalem be pleasing to God, as in days of yore and years gone by." (*Malachi* 3:4) This same verse is said immediately after the recitation of the passages summarizing the details of the incense offering in the first stage of *Shacharit*. The term *minchah* (offering) may be taken as an allusion to all offerings in the Temple, including the incense, which is the crowning glory of all the offerings. Hence, we may see in this final verse an allusion to the incense. How fitting that we conclude the *Amidah* with this verse, which hints at the ritual that allows us to attain *da'at Hashem*.[95]

Let us briefly summarize the entire spiritual journey. In the first two stages of the prayer, we focus on recognizing and appreciating God, insofar as He is manifest in one's body, and in the natural world. In the third stage of *Shacharit*, we focus on God as manifest in the heavenly bodies, and in the miracles of the redemption from Egypt. We also recognize God as the one King, and accept upon ourselves the commitment to respect and love God through keeping the *mitzvot*. In the third blessing of the *Amidah*, we recognize God's transcendence, or *kedushah* – the fact that despite all of those expressions, His essence is infinite and He is *not* totally manifest or expressed within the natural world. Throughout the bulk of the *Amidah* we cultivate *devekut* and *hitbatlut* of the will through petitionary prayer. We also contemplate God as manifest in eighteen fundamental ways. Finally, as we reach the end of the *Amidah*, that is, the tip of the *yod*, we strive to achieve that higher bond of "being exclusively with" God. We remain in that condition of silent devotion as long as we can. If we are fortunate, we experience some level of *da'at Hashem*, and we depart from that condition with fresh insights about how to improve our relationship with God in the future.

It turns out, then, that *Amidah* is not merely an end in itself, but also a vehicle for improving one's lower *middot*, and subsequently reaching higher levels of *hitbatlut* and *devekut* in days to come. After the *Amidah*, toward the end of *Shacharit*, we pray that it may be God's will that he should open our hearts in his Torah, and place in our hearts the love and reverence to do His will, and serve Him with a full heart. We also pray that we should observe His commandments in this world, and that we should merit life, goodness, and blessing during the days of the Messiah and the World to Come.

---

95. A similar point concerns the custom of reciting passages detailing the *pitum haketoret* (incense mixture) toward the very end of *Shacharit*. The preamble *Ein kelohenu* ("There is none like our God," etc.) states that although God transcends all, we can still have a relationship with Him. Thus, it starts with "There is none like our God, etc." but ends with "You are our God, etc." The switch from third person to second person is noteworthy. This is a fitting prelude to the recitation of the *pitum haketoret*. For, it is precisely this ritual that allows Israel to have an intimate religious experience of the infinite and transcendent God.

APPENDIX: SEVEN MEDITATIONS

MEDITATION HAS VARIOUS USES AND APPLICATIONS. The purpose of the following meditations is to cultivate the *middah* of *devekut* with God. One should have this intention in mind when practicing any of these meditations. All of the following meditations involve focusing one's concentration and indeed one's very being on God, insofar as He is manifest through the Name, י-ה-ו-ה. Hence, all of these meditations are variations on the same theme, and to some degree, they overlap. Practice in one meditation will strengthen and enhance any of the other meditations. All of these meditations are easy to do, for at least some short period. What is not so easy is to sustain the meditation for a lengthy period. As one grows in learning and understanding of the Name, and, as one follows the Way of the Name in one's everyday life, one's meditation and prayer are enriched and deepened.

These meditations can be done at any time, but they are especially appropriate to do shortly before *Shacharit*. One may thereby fulfill the *mitzvah* of "*shohim*," or silent preparation for prayer, as discussed earlier in this book. It is best to practice these meditations without interruption and in a place where one is confident that one will not be disturbed. Ideally, one begins by clearing the mind of distractions. A common way to do that is to focus on one's breathing (*neshimah*) for a few moments. This also brings a person in touch with one's soul (*neshamah*). Another helpful practice is to recite a Psalm or two as a preface, such as Psalm 16 or 27. Subsequently, one may spend as little as a minute or as long as an hour on any of these meditations. The more carefully and deliberately one engages in them, the more powerful will be their effect.

In meditating on God's Name, one may proceed either "from bottom to top" or "from top to bottom." That is, one may start with the lowest level and move gradually toward the highest level, or one may start from the highest level and move down to the lowest level. In doing the former, a person focuses on the human process of reaching up to God. In doing the latter, one focuses on the divine process of God's reaching down to us. Both are important. Most of the following meditations can be done in both ways. For each of the meditations below, there is a short introduction and then brief instructions in italics.

It is important to remember that the effect of meditation is not necessarily felt immediately. One should not expect to attain deep insights every time one meditates. Rather, meditation is part of a way of life that is God-centered. In time, meditation promotes *devekut*, *hitbatlut*, *da'at Hashem*, and indeed all the *middot*.

At first, it may be difficult to do these meditations on one's own. To hear guided meditations by the author, visit thewayofthename.com.

⇒⇒⊂⊂

1.   Letters of the Name

A verse in Psalms (16:8) reads, *Shiviti Hashem lenegdi tamid,* "I have set
ה-ו-ה-י before me, always." Focusing on the Name of God has a powerful
spiritual impact. In this relatively simple meditation, one focuses on
each individual letter of the Name, and then on the entire Name. One
may do this with eyes closed, while visualizing the letters. Or, one may
use a text that has the Name printed on it. One may use a *"shiviti,"* which
is a printed page that has the Name, together with other Kabbalistic as-
sociations. The table below (read from bottom to top) provides the order
of this meditation.

> י   *Chochmah, Keter* (divine wisdom and will;
> the maximal expression of Being in a finite World)

> ה   *Binah* (divine intelligence; the structure and pur-
> posefulness of the universe)

> ו   *Rachamim, Chessed, Gevurah* (the divine moral
> attributes; the divine ways)

> ה   *Malchut* (the Divine Presence as revealed in all
> things)

*Begin by clearing the mind of all distractions. Focus for some time on the
lower heh. Let your soul dwell on the lower heh and the sefirah that it represents, namely, malchut, or Shekhinah. Think of yourself as connecting
with the Shekhinah. When you feel ready, move up to the vav. Again, let
yourself dwell on the vav and everything that it stands for. This includes
the divine middot of compassion, benevolence, and justice. Connect with
God insofar as he manifests in these ways. When you feel ready, move
to the upper heh, which represents binah or divine intelligence. Dwell
there for some time. Connect with God insofar as he is manifest in the
structure and purposefulness of the world. Finally, focus on the yod, which
represents divine will and wisdom. When you feel ready, continue the
process in reverse. Focus on the yod itself, then yod heh, then yod heh vav,
and finally yod heh vav heh. Recall that yod heh itself constitutes a name
of God, and the vav connects the yod heh with the lower heh to make the
full Name. Conclude the meditation by dwelling for some time on the
entire Name.*

2. The Natural World and Colors

As explained in this book, different aspects of the natural world and different colors are expressions or manifestations of the infinite God or Being itself. Thus, certain aspects of the natural world and certain colors correspond to different letters of the Name. In this meditation, one focuses on each of these different aspects in ascending order. In each case, one contemplates a certain aspect of the natural world and its associated color as a manifestation of God. The table below (read from bottom to top) provides the order of this meditation.

> י Light, energy (white, shining light)
>
> ה Sky, the heavens (blue)
>
> ו Trees, vegetation, living creatures (green)
>
> ה Ground of the earth, fertile soil (reddish brown)

Start by visualizing or focusing on the lower heh, while thinking of the earth and its reddish brown color. Think of the earth and its fertile soil as an expression of God or Being. Think of its great humility and yet its great capacity to bear crops and to sustain life. Dwell on this for some time. Next, move up to the vav. Think of the wondrous and bountiful greenery that flows from the earth. Recognize that this too is an expression of Being. Dwell on this for some time. Next, move to the upper heh. Think of the blue ocean and the blue sky that surrounds the earth. Meditate on the fact that the earth is irrigated from the waters of the ocean and the seas, and from the rain that falls from the sky. It is with the energy of the sun that the earth produces all forms of life. Think of the sky and the ocean as expressions of Being. Next, move up to the yod. Think of light and energy itself. This too is a powerful expression of Being. Finally, meditate on the entire Name. Think of the world and all its contents as an expression of the infinite essence of Being, as manifest through the Name.

3.   *Middot,* or Spiritual Virtues

In this meditation, one focuses on the *middot,* or spiritual virtues, that correspond to each of the four letters of the Name. One begins with the lower *middot* and proceeds to higher *middot.* The purpose of this meditation is not simply to think about the *middot* but rather to focus on cultivating the *middot* in one's life. One may wish to use the chart on page 236 as one does this meditation. Or, one may keep one's eyes closed and visualize the chart while meditating.

 י   Bonding with God/self-abnegation before God

ה   Accepting the divine kingdom and the commandments, with love and reverence

ו   Compassion, benevolence, justice

ה   Receptivity, thankfulness, humility

Start by visualizing or focusing on the lower heh, while thinking of the middot associated with the lower heh. Feel yourself becoming receptive, thankful, and humble. Recall that the lower middot are the basis for the higher middot. When you feel ready, move to the vav, and the middot of compassion, benevolence, justice. Resolve to develop these active middot. Think about what it takes to be compassionate, benevolent, and just. When you feel ready, move to the upper heh. While visualizing the upper heh, resolve to accept the divine kingdom and the mitzvot, with love and reverence. Realize how challenging, but also how rewarding it is to keep the mitzvot. After dwelling on the upper heh for some time, move to the yod. While visualizing the yod, resolve in your mind to bond your will with God's will. Finally, experience the menuchah or repose of being with God. Dwell there for some time in wordless meditation. If you wish, continue the process in reverse, going back down to the lower heh.

4. *Mitzvot*

As explained in this book, different *mitzvot* pertain to different aspects of God and to different aspects of the soul. In this meditation one focuses on certain *mitzvot* that correspond to each of the four letters of the Name. One begins with lower or more physical *mitzvot* and culminates with more refined or spiritual *mitzvot*. One may choose any relevant *mitzvah* at each stage. The following table provides some suggestions.

י The *mitzvah* of keeping Shabbat

ה The *mitzvah* of Talmud Torah

ו The *mitzvot* of giving charity or helping people in need or carrying out justice

ה The *mitzvah* of putting on *tzitzit* or wearing modest clothing

Start by visualizing or focusing on the lower heh, while thinking of a relevant mitzvah. Say in your heart that you will fulfill that mitzvah in the best way possible. Bear in mind that by cultivating that mitzvah you are connecting yourself with a certain aspect of Hashem. When you feel ready, continue to the next level and repeat the process. Think of yourself as a person who will practice these mitzvot. Bear in mind that by cultivating these mitzvot, you are connecting yourself with Hashem.

5.   *Yedid Nefesh*

The poem *Yedid Nefesh* by Rabbi Elazar Azikri (16th century Kabbalist) is printed in some *Siddurim* as a prelude to *Shacharit*. It is more commonly found in the hymns for *Seudah Shlishi*, the third meal on *Shabbat* afternoon. Each stanza starts with one letter of the Name. The poem is laden with Kabbalistic allusions, many of which have been addressed in this book. For example, note the reference to *ratzon* (will) in the first stanza corresponding to the *yod*. Note the reference to *rachamim* (compassion) in the stanza corresponding to the *vav*. Note the reference to *ahavah* (love) for God in the stanza corresponding to the upper *heh*, and the reference to *aretz* (earth) in the stanza corresponding to the lower *heh*. The attentive reader will find other allusions as well. (Incidentally, a similar pattern is found in the popular *Shabbat* hymn, *Yah Echsof*, which may also serve as a basis for a similar meditation.) This is clearly a "top to bottom" meditation; it starts with the *yod* and moves down to the lower *heh*.

Read the poem aloud slowly, or simply meditate on its content. As you read or recite each stanza, consider that you are connecting the relevant part of your soul, to Hashem, that is, God insofar as He is revealed through each aspect of the Name. In sum, connect your entire soul with God as He is revealed in all of His aspects.

6. The Five *Halleluyahs*

The book of Psalms closes with five chapters that are known as the "five Halleluyahs" because they each begin and end with the exultation, *Halleluyah!* These chapters are incorporated into *Psukei D'Zimrah* (Verses of Psalms). A study of their content reveals that as one advances from the first to the final chapter, there is a progression from lower to higher levels. Each chapter corresponds to a certain aspect of the soul, starting with *nefesh* and culminating with *yechidah*. (Recall that there are five parts of the soul, and that the two highest parts correspond to the *yod* and the tip, or *kotz*, of the *yod*.) One may engage in this meditation while one is saying these psalms as part of *Psukei D'zimrah* or one may do this meditation silently, before or after *Shacharit*. The following table (read from bottom to top) describes some of the allusions in each chapter to a particular aspect of the soul.

י 5. *Halleluyah, Hallelu el bekadsho*, etc. – *yechidah* (God is transcendent, or *kadosh*, beyond description)

4. *Halleluyah, Shiru La'Hashem shir chadash*, etc. – *chayah* (reference to creativity or "new Song;" this hints at *chochmah*, or wisdom)

ה 3. *Halleluyah, Hallelu et Hashem min Hashamayim*, etc. – *neshamah* (reference to heavens, luminaries, and the angels)

ו 2. *Halleluyah, Ki tov zamrah*, etc. – *ruach* (songful praise of God insofar as He is manifest in nature; references to divine justice and providence on earth)

ה 1. *Halleluyah, Halleli nafshi*, etc. – *nefesh* (the mortality and frailty of humankind; note the allusions to some of the themes in the Morning Blessings such as *Pokeach Ivrim* and *Zokef Kefufim*)

Read or meditate silently on each Psalm. Connect each aspect of your soul to Hashem, starting with the lowest part, and culminating with the highest part of the soul.

⇒⇒⇐⇐

7.   Being with God, in the *Beit Hamikdash* (Temple)

In this meditation, one imagines oneself as present in each of four different locations of the Temple in Jerusalem. The four locations correspond
to the four letters of the Name.

In each place, one focuses on connecting with some aspect of God.
The outer realms of the Temple represent a more distant relationship;
the inner realms represent a more intimate connection. As one advances, one gets closer to the essence of the divine. Remember that it is
forbidden to enter the Holy of Holies, and many authorities at this time
prohibit entry on the grounds of the Temple. But no halachic source suggests it is forbidden to *imagine* oneself doing so. Still, perhaps one might
imagine going into the Holy of Holies only with trepidation and perhaps
with an incense offering. (See page 235.) If a person is in Jerusalem, the
first or lowest step can actually be done. One might do the rest of this
meditation while sitting in the area near to the Western Wall. No doubt,
at this stage, the reader does not require further instructions for this
meditation.

י   The *Kodesh Kodashim*; the Holy of Holies, or
    Inner Sanctum

ה   The *Kodesh*; the Holy area or Outer Sanctum

ו   The *Azarah*, or Courtyard of the Temple

ה   The *Har ha-Bayit*, or Temple Mount, outside the
    Temple grounds

===><===

יְהִי רָצוֹן מִלְפָנֶיךָ ה' אֱלֹהֵינוּ וֵאלֹהֵי אֲבוֹתֵינוּ

שֶׁיִּבָּנֶה בֵּית הַמִּקְדָּשׁ בִּמְהֵרָה בְיָמֵינוּ. וְתֵן חֶלְקֵנוּ בְּתוֹרָתֶךָ

וְשָׁם נַעֲבָדְךָ בְּיִרְאָה כִּימֵי עוֹלָם וּכְשָׁנִים קַדְמוֹנִיּוֹת.

וְעָרְבָה לה' מִנְחַת יְהוּדָה וִירוּשָׁלָיִם כִּימֵי עוֹלָם וּכְשָׁנִים קַדְמוֹנִיּוֹת.

LIST OF WORKS CITED

THE PRIMARY SOURCES OF THIS BOOK are the Hebrew Scriptures or *Tanach*, the Talmud, Midrashic literature, and the Zohar. The bibliography lists only the later rabbinic sources used in this book. Almost all of these texts are accessible on Sefaria.org or Hebrewbooks.org. Bibliographical information is provided only for those more recent texts that are not easily available on those websites. Alphabetical ordering sometimes follows a last name, sometimes a first name, and sometimes a place of origin.

YEHUDAH ASHLAG, *Hakdamah LaSefer HaZohar*

BAHYA IBN PAKUDA, *Chovot Halevavot*

YITZCHAK LEVI OF BERDITCHEV, *Kedushat Levi*

SHOLOM NOACH BERZOVSKY OF SLONIM, *Netivot Shalom*. Jerusalem: Yeshivat Beit Avraham, Slonim, 2000

NACHMAN OF BRESLOV, *Likutei Moharan*

MOSHE CORDOVERO (RAMAK), *Pardes Rimonim, Or Ne'erav*

MENAHEM AZARIAH DI FANO, *Asarah Ma'amarot*

SHLOMO GANZFRIED, *Kitzur Shulchan Aruch*

YOSEF GIKATILLIA, *Shaarei Orah*

YEHUDAH ARYEH LEIB OF GUR, *Sefat Emet*

AVRAHAM YEHOSHUA HESHEL OF APT, *Ohev Yisrael*

YAAKOV MOSHE HILLEL, *Petach Sha'ar Hashamayim*. Jerusalem: Ahavat Shalom, 2008

YOSEF IRGAS, *Shomer Emunim*

YOSEF KARO, *Shulchan Aruch, Maggid Mesharim*

MENACHEM KASHER, *Torah Shelemah*

AVRAHAM LANDAU, *Tzelosah D'Avraham*

YERUCHEM HALEVI LEBOVITZ, *Chever Ma'amarim*

YEHUDAH LOEWE (MAHARAL) OF PRAGUE, *Gevurot Hashem, Tifferet Yisrael, Netivot Olam, Ner Mitzvah, Drush Le'Shavuot*

MOSHE CHAIM LUZZATTO (RAMCHAL), *Derech Hashem, Mesilat Yesharim, Da'at Tevunot*

MENACHEM MENDEL (TZEMACH TZEDEK) OF LUBAVITCH, *Derech Mitzvotecha*

MOSHE BEN MAIMON (MOSES MAIMONIDES), *Guide to the Perplexed, Mishneh Torah*

MOSHE BEN NACHMAN (RAMBAN), *Commentary on the Torah*

SIMCHA RABINOWITZ, *Piskei Tshuvot*. Jerusalem: 2007

YAAKOV CHAIM SOFER, *Kaf Hachayim*

YAAKOV BEN ASHER, *Tur*

YISRAEL MEIR HA-COHEN, *Mishnah Berurah*

MOSHE DAVID VALLI, *Commentary on Chronicles*

CHAIM VITAL, *Kitvei Ari*

CHAIM OF VOLOZHIN, *Nefesh Hachayim, Introduction* to the Gaon of Vilna's *Commentary on Sifra Detzniyuta*

SCHNEUR ZALMAN OF LIADI (FOUNDER OF LUBAVITCH CHASSIDISM), *Tanya, Sha'ar Hayichud Ve-ha'emunah, Iggerret Hatshuvah, Likutei Torah, Shulchan Aruch Ha-Rav*

ZEDEKIAH BEN ABRAHAM ANAV, *Shibbole Haleket*